What ex-Californi~~~ /~~d
say about **The Califo**

I wish I had read the book before I m(
me was the common sense advice an
shock—wherever you move to—is a
book just for the information on getting over the culture shock.

The details on checking out schools and how to involve your children in a move are also essential information.

Margot Strombotne, Realtor
Las Vegas, Nev.

Mark Bacon has done his homework. *The California Escape Manual* is a most useful nuts-and-bolts guide to life beyond the Golden State. Web surfers will find its voluminous listing of Internet sites especially useful.

Ken Ward, Columnist
Las Vegas Review-Journal
Co-author, *The Insiders' Guide to Las Vegas*

As a corporate refugee who made his way to Oregon via the Golden State I am amazed at the thorough job Mark Bacon has done in his guidebook for the restless. Mark has left nothing out, from home financing to dealing with the weather! He even has sections on using the Internet to help plan your escape.

He did get one thing wrong: Portland is a terrible place to live, really. Everyone here is sick and tired of low crime, natural beauty and a strong economy. We're simply miserable.

Neal Maillet, Acquisitions Editor
Timber Press
Portland

This is definitely the book that will help you escape the California rat race. It gives you everything you'll need to succeed. The book gets five stars for research. It includes incredible details on Web sites, weather, schools, cost of living information and more.

Kevin Shaddy,
Relocation Manager/Realtor
All Star Realty
Reno, Nev.

I sat down one morning with the idea of reading it for an hour or so. Five hours later, I looked at the clock and wondered where the time had gone.

The book captures the essence of Nevada—where my family and I relocated from the Bay Area in 1991.

Angela R. Beard-Mann, Copy Editor
Reno Gazette Journal

The California Escape Manual

Your guide to finding a new hometown

Mark S. Bacon

Archer & Clark Publishing

The California Escape Manual
Your guide to finding a new hometown

Published in the United States of America by
Archer & Clark Publishing
Redlands, California

Cover design: Don Markofski

This book is designed to provide information in regard to the subject matter covered. It is sold with the understanding that the publisher and author are not engaged
in rendering legal, accounting, or other professional services. If legal advice or other
expert assistance is required, the services of a competent professional person should
be sought. While striving for accuracy, the publisher and author assume no responsibility for errors or omissions.

Library of Congress Catalog Card Number: 97-74889

Publisher's Cataloging-in-Publication
(Provided by Quality Books, Inc.)

Bacon, Mark S.
    The California escape manual : your guide to finding a new
hometown / Mark S. Bacon -- 1st ed.
    p. cm.
    Includes bibliographical references and index.
    ISBN: 0-9660000-2-1

    1. Relocation (Housing)--West (U.S.) 2. Moving (Household)--
West (U.S.)--Handbooks, manuals, etc.   I. Title

TX307.B33 1998   648.9'0979
                         QBI97-41008

Also by Mark S. Bacon

Do-It-Yourself Direct Marketing
Secrets for Small Business

Write Like the Pros
Using the Secrets of Ad Writers and Journalists in Business

Contents

Introduction xiii

    Who should read this book
    Purpose of this book
    Getting out

1. **Where's everybody going and why?** 1

    Come to California!
    Where are they going?
    Corporations moving too
    Curing Caliphobia
    How to use this book

2. **Your escape plan: priorities, finances, and family** 14

    Determining preferences
    Quality of life
    Plan B
    Financial review
    Involve your children
    Resources

3. **How to collect information (on destinations)** 28

    How to get started
    Gathering the facts
    Resources

4. **Digging deeper: Hunting for sources
    and hitting the road** 42

    Data: Climate to crime
    Making the trip
    Resources

5. **What to expect when you move: Culture shock and a
    collection of trade-offs** 60

    Life: Pluses and minuses
    Climate
    Public services
    Culture: Quality vs. accessibility
    Community involvement vs. privacy
    Big fish, small pond
    Realistic expectations
    Making a decision
    Resources

6. Finding a job out of state 77
Employment searching skills
Obtain a transfer
Get a new job in your field
Resources

7. Changing careers, starting a business 100
Find a job in another field
Start your own business
Take your business or profession with you
Learn before you leap
Resources

8. Selling your California home 119
On your own or with an agent?
Price it reasonably
Make your house memorable
Gain the widest exposure
Be creative with premiums and incentives
Be reasonable about negotiating
Understand financing options
If you're transferred
Resources

9. Buying a home out of state 139
To buy or rent
Gathering information
Finding an agent
Resources

10. Home financing, inspecting, and sweating the details 150
Applying for a loan
House-hunting via shoe leather
Sweating the details—country or city
Home inspections
New homes, bargain homes
Closing the deal
Resources

11. Ready for the movers? 167
Cleaning out
Working with movers
Doing it yourself
Hybrid do-it-yourself option
Sample moving schedule
Resources

12. Where to go: Southwest. **182**

Arizona
Colorado
Nevada
Hawaii
New Mexico
Texas
Utah
Resources

13. Where to go: Northwest **211**

Alaska
Idaho
Oregon
Montana
Washington
Wyoming
Resources

14. How to fit in, settle in (and avoid Caliphobia) **233**

Fitting in

Getting involved

Avoiding an attitude

First aid for homesickness

Staying for good?

Appendix A. Basic Internet research techniques **251**

Using a search engine

Capturing information

Web terminology

**Appendix B. Want to move your company
or get your company to move?** **255**

Why leave California?

Companies seek benefits

Incentives

Resources

Index **261**

Tables

1.1   Profile of California emigrants 3

1.2   Fastest growing states. 5

1.3   State populations and projections. 7

2.1   State tax rates. 24

3.1   Education ratings of states. 38

4.1   Crime: FBI reports (by city) 48-49

4.2   Crime: FBI reports (by city) 50

5.1   Climate for selected cities 64-65

5.2   Cost of Living Index (by city) 72-73

6.1   Per capita income (by state) 93

7.1   Labor union membership by state 109

8.1   Home-price index. 124-125

10.1   Median home prices (by city) 163

Acknowledgements

Hundreds of people contributed to the creation of this book by sharing their experiences, their expertise, and their opinions. I'm grateful to the California expatriates who took the time to tell their stories of moving out and settling in. My thanks also to the experts in real estate, relocation, economic development, moving, demographics, employment, and other specialities who answered my questions, explained concepts, and referred me to sources.

I thank my wife, Anne, for her significant contributions to the chapters on home buying and home mortgages. These chapters benefit from her more than 25 years experience in the banking business—much of that time in senior management.

Mark Charlet and Craig Holland were my sounding boards, critics, and supporters. Their suggestions helped improve both the content and organization of the book.

The research assistance of Roy LaBomme Jr. was invaluable in tracking down traditional and online sources of information. Thanks to the book's interior designer, Sue Knopf, who made these pages organized and attractive.

Thanks also go to Fred Jandt for his encouragement and expertise in Internet research and job hunting, to Marjorie Lewis for her advice on real estate transactions, and to Anne Smith for information and suggestions on state economic development and corporate relocation.

My deep appreciation to my editor, Gene Michals, whose insight, counsel, and insistence on clarity (among other contributions) were essential to the success of this book.

—M.S.B.

Introduction

Why leave L.A.? "It's the quality of life.
There isn't any." — James Garner (as Jim Rockford),
"Rockford Files" TV movie

Sitting in the nearly motionless traffic on the San Diego Freeway I looked out at the smoggy horizon. Out there somewhere, just a few miles away, sat Santiago Peak, all 5,687 feet of it. But I couldn't see it through the thick, brown atmosphere of Orange County. The dashboard clock told me I was a half hour late for an appointment with a client. As traffic inched forward, my car's temperature gauge inched upward. It was another 100-degree day, but I had to give the cooling system a break. I turned off the air conditioning and rolled down my window just in time for a Mercedes diesel in the next lane to belch a cloud of foul-smelling gas over my face and into my car. Over the radio I heard a news announcer say that a local jury had just handed down a guilty verdict in the multiple murder trial of Randy Steven Kraft. "Authorities believe he may be the most prolific mass murderer in U.S. history," the announcer said. Then he read an earthquake story.

That was the day I decided to leave California.

To my regret, I didn't keep on driving. In fact, it took two years before my family and I escaped. But escape we did.

Having spent most of my life in California, I had mixed feelings about leaving. My wife Anne and I still loved California, but most of our favorite areas of the state were far from the cities. Our California vacations were spent in places such as Mendocino or Crescent City or Lassen National Park. Every time we'd return, driving south through smoggy Los Angeles to smoggy Orange County, we'd swear that we had to do something. Had to get out.

Who should read this book

If this sounds familiar, if you can identify with my feelings, if you've ever thought about what life would be like outside of urban California, this book is for you. I wrote this book for people who:

• Are ready to leave, and want some help in planning,

• Have always dreamed of moving but are looking for help with the details, and

• Want some suggestions and ideas from people who have already escaped.

Like many expatriates, before we moved, Anne and I took vacations in places we thought we might like to live. There are so many factors to consider. We almost moved to Portland but the research turned out to be a trial run for our ultimate move to southern Nevada. When we made our escape, we thought we'd miss California. We were skeptical of finding an ideal community—as much as we wanted to—and our stereotypes of Las Vegas certainly colored our thinking. We wanted to escape, and yet California was still our home and, except for the overcrowding of its cities, a beautiful one. Two weeks before we left, we drove up the coast to Big Sur; no ocean in Nevada.

Moving brings change. And change can be threatening. Many of the things you take for granted in Woodland Hills or Oakland or Chula Vista may not exist in a small town in another state. Making a successful transition out of urban California, we discovered, requires a sense of balance, an ability to appreciate positive changes and accept some of the inevitable trade-offs. Rather than lament what you've left behind, focus on what you gain. Moving to another town in another state can be a positive change that will lead you in new, exciting directions. Many cities and towns in the West where Californians have settled offer spectacular scenery, uncrowded streets, decent schools, good jobs, and opportunities to become a part of the community. If you're looking for a place where the pace is slower and the costs are lower, just follow the example of thousands of other Californians who are resettling in other Western states.

Purpose of this book

The primary purpose of this book is to help you find a new place to live and help you acquire a sense of balance to go with it. So that you can evaluate your interest in (or tolerance of) significant changes in lifestyle and surroundings, this book is filled with suggestions for ways to look at the pluses and minuses of the many options before you. And what options you have.

The other purposes of this book are to provide advice and suggestions for:

• Finding employment out of state

• Developing a personal strategy for moving

• Tapping into the World Wide Web and other vast free sources of information on the areas where you might like to live

• Selling your house

- Buying a house out of state
- Picking a town and working with movers
- Making the most of your new hometown

Planning is essential. A successful move to another state, with its attendant changes in employment, climate, people, and housing, calls for organizing and priority setting. That's why this book is arranged into chapters that help you develop an escape plan, gather data, evaluate conditions, and make decisions. As this book will show, a little research and planning can not only help make your move a physical and financial success, it can help you mentally adjust to some of the changes that will be flashing through your life like sign posts on the interstate.

Getting out

Living in a crowded California city is like smoking. You know it's not good for you, but you try not to think about the dangers. They drift around in the back of your mind, only occasionally coming to the surface. When they do, you rationalize that the hazards will claim someone else.

We left California for a variety of reasons; change itself was one of them. When my wife was invited to come to Las Vegas to interview at a bank, we didn't take it too seriously. First, she thought that being a woman would work against her and second, we had a hard time imagining ourselves living in "Sin City." She was offered a terrific job, however, and we made a somewhat impetuous decision to move. Although some people questioned our sanity about moving to the gaming capital of the world, the town turned out to be a marvelous place to live. Las Vegas, we discovered, has friendly people, a sense of community that tourists don't see, low taxes, and beyond the strip, a surprising lack of pretension.

Moving to a new community in a new state brought changes and adjustments. It meant changing more than just our surroundings. It was a new start. I was a self-employed marketing consultant. I finished my masters degree and started teaching university classes. We made an effort to meet and get to know our neighbors. We joined civic groups and tried to become a part of the community. We supported local athletic teams, and even learned about the history of our new state. At first we had to push ourselves to meet people and find out about the area in which we lived, but soon it became fun. We admired the pioneer spirit that seemed to be a part of business and government in the sparsely settled state. We recognized that although Las Vegas and Nevada had problems too, they were manageable problems. In contrast to the urban problems of crime, pollution, and clogged transportation that plague California cities, the solutions to Nevada problems seemed within reach. Las Vegas exceeded our expectations in many ways and when Anne's bank was sold and she was out of a job, moving back to California never occurred to us. A remarkably good job offer in California appeared, however, and after one of the most difficult decisions in our lives, we decided to move. In a number of ways, coming back served to reinforce the reasons we left in the first place, and we agreed not to stay very long. We spent more than four wonderful years out of state. Our return helped me coalesce thoughts about this book which I began writing in Nevada and concluded in California.

What follows is based on our experiences leaving our home in California and learning about life in another state. It is also based on interviews with experts in various fields and on the experiences of dozens of ex-Californians who now make their homes Washington, Oregon, Arizona, and other states.

Although the reasons why people have left California are a part of their relocation stories, and are therefore sometimes included here, the purpose of this book is not to bash California nor to persuade you to move. The choice is yours.

1

Where's everybody going and why?

Larry Miller, owner of Sure Look Homes and Land in Fort Collins, Colo., receives more than 200 inquiries per year from Californians. It's a similar story for real estate agents in Scottsdale, Ariz., Portland, Ore., Henderson, Nev., and all over the West. Californians are moving.

"What Californians like," says Miller, "is getting to know their neighbors, feeling at home and getting a sense of involvement. That's what it's like here in Fort Collins." If that sounds good to you, you're not alone. Hundreds of thousands of people are outbound from the Golden State each year. Many more are thinking about it.

Chances are, you've entertained the notion of leaving your California city for a quieter, safer, or less expensive life somewhere else. After nearly a lifetime in California, my wife and I did too, and our move to Nevada was the genesis of this book. This chapter explores some of the background of the California exodus, explains where people are going, and previews some of the challenges you may face in getting settled out of state. It also gives you an outline you can use to plan your escape.

Dissatisfaction with California seemed to rise sometime in the late 1980s as the housing market peaked and people started complaining—more than just routinely—about smog, crime, and congestion. They started talking about escaping to Oregon or Washington. In cities throughout the state—at cocktail parties, water cooler conversations, chance meetings at the store—escaping California (for some ideal, non-urban setting) was a frequent topic. Some people talked of Idaho or Montana; others said they weren't going to leave the state, just relocate to a small town in the mountains or on the coast. The wishes and conversations led to action. Before long, articles appeared in California papers about ex-Golden Staters flooding Seattle and parts of Oregon.

Leaving California is not a recent idea. With a population larger than many countries in the world, California has always had people flowing both in and out. According to figures from the California Department of Finance and the Department of Motor Vehicles, an average of 344,000 people left California annually from 1970 to 1988. But in the late 1980s the number of escapees rose. It wasn't just talk anymore. By 1990, more than 480,000 people were departing the state annually. Within a year the figure reached well over a half million people: a 60 percent increase over the 70s and 80s in annual out-migration. This is not to say the population of the state started to decline. Immigrants from other states and other countries and a high birthrate has kept the population rising.

It's impossible to determine the exact number of people who leave California every year. The most comprehensive figures available come from the DMV. It tracks California drivers' licenses returned from other states. (When Californians relocate and obtain drivers' licenses in other states, they must surrender their California licenses.) But the licenses don't account for everyone. At the beginning of 1996, slightly more than 19 million people—about 59 percent of the state population—had drivers' licenses. Since DMV figures from other states show only licensed drivers who left the state, those figures probably need to be increased about 40 percent to account for the non-drivers who also left. That shows, therefore, close to 550,000 people left California in one year (ending June 30, 1996). That figure was typical for the prior three years as well—2 million escapees in four years. Recently, at least, people in their 30s and 40s made up the largest group of emigrants. (See Table 1.1.)

The reasons people give for leaving Los Angeles, San Francisco, San Diego, and other cities are similar. Matt Hunter, who worked for a large real estate firm in San Diego before moving to McCall, Idaho, (pop. 2,005) looked for a scenic location with outdoor recreation. "I was tired of the congestion and always having to wait in line everywhere." Maryann and Fred Sabatini left Anaheim where their condominium was burglarized and their van stolen. They wanted a place where they could afford a house of their own, so they moved to Michigan where they were raised. Expatriates also talk about declining faith in the state's educational system, from elementary school through the state's crowded public universities. Retirees say they're looking for lower taxes, reasonable housing costs, and a less frantic pace. "There's nothing wrong with California that 20 million fewer people wouldn't cure," says ex-Bay Area resident Julien Wagenet who moved to New Mexico after he retired.

Some people who left California focused on economic issues, but a surprising number say quality of life was more important. "People move up here because they want to get out of the rat race," says Portland real estate agent Debbie Bucher. People are looking for cleaner air, less congestion, a safer, quieter life. Some of the ex-Californians interviewed couldn't wait to get out.

Leaving the Golden State
Profile of one year's exodus

Number of persons leaving:	
546,635	

Percent of total by ages:	
18 - 24	15.3%
25 - 29	16.6
30 - 44	41.1
45 - 64	21.9
65 & over	5.1
	100 percent

Table 1.1 These figures are based on the number of drivers' licenses returned to California from other states. The figures include a 40 percent adjustment to account for non-license holders who also moved. The estimate for the number of people who left the state may be low; the California DMV reports four states, including Colorado and New Mexico, underreported the number of California licenses returned. Data cover 12 months from July 1995 to June 1996. Source: California Department of Motor Vehicles, September 1996.

Others say California is still their home but, not the place they want to live. "My heart is there, but I enjoy having my brain and my body here," says Las Vegan Bill Torres who moved from Orange County in 1993. Relocation specialists and economic development directors in other states confirm the emphasis that expatriates place on quality of life in their decisions to move.

Come to California!

California is a victim of its own success. The early developers, the motion picture and television industries, and promoters of all stripes painted such a glorious picture of the Golden State from the days of the 49ers onward that people just couldn't resist trying to get a part of the good life. Strangely enough though, most of the hype was accurate hype. From the railroad company advertisements of the 1880s, to the promises of suburban paradise in the 1950s and 1960s, people found what they were looking for. More or less. While some early promoters may have tried to make immigrants think oranges grew on Joshua trees and that a subway was soon to be constructed in Los

Angeles (70 years before the Metro Rail), the promises of open space, mild winters, and soft ocean breezes were legitimate. Easterners saw photos, and later television pictures, of the sun shining in Pasadena on New Year's Day. They looked out at the three feet of snow on the lawn, and decided to come to California.

In 1935, guide-book author Abrey Drury wrote glowingly of Los Angeles: "In the depths of a national depression, felt everywhere, a Los Angeles 'go-getter' was heard to admit, 'True, this is one of the smallest *booms* we have enjoyed in years." In 1953, John Crow's book, *California as a Place to Live*, said you could buy a home in a respectable L.A. neighborhood for between $10,000 and $15,000. One thousand could be knocked off the minimum price, he said, if you didn't mind living in the, "farthest outlying suburbs; for example parts of the San Fernando and San Gabriel valleys." And Crow was probably not stretching the truth when he described San Jose of the early 1950s:

> *San Jose is a city of small homes occupied by families who have deliberately sought to escape the crowds and traffic of the larger Bay cities, in a climate that is more enjoyable. It takes the average San Jose worker only ten minutes to get to his job; he arrives fresh and ready for a full day's work.*

And so they came: Midwesterners, tired of long, cold winters, packed up their belongings and headed out Route 66 or, later, one of the interstates. Mexican laborers looking for higher wages did everything they could to ride, walk, or crawl across the border into prosperous California. People came from Oklahoma and Ohio and Wisconsin. From New York, North Dakota, and places in between. And they came from the Philippines, Korea, Cuba, Great Britain, and dozens of other countries. As California's population multiplied, so did the problems. Many, if not all, of the adverse conditions expatriates cite as reasons for leaving can be traced to overpopulation. Or perhaps too little planning, too few resources.

It wasn't until 40 years after the discovery of gold, in 1848, that California's population reached one million. (The 1890 census listed California's population at 1.2 million.) Six more decades of Rose Parades and chamber of commerce hype increased the population more than eight fold to more than 10 million people in 1950. Twenty more years brought ten million more people so that by 1970 one in every ten Americans was a Californian. Today there are more than 32 million people in California, nearly 12 percent of the U.S. Some 27 million people will live in five Southern California counties by the year 2000 according to California State Department of Finance estimates. Within 20 years, according to the *California Almanac,* the Los Angeles metropolitan area will surpass metro New York as the most populous area in the United States.

Where are they going?

We moved to Nevada. The majority of Californians who move also stay in the West. According to California DMV figures, Western states draw most Californians. Nevada accounts for nearly 11 percent of the exodus, with Arizona, Oregon, and Washington each just slightly below that figure. Recently, Texas also started to attract a large number of Californians. Studies by United Van Lines show that the top five states with the highest percentage of net inbound moves (from all states) are in the West: Alaska, Nevada, Oregon, Arizona, and Idaho.

It's not difficult to imagine why people are staying in the West for work or retirement. Hundreds of scenic communities, from tiny Bandon on the rocky Oregon coast to the Rocky Mountain metropolis of Denver, beckon burned-out Californians. States from Alaska to New Mexico offer a relaxed, Western lifestyle without the teeming millions. Economically, and perhaps socially and culturally, the Western states other than California are experiencing a renaissance.

For the past several years, cities in the West have dominated the ratings of housing markets in the annual *U.S. News and World Report* "Hottest Cities"

Top ten fastest growing states
Percent population change

Mar. 1, 1990 to July 1, 1996	
Nevada	33.4%
Arizona	20.8
Idaho	18.1
Utah	16.1
Colorado	16.0
Washington	13.7
Georgia	13.5
New Mexico	13.1
Oregon	12.7
Texas	12.6

Table 1.2 During the same period, the U.S. population increased by 6.7 percent. Source: U.S. Bureau of the Census: Population Division, Population Estimates Program. Released Dec. 30, 1996. For population totals, see Table 1.3.

reviews. "Cities in both [population size] lists—Salt Lake City; Denver; Tucson, Ariz.; Albuquerque, N.M.; Colorado Springs, Colo.; Portland and Eugene, Ore.; and Spokane, Wash., continue to draw California escapees to a lower cost of living and a higher quality of life," the magazine said in its 1996 housing review. The year before, it praised Boise, Idaho, for low energy and real estate prices, Eugene for a high percentage of skilled workers, and Salt Lake City for a rock-bottom unemployment rate.

Seven Western towns were in *Money* magazine's 1996 top ten "Great Towns with Great Jobs." The listing, limited to cities under 50,000 in population, included Divide, Colo., Elko, Nev., and North Kona, Hawaii. In a *Forbes* magazine survey of job growth, six of the top seven cities were in the West. The survey compared net job growth from January 1990 to July 1996. Las Vegas; Austin, Texas; Boise, Idaho; and Provo, Utah, posted gains of 30 percent or more while San Francisco and Los Angeles showed negative numbers. The states with the highest percentage of annual job growth for the first half of the 1990s were Nevada and Utah, according to the U.S. Bureau of Labor Statistics.

Calvin Beale, who tracks rural migration for the U.S. Department of Agriculture, says he sometimes thinks of the historical movement of people as, "a wave of population growth going across the United States. When it comes to the Pacific Ocean, it's almost as if it hits a wall and then splashes back to Arizona, Nevada, Utah, and Idaho."

Among the trends Beale follows as senior demographer for the USDA is the growth of non-urban recreational counties. Almost all of the fastest growing ones are located in Utah, Colorado, and Idaho. For example, from 1990 to 1994 Summit County in northern Utah grew by almost 39 percent and San Miguel County, home of Telluride in eastern Colorado, grew by 31.3 percent. According to Beale, retirees and urban escapees seeking outdoor recreation account for much of the growth of these areas. Yavapai County, Ariz., home to Prescott and portions of Sedona, grew by more than 20,000 people since 1990 and Beale also notes a large percentage of growth in the three counties near Bend, Ore., where the dry climate and recreational opportunities have attracted many California transplants.

Overall, Nevada and Idaho are the fastest growing states in the U.S. with other Western states close behind. According to the U.S. Census, Nevada had the highest percentage of new home construction of any state from 1990 to 1997. Idaho ranked second. While congestion may be a concern in the future of Las Vegas, Idaho and Nevada still have plenty of space for growth. The two states' combined population is about equal to Orange County while their area is about 25 percent larger than California.

Corporations moving too

Economic growth and wide-open spaces are equally appealing to California companies. The downturn in the California economy in the late 1980s and early 1990s started many company officials thinking about relocating, and by some estimates, more than 700 companies have moved all or part of their facilities to other states since 1989.

Why do companies move? Many executives who have moved their businesses beyond the California borders cite high taxes, oppressive regulations,

State Population
Growth since 1990 and projections

	4/1/90	7/1/96	2000	2005
Alaska	550,043	607,007	699,000	745,000
Arizona	3,665,339	4,428,068	4,437,000	4,763,000
California	29,758,213	31,878,234	34,888,000	37,771,000
Colorado	3,294,473	3,822,676	4,059,000	4,309,000
Florida	12,938,071	14,399,985	15,313,000	16,347,000
Hawaii	1,108,229	1,183,723	1,327,000	1,436,000
Idaho	1,006,734	1,189,251	1,290,000	1,385,000
Illinois	11,430,602	11,846,544	12,168,000	12,417,000
Minnesota	4,375,665	4,657,758	4,824,000	4,986,000
Montana	799,065	879,372	920,000	962,000
Nevada	1,201,675	1,603,163	1,691,000	1,835,000
New Mexico	1,515,069	1,713,407	1,823,000	1,956,000
New York	17,990,778	18,184,774	18,237,000	18,348,000
North Carolina	6,632,448	7,322,870	7,617,000	8,002,000
Oregon	2,842,337	3,203,735	3,404,000	3,645,000
Tennessee	4,877,203	5,319,654	5,538,000	5,791,000
Texas	16,986,335	19,128,261	20,039,000	21,447,000
Utah	1,722,850	2,000,494	2,148,000	2,318,000
Washington	4,866,669	5,532,939	6,070,000	6,570,000
Wisconsin	4,891,769	5,159,795	5,381,000	5,528,000
Wyoming	453,589	481,400	522,000	559,000

Table 1.3 It's interesting to compare the projected population of California—more than 37 million by 2005—with that of popular destination states. Source: Population Estimates Program, Population Division, U.S. Bureau of the Census.

and tell how disagreements with various levels of government created huge legal bills and caused years of delays in expansion or construction. Jack Hileman, senior vice president of the Koll Real Estate Group of Los Angeles, explained the advantages of construction work in a smaller state:

Hired to build a 165,000-square-foot office complex in Las Vegas, his company obtained partial building permits in 90 days and was able to break ground. Four and a half months into the job, says Hileman, his company had final permits.

In contrast, says Hileman, his company was constructing a building in downtown Los Angeles.

"We were told by the L.A. Streets Department to remove two large ficus trees in front of our new office building and install new street lights. Unfortunately, the removal of the trees had to be coordinated with the L.A. Parks Department. After 18 months of negotiations between the two departments, we finally got approval to remove the two trees.¹

Company executives often find smaller state governments eager to please new businesses. For example, when Citibank wanted to locate a credit-card processing center in Nevada, a major obstacle was a state law that limited bank late fees to an amount lower than those charged by Citibank. Not a problem. A special session of the state legislature was called, and the law was changed. Now Citibank employs about 1,400 people at its facility in Las Vegas.

While Citibank didn't come from California, the flexibility and willingness to accommodate new business, evident in Nevada and other states, is still luring companies from California. The other Western states, eager to build their employment bases, actually conduct sales campaigns to convince corporations to find a home within their boundaries. Corporation raiders from organizations such as the Nevada Development Authority, the Portland Development Commission, and Arizona Department of Commerce try to woo companies from California. Nevada continues to be a recruiting leader, attracting dozens of California companies every year including Williams-Sonoma, the San Francisco home and garden products firm which recently opened a call center employing about 1,000 people in the Summerlin area of Las Vegas.

Factors unrelated to the business climate in California are also responsible for company departures. In 1993, Charles Schwab & Co., Inc. moved its data processing center from San Francisco to Phoenix. Economic factors were not as important as geologic ones. Since Schwab's computer center could serve the U.S. from anywhere, company officials decided they didn't want to worry about the risk of an earthquake disrupting their network.

If you have your own business, or if you work for someone who has thought about moving to another state, see Appendix B for details on corporate relocation.

Curing Caliphobia

A bumper sticker seen occasionally in Las Vegas says, "I don't care *how* you did it in California." Its sentiment is similar to a harsher slogan that used to be popular in another state: "Don't Californicate Oregon." Both sayings reflect one of the hazards of an out-of-state move: resentful locals. As Californians fill up the coffee bars in Seattle, push up home prices in Santa Fe, and contribute to traffic in Denver, some residents are rebelling.

In the late 1980s, when Seattle seemed to be the destination of choice for discontented Californians, *Seattle Times* columnist Emmett Watson became the unofficial leader of the anti-California movement. Although he says he was only joking when he wrote that Washington should impose a head tax for Californians, his columns spoofing Golden Staters found welcome readers among long-time Puget Sound residents. The *Los Angeles Times*, and other California newspapers, ran stories about the crusty columnist and the anti-California sentiments, alerting potential escapees of the problem. Maryann Sabatini and other expatriates interviewed say they crossed Seattle off their lists of potential hometowns because of the negative publicity.

Bonnie Fletcher, a relocation specialist with John L. Scott Real Estate in Seattle for more than 20 years, says of the anti-California sentiment, "You hear about it occasionally, but actually I don't think it's true." Just the same, when Dick and Sheila White moved to the Puget Sound area from Orange County in 1993 they not only exchanged their license plates quickly but Dick obtained license plate *frames* from a local car dealer.

Excessively high home prices in the Golden State in the late 1980s contributed to the start of various anti-California movements. Californians who had owned their homes for years saw their equities fatten, and many of them decided to move to areas where house prices were a fraction of those in California. In Seattle in 1989, says relocation specialist Fletcher, "Californians were coming in, driving the price of housing up—and truly they were . . . . They had a lot of money and when they found a house they wanted they would pay $100,000 more than a local."

Today, the atmosphere in Washington and other states is not as hostile— if it ever was as unfriendly as many Californians believed it to be. In many cities now, newcomers from California are not likely to be ridden out of town on a rail, because ex-Californians are part of the landscape. One Californian who moved to Idaho said she attended a local crafts class and found three-quarters of the people in class were also Golden State expatriates. Another reason why anti-California sentiment may not be as prevalent today is that home prices in many destination cities have increased—while prices in

California have decreased—somewhat reducing the disparity. By California standards, however, bargains are still to be found.

Dislike or distrust of outsiders is a complex issue. The amount of goodwill you will find when you move is dependent on a variety of factors—including your attitude and local conditions. For example, in Santa Fe, N.M., two issues rile locals. One is real estate, the other is culture. Longtime residents have seen real estate prices escalate over the last ten years as Californians, and people from other states, have bid up the price of homes so much that the upcoming generation of natives is being priced out of the market. This fueled the anti-California or anti-out-of-state sentiment, says a Santa Fe shopkeeper. She talks about the influx of well-heeled Californians as the "Range Rover syndrome," referring to the pricey sport utility vehicles that "you can now see lined up everywhere in town on Saturday night."

The Santa Fean, who asks not to be identified, also explains the second point of annoyance for locals. "Some people do not seem to have an interest in or respect for local history and traditions. They treat [local Native American customs] as if it's just part of Disneyland, 'and isn't it cool.' It's pretty frustrating."

She says she saw evidence of anti-California feelings in another state. "I was in Colorado Springs for a seminar and one of the jokes a speaker told was that there were more Californians at the program than anyone else and that they were all going to move to Colorado Springs. No one laughed."

Fortunately for Californians planning to move, Caliphobia is waning in many Western states. Remember though, the reception you receive also is up to you. Chapter 14 discusses ways to settle into your new community, but here's a hint taken from the mayor's "welcoming" message in the 1995 *Santa Fe Newcomers Guide*. Such letters are usually ebullient greetings overflowing with praise for local schools, recreational opportunities, and city services. Here's a part of what Mayor Debbie Jamarillo wrote in her brief letter:

Dear friend,

Welcome to the ancient and historic city of Santa Fe, crossroads of the cultures of the Southwest!

I invite you to learn about the unique traditions and life of this community. You will find that living here means more than just Pueblo style architecture and beautiful climate . . .

If you take care to learn our ways and our concerns, if you get involved with us in preserving a special way of life that has stood the test of many generations, then you will find yourself a very welcome citizen of Santa Fe.

How to use this book

This book is organized to help you develop and implement your escape plan—and make the transition from urban California to less crowded surroundings. For a complete relocation strategy, follow the chapters in order. As no one plan will fit everyone, some of the chapters—such as 12 and 13—are free-standing, allowing you to jump around to find the information that's most useful for your situation.

Elements of your escape plan:

A. Determine your priorities, review your finances, involve your children.

Use daydreaming and brainstorming to help you decide what you're looking for. What size city is best? What region of the country? Do you already have one or two specific cities in mind? Develop your wish list of hometown attributes. Decide what quality of life means to you. Review your finances. Consider how to involve your children in your moving decision. See Chapter 2.

B. Collect information.

Sources of information abound. Use the tables throughout this book to isolate factors that are important to you. Then call chambers of commerce, surf the Web, visit your library, talk with people out of state, etc. When you've collected the information, it's time to visit your potential hometowns. See Chapters 3 and 4.

C. Develop realistic expectations.

Your new hometown may be full of surprises and challenges. Explore the trade-offs: weather, transportation, entertainment possibilities, cost of living, and geography. To help you establish reasonable expectations, read Chapter 5 for previews of coming attractions.

D. Tune up your job search skills.

Are you planning to look for a new job out of state? Change fields? Start your own company? Chapters 6 and 7 help you explore employment options.

E. Decide where you're going to go.

Chapters 12 and 13 give you a look at the 13 other Western states and selected cities. Will your personal paradise be Provo, Prescott, Pueblo, or perhaps Puyallup (Wash.)?

F. Sell your California home.

Easier said than done? Maybe. Chapter 8 is filled with professional marketing ideas and (slightly) devious ways to perk up and peddle your property.

G. Buy a home in another state.

Whether you buy right away or rent temporarily, the housing market outside California is definitely unlike what you're used to. Will you need an agent? Can you use the Web? Should you obtain an adjustable rate mortgage? See Chapters 9 and 10.

H. Call in the movers.

Packing up can be hard to do, properly. If you haven't moved in a few years, here are some suggestions. See Chapter 11.

I. Settle down. Enjoy. Get involved.

Becoming a part of your new community could be the start of a wonderful new life for you and your family. Chapter 14 has suggestions for settling in.

J. Learn Internet research techniques.

The brief outline and glossary in Appendix B is a beginner's introduction to doing research on the Internet and World Wide Web.

K. Want to move your company?

See Appendix B for company relocation information.

At the end of most chapters are resource sections. They contain names of books, articles, organizations, Web sites, and government agencies where you can find additional information on the topics discussed in the chapter.

About the tables in this book

Tables throughout this book provide information on various quality-of-life factors, such as the cost of living, housing prices, and weather. As the vast majority of California escapees relocate in the West, the tables focus on Western cities and states. Data for selected Eastern, Midwestern, and Southern cities and states are also included for comparison.

Most, but not all, of the same cities are represented on each table. Not all data for each category were available for all cities.

Consider the information in the tables as a general guide, a beginning point for your own, individual research. Keep in mind the relative value of statistics and averages as well. See the discussion about averages in Chapter 12.

References

California population figures come from the California State Department of Finance. Population projections come from the *California Almanac*, sixth edition, Pacific Data Resources, 1993. According to the almanac, in the 1980s, 70 percent of the newcomers to California came from outside the United States.

John Crow wrote *California As a Place to Live*, published by Charles Scribner's Sons, copyright 1953. In the book, he also said a lot in a medium-priced Los Angeles neighborhood costs between \$2,000 and \$4,000. Abrey Drury's *California, An Intimate Guide,* was published by Harper & Brothers, copyright 1935.

In the *U.S. News and World Report* review of housing in the West, published, April 1, 1996, Salt Lake City, Denver, and Portland were the top three cities. Las Vegas, Phoenix, and San Antonio were also in the top 20. In the *Forbes* magazine survey, published Oct. 21, 1996, nine of the top 17 cities with the highest job growth were in the West.

Population growth figures come from the U.S. Census Bureau.

Santa Fe Mayor Debbie Jaramillo's advice for prospective residents came from the *Santa Fe Newcomer's Guide,* published by Starlight Publishing, Inc.

2

Your escape plan:
priorities, finances, and family

Daydreaming is the first step in your great escape.

You don't need to decide immediately where you want to go. Think instead about what you want to find when you get there. Cool weather? A small community? Near the ocean? The mountains? Close to a large airport? Near relatives? What about recreation opportunities, schools, shopping?

If you've daydreamed about an existence outside California, you already have some of the raw material you need to get started, but the more ideas the better.

This chapter shows you how to build an escape plan by determining your priorities, reviewing your finances, and looking for ways to include your children in your relocation activities. Succeeding chapters show you how to collect information and put it to use.

Determining preferences

Daydreaming is helpful because it uses your imagination to provide insight into your inner desires. You can expand your daydreaming and tap into your inner thoughts through brainstorming, a sort of formalized daydreaming. (The term *brainstorming* was coined by advertising people who used it as a way to open their minds to new ideas, which is exactly what you want to do.) Your brainstorming will focus on places to live and your likes and dislikes. By examining your preferences (and those of your spouse or partner) you can come up with a list of priorities—your relocation wish list—that will help you find your ideal location.

To make brainstorming work, don't be practical or logical. Just think out loud and write down what you say. Sit down with your spouse or a friend and just start talking about moving out. At least one of you, perhaps both, should have a pad and pencil for recording what you say. You might start with a few of the things you want to be rid of, such as traffic jams or smog. Let your mind wander. Say the first thing that occurs to you, somewhat like a word association test. Now is not the time to evaluate or put things in priority order, just record your thoughts. Write down every idea and comment. The more random and unstructured your ramblings, the more material you'll come up with, and the greater the likelihood of writing down new and useful ideas. Here's an example of one short brainstorming burst, where one idea leads to another:

> *One-hour drive to work . . . small town with no freeways . . . lots of trees, hiking trails . . . need cell phones for communication . . . why take civilization with us? Slow down and enjoy the view. Ocean views. A house on a hill. Sweeping vistas, watching storms. Neighbors close but not too close. Fireplace for warmth. Forced air furnace. Repairs? Not too remote, need services, repairs. Isolation breeds mechanical breakdowns. Need city services, but how big? Half a million? Fifty thousand? Need customers for my business. Groups of smaller towns— sales routes pretty but long . . . too long in winter?*

Try brainstorming now, even if you're alone. Say your ideas out loud. Spend at least five minutes writing down as many ideas as you can. Later you can brainstorm with someone else.

If possible, hold a brainstorming session before you read on. If you have trouble coming up with things to say, you're probably being too formal, too structured. Relax. Write down anything that comes to mind. You don't need complete sentences. Only after you've filled a few pages with notes should you give any thought to making sense out of your brainstorming. Did you write down any ideas or descriptions about ideal locales that you hadn't considered before? Did you focus mainly on work, family, or leisure-time activities? You could conduct separate brainstorming sessions on each topic, although it's important to keep your brainstorming as unstructured as possible. If you plan to focus on business/work relocation ideas and wind up talking mostly about weather, keep going. Let your mind wander across the plains and up the mountain peaks of your mind.

While you're thinking about moving is a good time to consider your lifetime goals—even those that may not be connected to relocating. Moving out of California is a consequential decision and if you're interested in changing your surroundings you may be interested in other changes. Transplanting yourself and your family to another state can afford an opportunity to do things differently. You can make changes in your life more easily when you don't have familiar surroundings and routines reinforcing old habits. Moving is exciting, and sometimes formidable—because so many things in your life change at once. You can change with them, if you want to. In a sense, you can leave your past behind and start over.

If employment, educational opportunities, or social conditions are among your reasons for moving, then you're seeking more than just escape from the freeways. Many people who left California did so with lifestyle and personal priority changes in mind as well. They examined their values as much as they did their road maps. So, before you plot an escape route, consider more than just a physical destination.

One of the best ways to evaluate your goals is to do a series of exercises you'll find in the book, *How to Get Control of Your Time and Your Life,* by Alan Lakein. The author's premise is that you can't make wise use of your time if you don't know where you're going or what you want to accomplish. Through a series of short, timed idea sessions you write down personal objectives and then rate them. Lakein's method is a form of focused brainstorming with a goal of bypassing your conscious, judgmental self and getting down to what's most important to you, inside. Says Lakein: "Your perceptions will come directly, unfiltered by your reasoning processes." The innovative book, originally published about 25 years ago, is available in bookstores.

Even if you think this form of introspection may not be for you, a little time spent evaluating your goals may help you personally and professionally. While you may want to leave California to get off the fast track and diversify your life, you don't have to sacrifice career advancement. Just find a smaller city in which to excel. As we'll see, moving to a smaller state and town may give you business advantages.

This book is designed to help you find a new hometown and to provide suggestions for making a successful transition out of California and into a more satisfying state (of mind). One way to make the jump out of your urban surroundings is to be open to new ideas and ways of doing things. Try to look at life a little differently and not take all your California predispositions with you. For example, one of the most important criteria to your happiness and satisfaction with your new hometown will be the people who live there and your success at making friends with them. Fitting in may require new social techniques or new attitudes. People are, in fact, so important to your enjoyment of your new community that opportunities to meet and get to know people should be a high priority. For some, the way to find people will be through a church, fraternal organization, or professional group. For others it will be their job or neighborhood. However you do it, connecting with people should be high on your list.

Quality of life

As you develop your hometown wish list, you get closer to identifying your *driving forces,* your most important considerations in moving. Many expatriates and would-be ex-Californians talk about improving their *quality of life*. The term is expressed often, rarely with the same definition in mind. For some people it reflects physical or monetary concerns; for others, quality of life denotes spiritual values; for still others, QOL is a combination of elements.

Here is a list of qualities, capabilities, and facilities to weigh before you weigh anchor. Only two or three may be driving forces for you. Everyone's vision of heaven, and quality of life, is different.

QOL factors

Climate Consider not only temperatures, but also the amount of rain and snowfall, prevailing winds, humidity, and average number of sunny days.

Pollution The cleanliness of air and water are prime concerns. Public and private agencies offer benchmarks and surveys.

Crime FBI and Justice Department reports are ways to evaluate incidents of crime and compare one city with another.

Local economy/employment Statistics about the growth of jobs and unemployment indicate the general economic health of an area, but you also must investigate the market for jobs in your field or specialization.

Topography/geography Choosing to live in the mountains, the desert, or the seashore is a fundamental decision, but its importance could be overshadowed by climate, job opportunities, and other factors.

Heath care facilities Your age and health may dictate specific needs. If you are retired from the military you may want to live near a base for subsidized health care.

Education Quality instruction for your children, continuing educational opportunities for you or your spouse, and the benefits of a university will be a priority for some.

Entertainment, spectator sports If you're going to miss the Chargers, Giants, or Lakers, will the Cardinals, Rockies, or Trailblazers do? What about minor leagues and college teams?

Culture How important are theatres, museums, and galleries?

Outdoor and recreational activities Instead of traveling hours to hiking/biking trails, you could live next to one.

Housing Enterprising real estate companies and agents make information overload your only problem here.

Convenience of shopping Can you settle for Dillards or J.C. Penney when you're used to Nordstrom or Neiman Marcus?

Cost of living/tax structure Lower state taxes are easy to find. See Table 2.1 for state tax rates, Table 5.2 for cost-of-living figures.

Transportation The availability of airports, highways, and waterways may be important to your business.

Proximity to a larger city Living on a city's edge can give you combined rural/urban benefits.

Population/congestion potential They complain about crowds in Boise and Bellingham, but you know better. Phoenix is another story.

Demographics The mixture of ages, races, and socio-economic levels varies greatly across the West.

Unique local conditions Can you tolerate mosquitoes or other pests, swamps, military aircraft noise, toxic or nuclear waste storage? What if local politicos are too liberal or too conservative for you?

Plan B

Many people are looking for new places to go, but you may already have your eye on a destination. If so, your planning and research will proceed differently, hence, *Plan B*. With a potential anchor in another state you will conduct *Plan B* under a variety of circumstances:

• You're thinking of moving to Galveston, Texas, Bend, Ore., or another place, because your family lives there.

• You've always vacationed in Sun Valley, Idaho, (or Wickenburg, Ariz., etc.) and it's your ideal community, where you simply must live.

• You have a job possibility in some place called Federal Way, Wash. You've never even heard of it. Or perhaps your company wants to transfer you to its plant in Colorado Springs, but you've never been there.

• Your brother-in-law owns a business in Salt Lake City and wants you to move there and help him run the company.

No matter what the reason, if you already have one destination in mind, no search is needed. But examining the quality of life in your potential destination still may be important; it may lead to a yes-or-no-decision. Alternatively, your research may help you find ways to take best advantage of your opportunity and develop reasonable expectations. Once you make a decision about location, your plan jumps ahead to the next requirement, be it a job, a house, or a moving company.

Financial review

At the opposite end of the spectrum from daydreaming is sound financial planning. You'll need to do some of that too if you are to succeed in your escape from urban California to a smaller community with a better quality of life. Of course you don't have to plan your entire life before you move. Much of the attraction of moving is the unknown. A surprising number people leave California with little idea of where they're going, or what they'll do when they get there. So if you're planning to load up the U-Haul and hit the highway tonight, you might want to skip to Chapters 12 and 13. They describe other cities and states. If you want to be more organized, however, and stick with a more methodical escape plan, you need to consider your finances.

Moving may bring on a host of financial changes and challenges (depending upon your situation). Even if you keep the same job with the same company, your financial circumstances will change with the landscape. Other states have different tax structures, different costs of living, different demands of climate. When you factor in expenses for buying and selling a home, job hunting (for you or your spouse), and relocating your household, expenses and financial uncertainties add up. Before you move, rather than just checking out the costs of relocation, give yourself a financial checkup too. Figure 2.1 shows a list of tasks and considerations. You may already have done some of this reviewing; some can be done only after you learn the laws in your destination state.

Pre-move financial checklist

- ☐ Computerize your family finances
- ☐ Examine tax liabilities
- ☐ Make tax projections, evaluate your withholding
- ☐ Investigate cost of living in new state
- ☐ Estimate relocation expenses
- ☐ Prepare budget showing expenses now and in your new town
- ☐ Evaluate potential costs, profits in selling your home
- ☐ Consider consolidating debts
- ☐ Review insurance coverages
- ☐ Revise wills and trusts as necessary
- ☐ Examine investments
- ☐ Find a competent financial advisor

Figure 2.1

Dollars and sense software

To make sense of your finances and organize the information all in one place, nothing beats family financial software. Putting our family books, including our checking account, on our computer was a time-consuming task at first. Once we were computerized, however, it was, at last, easy to understand our finances. Not that we have a massive portfolio, nor staggering indebtedness, but even with our few investments the paperwork can get confusing. Now that we have everything in one place, updating our records is simple. The software computes interest, draws pie and bar charts to show us just where our money is going, and makes it easy to experiment: What if we moved to . . . and our expenses went down by . . . but our moving costs were . . . ? Doing financial projections can take some of the uncertainty out of a move.

Even the daily or weekly chore of entering checks is not as tedious as it might sound. The computer remembers all recurring payments. Just press a few keys and the computer completes the entry for you. Taking this first step to modernize your record-keeping can make the rest of the steps in your income-and-expenses checkup flow smoothly, whether you review your finances yourself or hire a specialist.

Financial planner Suzzanne Brubaker says that she frequently helps people review their finances when they have what she calls a "life event"—a retirement, the birth of a child, or a relocation. When Brubaker had her own life event—a corporate relocation from Los Angeles to Las Vegas in late 1996—she took stock of her own personal finances.

"One of the first things on my mind was the difference in tax rates," she says. "The other thing I gave a fair amount of consideration to was the cost of living."

Although it's generally cheaper to live outside the urban centers of California, Brubaker warns that not all costs are lower. Her utility rates, she says, are higher in Las Vegas than they were in the Los Angeles area. But state income tax is substantially lower. (Nevada doesn't have any income tax.)

With costs of living in mind, pro forma budgets came next. (Developing budgets is a natural for Brubaker; she is a division director in Las Vegas for Arthur Andersen & Co., a major national accounting firm. But it is important for anyone planning a relocation to develop a careful budget.) Brubaker says she noted what all her expenses were in Los Angeles and on that basis tried to budget what her expenses would be in Nevada. In addition, she added up the costs she might incur to move her household. This helped her negotiate with her employer for her moving expenses.

Even if you can only estimate what a portion of your living costs will be in your new hometown, that will be a useful place to start. Chambers of commerce, utility companies, and other sources can provide information to help you plan your budget before you move. Housing costs will be a large part of your living expense, but you will have some control over how much you will pay. How quickly you can sell your California home, and the price you get, is not out of your hands, but the condition of the market is a controlling factor. (See Chapter 8.) Estimating your taxes may be slightly easier. But Brubaker says that after she relocated, she incurred expenses that she hadn't anticipated. So she revisited her original budget to see just how realistic it was. "You should not just *do* a budget," she says, "but *use* it, especially for the first couple of months."

Bills, insurance, investments

"Organize, simplify, and consolidate," advises Brubaker. These words are well applied to your consumer credit. Look at all the credit cards you have with outstanding balances. Are you making car payments? Home-improvement payments? Student loan payments? All these liabilities will follow you out of state. If you can pay off some loans and consolidate others at lower rates, you'll be in a better position to handle unforeseen expenses in your new location.

When Andy Schneider moved his family *and* his company from Orange County to north Idaho, it took more than two years of planning. An important step he took was to consolidate both his business and personal debts. "In the last two years before we moved, I paid every bill that came in within two weeks," he says. "I practically had no accounts payable. I consolidated every debt I had. The only personal debt I brought with me was the mortgage to our new home." Schneider's conservatism helped him deal with the inevitable business challenges of moving a company out of state.

One element you may not normally include in your financial planning, but that can be critically important, especially if you or your spouse is changing jobs, is insurance coverage. If you change employers, you may have a gap in health, life, or disability insurance, between the time your old insurance coverage ends and your new employee coverage kicks in. To fill that gap, you may have to obtain coverage from a local California agent before you move, or get a referral from your local agent to someone in your new hometown. You are more likely to become disabled than to die, says Brubaker. So, depending on your age and general health, disability coverage could be more important than life insurance. Short-term disability coverage is offered through states and paid for via withholding taxes. For long-term disability coverage and life insurance, a good agent or financial planner can help you determine what makes the most sense in your situation.

If you have a will or trust, you will need to make changes or at least review the documents to be sure they comply with the laws when you move to another state. Visit a local estate attorney or use one of the will-making software packages that, Brubaker says, are becoming increasingly popular.

Young couples are less likely than, say, baby boomers, to have a will, but, says Brubaker, one strong incentive to have a will is that you will be able to designate who will be the guardians of your children if you and your spouse both die. It may be a difficult decision, she says, but it's better for you to leave your wishes in a will than to leave the future of your children to the courts.

As long as you are reviewing your fiscal standing, you need to look at your investments, reminds Brubaker. Your age and investment goals will be crucial factors in your investing strategy. And as many people have discovered, any investment plan is a balance between your financial needs and your ability to handle risks.

Brubaker's advice is to pay attention to the balance of your portfolio, rather than focus on individual investments, as some people tend to do. "In the long run," she says, "90 percent of your portfolio's performance is determined by how your assets are allocated among classes, i.e. stock and bonds, real estate, bank accounts." Over time, the percentage of your money in the various categories of investments is a more critical factor to your success than your choice of one stock over another, she says.

This good advice is obviously for those fortunate enough to *have* investments. Generally the older you are the more likely you are to be saving for the future. As you get older, your investment goals change—particularly as you approach retirement. If you're planing to retire when you move to another state, a review of your personal finances and investments is definitely in order. One of the advantages you'll find to exiting the Golden State when you start to withdraw from retirement accounts is that you can take your gold with you. Prior to 1997, people who maintained tax deferred retirement accounts or pensions in California, then retired in another state, found that California was sorry to see them go. So sorry, in fact, that the state dinged them for California income tax on withdrawals. The state wanted its once-deferred tax bite, regardless of the fact that the taxpayers were no longer residents of California.

"That was a bone of contention for an awfully long time," says Brubaker, "especially with the high-income-tax states such as a California and New York. And what you see is that people leave high-income-tax states when they retire."

The issue was settled in 1996 when Public Law 104-95 was approved by Congress. It says that you will have to pay state tax in the state in which you're living when you withdraw from your retirement account. So if you establish residence in Nevada, Washington or a few other states, your state income tax will be zilch.

Table 2.1 shows the income and sales tax rates for California and other states. These rates are just a starting point for you to determine your potential tax liability. First, the sales tax rates do not include local levies found in many cities and counties. For example, the table shows the California sales tax at 6 percent, but few people pay only that amount. Counties and other taxing districts throughout the state add local rates on top of the state rate. Second, other factors dictate which tax rate you will pay.

Verenda Smith, Governmental Affairs Associate for the Federation of Tax Administrators, says that to determine your income tax liability you must consider the source of your income, e.g. retirement accounts, wages, investments, Social Security. (Retirement income, wages, and income from the sale of some investments may be taxed at different rates.) In addition, people who move out of state but return to the state to do work for California clients, will be liable for local income taxes on money earned in California, she says. Further, property taxes account for a large portion of state and local revenue.

To get a better idea of what your combined tax bite might be, refer to the Web sites for the taxing agencies in your target destinations. If the site(s) do not contain the information you need, call the specific government agencies involved. (Web sites cited at the end of this chapter contain links to all state tax agencies.) You also can call county tax assessors' offices for property tax information. Real estate agents also have information on property tax rates and chambers of commerce can tell you about local sales tax rates.

This brief financial discussion is no substitute for professional advice from a financial planner (such as Brubaker), a tax accountant, or attorney. If you have concerns or questions about any financial aspect of your move, from insurance to debt consolidation, get professional advice. Brubaker recommends fee-based financial planners. In a new town, she says, you may come in contact with insurance or investment people who promise they will do a complete financial plan. But for these advisors to make money they have to sell a product. Fee-based advisors such as Brubaker sell only their time and do not have to recommend a particular product or investment.

Involve your children

Your children have a big stake in what will happen when you move. It's important to involve them in the plans and discussions about your possible relocation.

One of my strongest memories in my younger daughter's life was her first day in third grade. We had moved from Los Angeles to Orange County, and

State tax rates
(Percentages)

State	Sales tax	Personal Income Low High	Corporate Income Low High
Alaska	None	None	1.0 - 9.4
Arizona	5.00	3.0 - 5.6	9.00
California	6.00	1.0 - 9.3	8.84
Colorado	3.00	5.00	5.00
Florida	6.00	None	5.50
Hawaii	4.00	2.0 -10.0	4.4 - 6.4
Idaho	5.00	2.0 - 8.2	8.00
Illinois	6.25	3.00	7.30
Minnesota	6.50	6.0 - 8.5	9.80
Montana	None	2.0 -11.0	6.75
Nevada	6.50	None	None
New Mexico	5.00	1.7 - 8.5	4.8 - 7.6
New York	4.00	4.0 - 6.85	9.00
North Carolina	4.00	6.0 - 7.75	7.50
Oregon	None	5.0 - 9.0	6.60
Tennessee	6.00	Dividends/int.inc.only	6.00
Texas	6.25	None	None
Utah	4.875	2.3 - 7.0	5.00
Washington	6.50	None	None
Wisconsin	5.00	4.9 - 6.93	7.90
Wyoming	4.00	None	None

Table 2.1 This table provides an abbreviated overview. All figures are subject to change and qualifications. Sales tax rates do not include local levies, e.g. county sales taxes. Contact the specific taxing entities for current rates and requirements. Source: Federation of Tax Administrators. Used with permission.

while the 40-mile distance had little effect upon my wife and me, as far as Angie was concerned we may as well have moved across the country. She was removed from her neighborhood and friends and enrolled in a new school in a new town. I walked her to school the first morning and held her hand as we looked around for her classroom. I knew what it was like to be the new kid in school because when I was growing up my family had moved frequently. I had spent six years in six different elementary schools in three states. I introduced myself and Angie to her new teacher and saw Angie glancing expectantly around the room at the other students. Because we had moved over Labor Day, Angie started school only a few days after the moving van had left. We hadn't planned it this way, but beginning school when she did gave Angie an immediate chance to meet other children. As I walked out the classroom that day she was already talking with another student.

Dealing with the concerns of your children can be the toughest part of a move. For you, getting out of California means less congestion, lower home prices, shorter commute times, and perhaps a lower cost of living. For your son or daughter it means being snatched away from friends and familiar surroundings. Depending on their age, your children may not even fully understand what it means to be out of California, especially if they have lived in the Golden State all their lives. Ultimately your relocation can be loaded with benefits for your children, but initially it can be scary. One of the best ways to ease your children's apprehension is to include them in your discussions and research about your move.

According to Pandra Dickson, a Raleigh, N.C., real estate agent, you shouldn't expect much help in this aspect of your move from real estate companies or corporate relocation staff. Dickson, vice president of relocation services for Howard, Perry and Walston, is an advocate for helping children understand an inter-city move. Through industry presentations and trade journal articles, Dickson has been campaigning for companies to provide more assistance to parents and children. The young people's relocation program she created for her company could be a model for others.

When Dickson is working with a family relocating to her area, she finds out the names and ages of the children in the family and sends them a "kids' relocation package." The brightly colored folder includes a story book, crayons, a bank, activity book, map, and brochures on places of interest to kids such as parks and the local planetarium. "It's their own relocation packet and we try to send it addressed to them."

In addition, Dickson finds local pen pals for children who are moving to Raleigh. "We find out about their age and interests and where they might settle and try to match them up with somebody," says Dickson. The purpose is to let young people connect with someone in their new hometown even before they arrive. Says Dickson, "It gives them a chance to ask about hair styles and clothes. To ask, 'what's cool' and 'what's not.'" In some cases, students exchange phone calls. Dickson said she also has local Raleigh area children willing to correspond via the Internet.

While Dickson's program is only available if you're working with her firm, you can do some of the same things yourself. Rand McNally has state maps geared to children, she says, and van lines, insurance companies, museums, and zoos may have child-oriented materials. You can usually obtain brochures on places of interest to your children as easily as you acquire chamber of commerce booklets. Destination-oriented Web sites (discussed in the next chapter) let you print custom maps of the areas you want to explore. Share the maps with your kids.

Dickson, a 14-year real estate veteran who has specialized in relocation for the past nine years, says she only came to realize how important it is to include children in moving plans when she and her husband moved from Dallas to Raleigh a few years ago. Finding new employment and relocating the family were their priorities, she says. She and her husband didn't give enough attention to the concerns of their oldest son who was 12. He was adamantly opposed to moving, primarily because he would be leaving his grandparents. When Dickson and her husband visited Raleigh, travel expenses for her children were not covered, so they left the children at home. This, she says, was a mistake.

Dickson says that involving children in the early stages of planning helps them feel a part of the move and lets them express their concerns and ask questions.

Several aspects of moving, reviewed in this book, contain opportunities for you to work with your children. They range from gathering research on the Web to having your children help pack their belongings for the movers. Talk with your kids about the move. They may surprise you. At 14, my daughter Angie understood the reasons for our growing dissatisfaction with life in California and was not surprised when we started seriously discussing a move. She could cite the litany of smog, crime, and traffic. The more Anne and I talked about moving, the more Angie seemed to be interested.

Many of the California expatriates interviewed said they considered their children. In fact, their children often were the main reason for moving: the parents were looking for better schools and more friendly neighborhoods. Many said they moved before their children were in high school, because they knew moving with teens could be far more traumatic. Dickson, too, says younger children often have fewer problems in a move than those 12 and up.

When is the best season to move? Conventional wisdom says it's best to move in the summer. Summer is by far the busiest time of the year for van lines. "We heard for so many years to move in the summer time, but I think that's a mistake," says Dickson, "You need to move and get your children started in school immediately."

If you move during the summer it may mean your children will have a month or two of reduced opportunities to make friends. Yet making a friend soon in a new town is essential for most kids, says Dickson. While a new school may place some academic and social pressures on your children, depending on their ages, it also guarantees them opportunities to establish friendships. If you do move during the summer, Dickson recommends you enroll your children in local activities at Y camps, parks, or pools. Give them plenty of opportunities to meet other children their ages. "Get them onto the tennis court, into the pool, and around other kids," she advises.

But before you leave California, you have lots of work to do—and your children can help. The next chapter has suggestions for family destination research.

Resources

How to Get Control of Your Time and Your Life
Alan Lakein
New American Library, 1996

The Advisor *http://www.Americanexpress.com/advisors/assess*
This Web site, operated by American Express, contains calculators to help you determine your savings and investment needs.

Federation of Tax Administrators *http://www.sso.org/fta/fta.html*
This web site is designed for state tax agency employees, not consumers, but it contains comparative details on tax rates for every state, plus links to individual state tax agencies.

Tax Web *http://www.taxweb.com/research.html*
A great resource for state tax information, the site maintains separate pages for each state's tax rates and provides links to various taxing agencies. The site's master list of tax links is designed to help you research individual topics.

3

How to collect information

Scott Sullivan of Bakersfield had never been to Estacata, Ore., when he
visited the town for a job interview on Father's Day a few years ago. He
stopped in a real estate office to gather information and ask about a place
where he could get lunch.

When he finished his meal at a nearby bakery restaurant, and walked up
to the cashier, he was told his bill had already been paid.

"They told me: 'Somebody said you looked like a lonely father on Father's
Day, and bought your lunch,'" says Sullivan. "That's how I was introduced
to this town." His favorable first impression proved prophetic. He landed a
job teaching high school in Estacata and moved his family there.

Not all relocation search experiences are so positive. Vermont was high
on the list of new locations for Glenn and Sheri Sweitzer when they sought
escape from Burbank in 1993. "We looked in Vermont because we had so
many pictures in our mind of what it would be like there: Get out of the big
city, buy a farm and watch the deer." Their first impression of the small New
England state, however, was considerably less appealing than the calendar
photos. The couple soon discovered, "We would never fit in with the locals;
they don't like Californians much."

New-town searches involve more than just finding scenic spots. Pursuing
your personal utopia can be complex and time-consuming. It's an inexact
process that can pit your intellect against your emotions. Some people spend
months or years gathering information and impressions. Thanks to the World
Wide Web and other resources, however, you can collect volumes of information on other states and towns before you start to spend money on
exploratory trips. Many research suggestions in this chapter come from
California expats who used various techniques—from the telephone to networking—to track down information on potential hometowns. Most people
combined library-style research with family vacations.

Vern and Pattie Hesson took a meandering approach. When the Orange

County couple retired in the late 1980s, they put their furniture in storage, bought a motorhome, and set out to find a new place to live. They didn't particularly want to move to the desert, in part because Pattie worried about tarantulas and scorpions, so they focused their search on five states: Washington, Oregon, Idaho, Wyoming, and Montana.

Their envisioned ideal was a small town—about 5,000 people—but one with a hospital. Neither was ill, but they wanted to be prepared. They looked at towns as small as 2,500 to 3,000, rejecting those that didn't have a large supermarket—they didn't want to drive to the next town for groceries. Taxes also figured in their formula, and that made Idaho and Montana especially appealing.

How to get started

How you do your research is a personal choice. You can hit the road as the Hessons did or compile detailed files on towns before you ever leave your driveway. Or you can combine the Information Highway with interstate highways. This chapter introduces ways to collect information via the telephone, mail, and the Internet. The next chapter shows you how to dig deeper for data, and it concludes with ideas for intelligence-gathering trips to potential hometowns.

To start, look at your criteria for a new place to live. Use your wish list or quality-of-life factors as a guide. Review the tables throughout this book, such as the weather statistics (Table 5.1) or home prices (Tables 8.1 and 10.1), as well as other sources. Or pick cities you already know match at least some of your criteria—such as geography and size. Once you have a few candidate communities, gather more specific details on those specific locales. Many expats started their research with cities and towns they had visited on vacations or business trips.

For Scott Gordon and his wife Perla Pesciatini—who moved from San Juan Capistrano to Ft. Collins, Colo., in 1994—several factors were important. Gordon says he became disgusted with congestion in southern Orange County. It took him an hour to drive 13 miles to work. On weekends, beach traffic thwarted family freeway forays. "I'll never live in a big city again," says Gordon, who quit his job, moved, then started looking for work. The Gordons' search for a new hometown began with these initial criteria:

• A small town, but not too small (at least 50,000-60,000 people, to minimize culture shock).

• A university town. (Gordon says a college provides cultural and entertainment opportunities and generally indicates a level of sophistication in a community. "There are some dust specks out [in the West] without a college that make Riverside [Calif.] look appealing," he says.)

• Proximity to a larger city. (Amenities such as a regional airport and expanded shopping opportunities come with a city.)

Fort Collins, Colo., fit the Gordons' guidelines. About 60 miles north of Denver, this city of 104,000 people is home to Colorado State University.

Smaller towns within easy driving distance of major cities are appealing because they allow an escape from metropolitan congestion and still provide access to city conveniences and employment possibilities. (Gordon, for example, found a job in Fort Collins working for a Denver-based firm.) If this town-near-a-city strategy interests you, identify the largest cities in your target states, then look beyond the suburbs. How far out should you go? You're from California, so you probably don't mind driving 90 minutes round-trip for dinner, or an hour one-way for shopping or entertainment. The farther you settle from a big city, the more likely you will find less traffic, lower home prices, larger lots, and more open space. Besides, what's an hour's drive if you're rolling down country roads or nearly-empty highways?

Circle the city

Make a game out of finding promising hometowns. Involve the whole family. Use a large state map and pick a city, Seattle, for instance. Now find the map's scale of miles and cut a piece of string to equal 50 miles. Use the string to draw a circle with a 50-mile radius around Seattle. Now, how many communities do you find inside your circle? Close to Seattle are the suburbs of Bellevue, Redmond, and Kirkland—all a part of the same metropolitan area.

South along Interstate 5, on the other side of the Seattle-Tacoma Airport, are Federal Way, and the much larger Tacoma. The latter city is lumped in with Seattle for purposes of population statistics, but it has about 177,000 people all by itself. Southwest of Tacoma, the 50-mile radius includes such tiny communities as Buckley and Wilkeson.

To the north are Everett, and the fast-growing—but still relatively rural—community of Mount Vernon. To the east and northeast, the circle takes in a variety of small, water-oriented towns near Puget Sound, including Oak Harbor, Freeland, and Poulsbo (a Scandinavian community).

The circle method is fun to do with your kids, but of course it's imprecise because it measures air miles, not highway distances. The 50-mile circle around Seattle, for example, takes in Dungeness. But that small community, named for the crab of the same name, is more than 60 road miles from Seattle and requires a ferry ride across Puget Sound. So, you need to be more exact about road mileage. You can make reasonable estimates by using the mileage figures written on most maps or you can invest in a gadget that you roll over maps to measure distances. One such device is the Roller Route Map Measurer (about $7 retail). Your kids will have even more fun with the Map Measurer than they did with the string.

This particular measuring gizmo looks like a fat pen, except it has a small metal wheel where the pen point would be. You set the scale of miles on the barrel of the device according to the scale on your map. Then you simply roll the wheel along the roads leading out of Seattle until you reach 50 miles (or whatever distance is comfortable for you).

But maybe Seattle's average of 37 inches of rain per year sounds too wet to you. Try another example. Pull out a Nevada map, adjust your mileage gizmo, and zero in on Las Vegas. You'll find that if you want the advantages of the state's largest city, without living in the metro area, you have few choices. Boulder City—a quiet town of 12,000 people, where gaming is banned—is only a 24-mile drive to the center of Las Vegas, even fewer miles to suburban employment centers. But all the other towns within the 50-mile radius are either contiguous suburbs (such as North Las Vegas and Henderson), or tiny communities with few services (such as Blue Diamond or Glendale). Mesquite, Nev., St. George, Utah, and Bullhead City, Ariz., are the closest towns large enough to have the "Welcome to" and the "Now Leaving" signs on different posts.

The Circle the City game doesn't suit everyone or every city—and mapping software programs will do it for you—but it's an easy, inexpensive way to start your search. Another way to add to your list of place names, used by several expatriates interviewed, is to read directories—such as the *Places Rated Almanac,* or special issues of magazines that regularly rate cities. As mentioned in Chapter 1, *U.S. News and World Report* and *Money* magazines annually rate U.S. cities. The Sabatinis, who eventually moved to Michigan from Anaheim, started their search with Charleston, S.C., at the top of their list. It got their top ranking based upon an article on the best places to live. (See the end of this chapter for more directories of cities.)

No matter how you build a list of possible hometowns—from recommendations from friends to tossing darts at a U.S. map—once you have a few promising candidates, it's time to start collecting data. Even if you've been offered a transfer, are thinking about moving closer to relatives, or otherwise have but one destination in mind (Plan B), it's still wise to collect and evaluate information.

Gathering the facts

The advent of the Internet, and especially the World Wide Web, made research of nearly all types easier and cheaper. Much of the information you're looking for on cities and states is available on the Web. If you don't have access to the Web, or are not interested in collecting information via cyberspace, traditional methods work just as well. And they have benefits of their own, such as the opportunity to ask questions of live sources.

First we'll review techniques for conventional research, then look at ways to gather material online.

Collecting written information

Chambers of commerce should be first on your list. What you receive from them, and how much it costs, depends upon the city. Many medium-to-large cities offer free booklets or brochures and have other materials for sale. For example, the Phoenix chamber offers a $10 relocation guide book; a $35, 40-minute video; and a $3.50 map. The Boise, Idaho, chamber has a $12 booklet and $20 video. Some chamber packages include lists of local industries, demographic reports, real estate information, employment agency directories, and more. Chambers in smaller cities may send free chamber-produced booklets or brochures and include materials from local real estate firms, hotels, and other merchants. (Smaller chambers may include a request for a donation.)

By the way, don't be surprised if you start receiving materials from various companies after you've requested a chamber of commerce packet. In the weeks after I called Las Cruces, N.M., for instance, I received material from three real estate companies, two banks, a company that builds manufactured homes, a hotel, and a local shuttle bus service.

When you call a chamber, you may request *additional* information on housing, transportation or other areas of interest. Be sure to ask questions. Chamber employees and volunteers are local boosters, not necessarily objective third parties, but you can learn by asking and listening. When I called the St. George, Utah, chamber I talked with someone who had recently relocated from the San Bernardino area. She told me about the housing development where she lived in St. George, the size of lots, and the fact that ex-Californians were so plentiful in town she felt at home.

State chambers or travel bureaus also dispense information. In exchange for a phone call, any Western state will send you a free, color magazine-style booklet with enough breath-taking pictures to make you want to ditch urban California immediately. Materials from Arizona, Alaska, and Oregon are the most lavish, Utah's most informative. But don't judge a state by its brochure cover.

Real estate agents, particularly those who specialize in relocation, can be a pipeline of almost endless information on everything from school-district rankings to weather. But how do you find an out-of-state real estate agent without going out of state? The World Wide Web and out-of-town phone books are two ways. Pick one or more agents in each town and get on their mailing lists. Explain that you're considering moving, and are in the preliminary stages of picking a new hometown. Correspondence and phone conversations with an agent over a period of time can help you decide if an agent is someone with whom you would like to do business. (For detailed information on working with an out-of-town agent, see Chapters 9 and 10.)

Real estate agents are just one source of information. Others include insurance agencies, utility companies, and visitor and convention bureaus. Helpful chamber people can refer you to these and other possibilities—such as local newspapers and city magazines. The latter source may be of lesser value as city magazines often focus on fashion, entertainment, and local celebrities.

A visit to your local (California) library also can be time well spent. A large college or public library will likely have books and possibly videos on the states and cities that interest you. Travel and vacation guides also can be helpful, as can a variety of directories and atlases.

Be sure to check out the *Statistical Abstract of the United States,* the reference source for several of the tables in this book. You won't find detailed information on any one city in the *Statistical Abstract,* but rather page after page of comparisons. Among the interesting tables:

- the annual expenditures of local governments.
- political preference of voters in each state.
- number of miles of urban roadway (California has 81,000, Utah, 6,000).
- the number of hazardous waste sites on the national priority list (California has 96, Oregon, 12, Nevada, 1).

Libraries also contain periodical guides—both printed and electronic—that can lead you to magazine articles on cities and states and other moving-related topics. Business, travel, and general news magazines probably are the most helpful. Some libraries also have out-of-town phone directories, often on microfiche. Ask the librarian for help.

Online searching

To supplement conventional research you can explore the vast resources of the World Wide Web and communicate online with locals in your target areas. If you're a novice at navigating the Web, see Appendix A for information on Internet basics. If necessary, have a knowledgeable friend (or your 12-year-old) help you get started. The mass of free information on the Web makes it well worth the time to learn the system. It's not difficult. One note about Web research: The online world is constantly evolving. All the Web information and sites discussed in this and other chapters, therefore, are subject to change. When searching the Web for relocation help, you will find vast resources beyond the specific Web pages referenced in this book. The Web itself, including its search engines and directories, is the best guide to the information on the Web. Addresses for all Web sites, and other resources mentioned, are listed at the end of each chapter. Explore a little on your own, and you'll be able to download until your hard drive is swimming in data.

Novice or expert, one of the best places to start is with the home page(s) of the state(s) you're interested in. Most of the official state home pages, operated by state governments, have similar Web addresses which are easy to remember. Nevada's home page, for example, is *http://www.state.nv.us/*. The Web address for Washington is similar: *http://www.state.wa.us/*. You generally use the two-letter postal abbreviation for a state to create its address. (Montana's address is slightly different: *http://www.state.mt.gov/*.) To see what you can find on a typical state home page, take a brief (virtual) fact-finding trip to Oregon at *http://www.state.or.us/*. That address leads you to a spectacular picture of Crater Lake. Floating over the lake are four buttons labeled: Government, Community, Commerce, Education. A click on any one leads you to several layers of sites. Since you're interested in city information for now, click on "Community." You'll see a list of links to more than 50 Oregon cities and towns.

This page of links alone could keep you busy for quite a while (if you have Oregon towns in mind). For an example, click on "Eugene Home Page." The page is devoted primarily to links to other sites. Rather than being shown in list form, the links are highlighted in text about city services, special events, and other topics.

In the paragraph describing community resources is a link to the Eugene Chamber of Commerce. Click over to the chamber's home page and you can jump to pages on a variety of topics including retirement, economy, recreation, culture, and housing. To find background information about Eugene, click on the chamber site's link to "demographics & other statistics."

You've finally reached a site with meaty information, rather than lists of links. Scroll down and you'll find several pages of statistics and information on the climate, schools, industry, and population of Eugene. If Eugene's one of your choice cities, you should print or download these pages. (You will discover that the average rainfall is 46 inches, Weyerhaeuser Co. is the largest local manufacturer, and the town is home to the 17,000-student University of Oregon.)

Backtrack one level to the chamber of commerce links and click on another option: "Order Information." You'll see an order form to complete and fax back along with a credit-card number. Among the materials you can buy are a report and directory of high-tech businesses in Oregon, plus two detailed relocation packages. Before you buy, call to request free information and scour the Web. In some cases, chamber information for sale is duplicated on the Web.

From the Eugene Chamber order form, backtrack to the chamber site that led you to the demographics. If education is important to you, click on "Schools and Education." What you see first is the chamber's summary of schools and school districts in the area. You can then click on a particular district, Eugene 4J, for example.

If your mouse clicking finger is getting tired, take a break. The district's first screen is simply a list of district links. Information on individual schools is still several clicks away.

Don't expect a hoard of useful data in school-district sites. From the many selections available on the main menu, the Eugene 4J School District site would seem to be packed with information. Instead it includes such platitudes as: "This is a student-centered district; everything we do must be good for children." On another page the district advises: "To the extent possible, our resources will go directly into the instructional process." Such trivial generalities give you no clue about the education you can expect for your children. Some districts are more forthcoming; many are not. You will have to look elsewhere for meaningful school information. (Start with Table 3.1.)

This brief tour of Eugene shows just a fraction of the online information available. It also points up two drawbacks to Web research: First, it's time consuming. Even if you have a state-of-the-art browser and modem, you will still wait for pages to download on your screen. Second, Web sites often emphasize form over substance. To find just a few paragraphs of useful narrative on a topic, you may have to click through several levels of menus and directories. The mammoth amount of free information on the Web, however, usually is worth the wait—especially since you can do your research from the comfort of your home (with an adult beverage at hand to help you through the dull moments).

Sites to see

When you're Web surfing, state home pages are good jumping-off points. But other online ways to investigate cities abound. For example, four Web companies—three of which operate search engines—offer city networks. These are labyrinths of sites filled with specific information and links. Check out these sites:

Excite City.Net This network is part of the popular search engine, Excite. In addition to travel articles and lists of links, City Net lets you download city maps, pinpointing any address you specify. The maps can zoom to surrounding towns, landmarks, and highways.

Lycos City Guide Among the many links offered are ones that let you discover "hot spots" and "local flavor." Albuquerque's hot spots, for example, include the International Balloon Fiesta and Sandia Peak. Examples of local flavor include the Indian Pueblo Cultural Center and the Art Collectors Guide. Some maps are also available.

USA City Link claims to be the "Internet's most comprehensive listing of Web pages featuring U.S. states and cities." But its list of cities for some Western states is skimpy. There are, however, feature stories on cities throughout the U.S.

Yahoo Regional: U.S. States Lacking the flashy graphics and pictures of the other sites, this series of directories is straightforward and easy to use. You can select from city- and state-oriented links, and then choose from a hodgepodge of other sites covering such things as gardening, road conditions, and local newsgroups.

What you'll discover, using a couple of these city directories, is that sites are interconnected. Whether you start out on the Yahoo directory or City Net, you'll eventually find most of the same Web pages. Spend time exploring one or two of the directories and you'll have a good idea of the city resources and information available on the Web.

You may also see references to online travel services. These sites also are worth visiting, even though they focus more on reservations and accommodations than on destination information. Agencies such as Travelocity and TravelWeb have complex sites with useful links.

As you navigate around the Web, here are the types of location-oriented sites you may find useful:

Chambers of commerce The mainstay of a city's online promotion, chamber sites come in all sizes.

Visitors and Convention Bureaus Even some small cities have visitors bureaus that can provide useful information. In Flagstaff, Ariz., for example, the Convention and Visitors Bureau has an appealing site with cartoons, photos, and good ideas. (The local chamber is found elsewhere.)

Municipalities Depending upon the city, you'll find information about anything from trash collection to parks and recreation.

Counties Sites for counties tend to include more statistics and fewer promotional messages than city and chamber sites. You can read about topics from road work to social welfare services to demographics. On the site for Larimer County, Colo., for example, is a lengthy health-indicator report, with information ranging from the local level of food safety to instances of diseases (including cancer and AIDS). To locate county sites, look for links on other pages, check the National Association of County Governments at *http:www.naco.org/links/counties.html,* or use Yahoo Regional.

Schools Universities usually have detailed, well-designed sites rich with information including community activities. School district sites are less available and generally contain less information.

Real Estate Do a search-engine search using just a city name and chances are the majority of sites you find will be sponsored by real estate firms. Real estate sites range from unintentionally comical (and useless) to invaluable. They frequently contain community information. They're discussed in Chapter 9.

Commercial/community Obviously you can find sites for many local merchants in your destination cities. In addition to one-company sites, many community pages are put together by groups of merchants. An example is *Colorado Links.*

Cooperative As communities have become aware of the possibilities for online communication, organizations have started public Web sites to promote community service. The *Eugene Free Community Network,* a service of Oregon Public Networking, is an example.

Malls If you're seriously interested in local shopping opportunities, you may find online malls originating from local areas. For example, the *Pan Handle Pages* serves residents of north Idaho.

Most of the sites and services mentioned are promotional as well as informational. To get a second-party view of your target towns, you can use the Web to locate magazine and newspaper articles about your proposed destinations. One place to look is *Pathfinder,* the home of Time Warner Communications and CNN. Here you can search back issues of *Money, Fortune, Time* and other publications.

Newspapers are a valuable resource. Most dailies have online versions that let you read about local issues and conditions. Many large online papers also feature links to local and regional Web sites. The Denver *Rocky Mountain News,* for example, features links to interesting Colorado sites. At the end of this chapter is an additional resource for finding online papers. You can

Education ratings by state

State	Pupil-teacher ratio	4th Grade reading	——SATs—— Verbal	Math	Percent taking SAT
Alaska	17.6	n/a	445	489	47
Arizona	19.3	206	448	496	27
California	24.0	197	417	485	45
Colorado	18.4	213	462	518	29
Florida	19.1	205	420	469	48
Hawaii	17.9	201	407	482	57
Idaho	19.1	n/a	468	511	15
Illinois	17.3	n/a	488	560	13
Minnesota	17.5	218	506	579	9
Montana	16.3	222*	473	536	21
Nevada	18.7	n/a	434	483	30
New Mexico	17.2	205	485	530	11
North Carolina	16.2	214	411	454	60
Oregon	19.9	n/a	448	499	51
Tennessee	18.6	213*	497	543	12
Texas	15.7	212	419	474	47
Utah	24.3	217	513	563	4
Washington	20.2	213	443	494	48
Wisconsin	15.9	224*	501	572	9
Wyoming	15.0	221	476	525	10
United States	17.3	212	428	482	41

*Did not satisfy one or more of the guidelines for school sample participation rates. The data are therefore not reliable.

Table 3.1 Here are three different ratings for state educational systems. The first column shows the ratio of students to teachers for 1994. From the U.S. Department of Education, National Center for Education Statistics, Common Core of Data Survey. The second column shows average proficiency in reading for fourth graders. From the National Assessment of Educational Progress. The last three columns show Scholastic Assessment Test scores (formerly called the Scholastic Aptitude Test), for 1994-95. Note the last column shows the percentage of high school graduates per state who took the test. SAT scores Copyright 1995 by the College Entrance Examination Board. Reprinted with permission.

also search back issues of large California newspapers for stories on relocation. If you search the *LA Times* back issues, however, you'll find articles showing the perils of an out-of-state move, but few success stories. Don't be dis-
mayed. (See Chapter 14.)

Another source of online information is your Internet service. If you're
hooked up to the Microsoft Network, America Online, or a similar service,
you may find information without having to browse the Web. As an example, AOL offers Digital City—individual views of cities, similar to the commercial city sites such as City Guide. AOL subscribers also can access an online
version of the book *Retirement Places Rated* and they can see links to real estate
information from Century 21.

Talking to locals

In addition to providing information for you to read, the Internet also
contains opportunities for you to communicate (more or less directly) with
residents of your target cities. For example, to find out more about what it's
like to live in the Portland area, Sullivan, (while still in Bakersfield) spent
time in AOL chat rooms "talking" with Oregonians. AOL, like the other
online services, has chat areas organized geographically.

Sullivan says he used the Portland area chat rooms to ask questions about
weather, crime, and other topics. After Sullivan moved to Estacada, he
attended a gathering of his online friends at a Portland pub. Also, since he's
an avid ocean surfer, Sullivan surfed the Web to find information about surfing the Oregon coast.

The most popular way to exchange messages on the Internet is via usenet
newsgroups. You can search newsgroup messages (called postings) looking
for discussions on relocation or on the cities that interest you. You can even
find newsgroups devoted to individual cities.

To read and post messages, you need special software called a reader.
Your Internet service provider may offer this software, or you may be able
to download it from the Internet. To locate and search newsgroups, try the
search engines *Deja News,* or the *Liszt Directory.* Each engine will search for
names of specific newsgroups or will search the texts of newsgroup postings looking for the key words you enter. The easiest way to locate people
in or near your target city is to find local newsgroups. Of the thousands of
online newsgroups, many are devoted to discussions of local areas and issues.
Once you locate a useful group, monitor the messages to get an idea of the
topics discussed before you post questions. Bear in mind, the response you
get may not be the absolute, accurate answer you need, but simply a person's opinion.

For example, a woman interested in moving from San Francisco to Austin, Texas posted questions on the *Austin.Talk* newsgroup. When she asked about housing prices, she received replies from several people eager to help. Trouble was, she got conflicting information. "Expect to pay S.F. prices," wrote one Austin resident. "I don't think so," wrote another. The second contributor said prices were lower than San Francisco; he suggested she read the *Austin American Statesman* to discover rental prices. A later posting from someone else told her how to find *Statesman* classified ads on the Web. The potential San Francisco escapee also received advice on weather, night life, and the best neighborhoods in town. "Weather," wrote one respondent, "that's the shock you'll really feel, not culture shock—except fo' the way we-all tawk."

Another way net surfers communicate is mailing lists. These are similar to newsgroups, except all messages are sent to list members via e-mail. Usenet search engines also provide information on mailing lists.

These information sources are just the beginning. Chamber of commerce brochures and city Web sites should sharpen your appetite for more. When you start asking: "How much rain do they really get?" and "How good are the schools?", it's time for your graduate-level lesson in city research. That comes in the next chapter.

Resources

Useful Web sites
For the address of most states, fill in the blank with the state's two-digit postal code: *http://www.state.__.us/*

Lycos City Guide *http://cityguide.lycos.com*

Excite City Net *http://city.net/regions/north_america/*

USA City Link *http://www.usacitylink.com/citylink*

Yahoo Regional *http://www.Yahoo.com/Regional/U_S_States*

City of Eugene Home Page *http://www.ci.Eugene.or.us*

Eugene, Ore. Chamber home page *http://www.eugene-commerce.com/*

Travelocity *http://www.travelocity.com*

Flagstaff Convention and Visitors Bureau
  http://www.Flagstaff.az.us/v&c.html

Colorado Links *http://www.entertain.com/wedgwood/colinks.html*

National Association of County Governments
  http://www.naco.org/links/counties.html

Eugene Free Community Network *http://www.efn.org*

Panhandle Pages *http://www.northernwebs.com/ppages*

Boise, Idaho Chamber *http://www.boise.org*

Pathfinder *http://www.Pathfinder.com*

Rocky Mountain News *http://www.denver-rmn.com*

Links to online daily newspapers in the U.S.
http://www.potter.net/mediasite/newspaper.html

Deja News *http://www.dejanews.com*

Liszt Directory *http://www.liszt.com*

Books and directories

Retirement Living Communities
Deborah Freundlich
Macmillan, 1995
   Described here are more than 400 retirement communities in 39 states offering independent living and a variety of health-care services.

Everything You Need to Know About Retirement Housing
Joan Cleveland
Penguin, 1996

Green Index: A State-by-State Guide to the Nation's Environmental Health
Bob Hall, Mary Lee Kerr
Island Press, 1991

Places Rated Almanac, 5th ed.
David Savageau, Geoffrey Loftus
Macmillan, 1997

Rating Guide to Life in America's Small Cities
G. Scott Thomas
Prometheus Books, 1990

*Retirement Places Rated: All You Need to Plan Your Retirement
or Select Your Second Home*
David Savageau
Prentice Hall, 1995

The 100 Best Small Towns in America, 2nd ed.
Norman Crampton
Arco Pub., 1996

Facts About the Cities, 2nd ed.
Allan Carpenter, Carl Provorse
H.W. Wilson Co., 1996

4

Digging deeper: Hunting for sources and hitting the road

A s you get more serious about your move, you may have second thoughts about your priorities. Your investigations may bring up new issues. In that case, dig deeper. Review the data you've accumulated and look for esoteric sources. Collecting detailed weather information, for example, is one way to expand your research.

Michael McKown, who moved from the East Bay to Douglas, Wyo., started his research at 10 p.m. one evening in Oakland; he bought out-of-town newspapers at a newsstand. Like many people, his research expanded and he eventually acquired "pounds and pounds of information"—including newspapers, real estate brochures, and videos from real estate agents. McKown, publisher of a small periodical, *Dog Sport Magazine,* said he asked his readers if they liked the places they lived, and if they had suggestions on moving.

One of McKown's priorities was weather. He has asthma and wanted a place with constant low humidity. When his preliminary research didn't provide the detail he wanted, he investigated further and discovered the National Climatic Data Center in Asheville, N.C. It's a treasure trove of weather information, available at nominal cost. Weather data that McKown received on temperature, precipitation, and humidity led him to eastern Wyoming.

Data: Climate to crime

National weather information

Noel Risnychok is a meteorological technician at the National Climatic Data Center in North Carolina. He says the center receives a steady stream of calls from people, like McKown, who are thinking of relocating. A mass of printed and CD-ROM weather information is available. But unless you're a meteorologist, you probably will be content with a few of NCDC's publications. Two large booklets, for example, provide an overview of climate for nearly 300 towns in the U.S. (They're the source of the information in the weather table in this book.) You can order weather booklets for each state, giving you detailed data for dozens of cities. When you call the NCDC, talk with a technician and carefully explain what you're looking for—whether it's an overview of U.S. climate, or specific information on a small area. (Risnychok says NCDC employees usually ask questions so they can recommend the right source.) Sometimes, he says, the technicians will refer a caller to sources available in local public libraries, such as *Climatology of the United States,* published by Gale Research.

Table 5.1 shows selected climate figures, giving you an idea of what weather is like in a variety of cities. The table shows the average number of sunny days, partially sunny days, and cloudy days for each city. (See the end of this chapter for more information on ordering weather data.)

Temperature and precipitation are important, but the amount of sunshine may overshadow the other figures. In Flagstaff, Ariz., for example, where winter temperatures fall below those of other Western cities, the sun shines a majority of the time. It may be easier to cope with snow in Flagstaff if the sun is shining.

Phone Books

Many California expats used the simple expedient of phone books to check out community resources. Some picked up phone books on visits, some found them in their local California libraries; some had phone books sent to them. More and more chambers of commerce are now selling local phone books to people interested in relocation. No matter how you get your hands on phone books, you can deduce many things about communities by flipping through the pages.

Take Boise, Idaho, for example. If you've received mixed reports about snow in the winter, the phone book may provide a hint. The Boise book has 20 listings under snow removal services and features a full page of snowboard and snowmobile dealer listings. Sounds like Boise gets more than just a light dusting occasionally. But it could also indicate that mountain ski areas are close by.

In the summer, boating is apparently popular; ads for boat dealers take up three pages. Indoor activities? Boise has 15 health clubs. Computer service or sales? The book has more than 11 pages worth. Will you be able to get service on your foreign car? Boise boasts dealerships for Kia, Saab, Land Rover, Isuzu, and even Ferrari—in addition to more common foreign makes.

In case you are concerned there won't be enough lawyers to serve you in Boise, flip through the A's. Thirty-eight pages of attorneys. Too many? Try a Phoenix phone book. It contains nearly 150 pages of attorneys.

You can even discover inter-community relationships via the phone book. Under many categories in the Cheyenne, Wyo., book, for example, are listings for companies and services in Fort Collins, Colo. Half the golf courses in the Cheyenne book are across the border—about 40 miles away in Fort Collins. What you can't find in Cheyenne you may find in Colorado.

Look at any letter of the alphabet, and a phone book can tell you about products or services that may be important to you. The H's, for example, will tell you about hardware stores, health clubs, health food, hearing aids, hobby shops, home health services, horse stables, hospitals, and house cleaning. Many telephone directories also now include color-coded community pages, containing maps and information on local shopping, events, and parks.

The size of phone books can give you an idea of how much smaller your prospective communities really are. Many out-of-state books covering vast geographic areas may be about as slim as neighborhood directories in California. At the other extreme, you can spot the growing cities by their books, too. The listings in Las Vegas recently got too large to fit in one book; now there are two, issued every *six months* to keep up with the growth. And if you had doubts about the weather there, look up air conditioning companies. You'll find 18 pages of listings.

Newspapers

When my family and I were considering moving to Portland (before we settled in Nevada) we subscribed to the *Portland Oregonian* by mail. Short of visiting a community, reading its newspaper is one of the best ways to collect both quantitative and qualitative information. News sections tell you about local crime, municipal issues, and which political party seems to have the most influence. You can read about the activities of charities, street gangs, schools, clubs, state agencies, community groups, and merchants. Articles may tell you about race relations, environmental issues, funding for education. Weather reports provide insight into local conditions. The sports pages may give you a hint about the amount of support given to local high school and college teams.

One ex-California couple said they even selected a church from an out-of-town newspaper. A feature article on a local pastor attracted their interest. When they moved, they attended one of his services and eventually joined the church.

Newspaper ads can be as valuable as the stories. Ads for supermarkets and department and discount stores tell you the variety of these outlets available and give you an idea of prices. Classified ads tell you the number and types of jobs listed in town. Real estate ads offer a way to evaluate property values. Also of interest may be ads for sporting goods, movie theatres, restaurants, clothing stores, office supplies, and automobiles. Many papers also feature business directories where you find small ads for handyman services, home cleaning, gardeners, and painters.

The number of local newspapers and other publications in an area may tell you something else. Few towns today support two daily newspapers, so the presence of a second paper, or of community papers competing with a larger daily, may indicate a vigorous economy with enough advertising to go around. It could also be an indication of the locals' literacy. In Sun City West, Ariz., a retirement community near Phoenix, the abundance of newspapers and other local periodicals is indicative of (1) the steady economy, (2) the locals' interest in reading, and (3) their amount of free time (to read). The small community has at least two weekly newspapers, a small daily and a variety of free, advertising-supported publications. This is in addition to the giant *Arizona Republic* that covers the entire Phoenix metro area.

School districts

Collecting information long distance is the first step in investigating school districts. The amount and usefulness of information available via the mail and the Web will vary greatly from one state and district to another. A place to start would be a state's department of education, or office of the superintendent of public instruction. Ask for the public information officer. Find out if the state provides comparison information on districts or schools. Most states have statewide testing programs—usually called assessments—and have scores available in some form. In Washington State, for example, the office of the state superintendent of public instruction recently published a booklet showing five years' worth of achievement tests for grades 4, 8, and 11. The comparison tables show the highest-ranking districts.

Usually districts or individual schools will send out packets of information upon request. The material typically includes school addresses and phone numbers, district/school boundaries, an academic calendar, statement of educational philosophy, and details on the school board, budget, food service, and bus transportation. Test scores may be included. Sometimes state school officials may refer you to a district or county schools office. That is the case in Albuquerque, where the Albuquerque Public Schools District covers Bernalillo County and portions of an adjoining county. The district sends out 5,000 information packets annually in response to inquiries from potential residents.

In contrast to other states, Arizona has open enrollment, meaning students do not have to reside in a particular district in order to attend a certain school. The state legislature mandates that each school provide its own "report card" showing such things as teacher-student ratios, test scores, and even the number of times the police have been called to the campus. The school reports are available from individual schools or from the state education department. The open-enrollment policy promotes competition; school report cards include messages from principals telling you why your children should attend his or her school. Added to the competitive mix are more than 100 charter schools—privately operated but publicly funded institutions—that are usually smaller than traditional public schools.

To complete your education research you can visit schools and talk with officials. According to experts, here are some of the details you should ask about:

Test scores For high schools, ask for the average scores on SAT and ACT tests and compare them with local and national averages.

Average class size This is a more helpful figure than a student/staff ratio; the latter may include administrators as well as teachers. Class size may be more critical in elementary schools. For a rough comparison see Table 3.1.

Placement in local competitions Districts may have math bowls, Shakespeare Festivals, Constitution Day, or other inter-school competition. Find out which schools or districts consistently place first.

High school graduation rate Depending on the schools' standards, or lack thereof, this figure could be deceiving.

Percentage of students going on to postsecondary education

Magnet schools, enrichment programs, foreign languages Ask about programs your son or daughter may be interested in. Does the high school have a variety of foreign languages from which to choose?

Double sessions In the fastest growing areas of the West some districts are so severely strained they're forced to hold double sessions. Ask bluntly.

School site councils Many schools have these councils, made up of parents, teachers, and administrators. (They've been a part of some California schools for more than 10 years so you may be familiar with them.) Parents generally reach council positions through elections. Councils vary, but they usually have authority in how some funds are spent, thus giving parents a measure of local control over education.

In addition to gathering school information yourself, you can enlist the help of SchoolMatch, a Westerville, Ohio, consulting and research firm that will provide you a detailed report on the schools in the area(s) you select. The SchoolMatch Web site, at *http://www.schoolmatch.com,* is worth visiting. It contains articles that explain the differences among school districts in different states and shows you a sample of the school ratings reports they sell.

Another online resource is the School District Data Book, from the National Center for Education Studies. It contains statistics on all 15,274 districts in the U.S. It's available on the Oregon State University site mentioned later in this chapter.

To explore private schools, visit the Web site of the National Association of Independent Schools. The site features articles on choosing private schools, lists of school directories, and a searchable school database.

For out-of-state colleges and universities, request a catalog and study it. Review the sections on accreditation, academic programs, athletics, costs, entrance requirements. Various directories that rate and evaluate universities are available in libraries and bookstores. When you get serious about a particular college, arrange a visit with an advisor in a specific field of study. Be sure to ask about the requirements to qualify for residents' tuition. It's likely you won't be able to move to a community and immediately enroll your child or yourself at the resident-tuition rate. Ask about the waiting period and other restrictions or exemptions.

Crime rates

Along with superior schools, a low crime rate is high on many families' priority lists. The most accessible crime rate figures that permit you to compare cities against each other come from the FBI. The Bureau's Uniform Crime Report, issued annually and available in many libraries, lists a variety of crime figures—for both violent and property offenses. Selected figures from the FBI report are listed in Tables 4.1 and 4.2.

The crime figures can be misleading and should be used only as a general guide. For example, the bulk of the data is organized by Metropolitan Statistical Areas. Central city areas are averaged with suburban and rural county areas to come up with one set of figures for each MSA. The resulting figures, therefore, are averages, not necessarily indicative of the crime rate for any one neighborhood in an MSA. The MSAs are compared on the basis of number of crimes per 100,000 people. For many areas, particularly small towns, the FBI reports the raw data only, without comparison rates.

Methods of reporting and classifying crime also may vary from one jurisdiction to another. Unique local conditions, which may have little effect on residential crime, can alter results. In small towns, just a few additional crimes above the average can, statistically, seem like a crime wave. In addition, the

FBI Uniform Crime Report per 100,000 inhabitants

Metropolitan Statistical Area	Crime Index total	Violent crime	Property crime	Murder non-negligent manslaughter	Forcible rape	Robbery	Aggravated assault	Burglary	Larceny theft	Motor vehicle theft
Albuquerque, N.M.	7,521.9	879.4	6,642.5	9.7	56.2	265.6	547.9	1,584.9	4,228.3	829.3
Anchorage, Alaska	7,220.9	990.1	6,230.8	11.4	95.5	306.5	576.7	994.5	4,399.2	837.1
Austin-San Marcos, Texas	6,051.2	579.6	5,471.6	5.6	50.3	154.2	369.5	1,157.5	3,873.2	440.9
Bellingham, Wash.	5,715.1	332.2	5,382.9	3.4	77.1	50.1	201.6	983.7	4,171.8	227.3
Boise, Idaho	5,165.6	366.4	4,799.1	3.1	31.1	32.8	299.5	835.1	3,666.6	297.5
Boulder-Longmont, Colo.	5,328.5	247.4	5,081.0	3.5	44.2	40.7	159.1	993.7	3,851.6	235.7
Bryan-College Station, Texas	6,028.1	502.8	5,525.3	4.5	65.5	88.8	344.0	975.6	4,293.0	256.7
Casper, Wyo.	6,336.4	336.8	5,999.6	7.8	23.3	35.7	270.1	1,162.7	4,456.6	380.3
Charlotte, N.C.	6,703.2	1,038.6	5,664.5	11.5	42.6	291.2	693.3	1,374.8	3,895.0	394.8
Cheyenne, Wyo.	4,097.2	166.4	3,930.8	0.0	38.1	33.0	95.3	403.9	3,392.3	134.6
Colorado Springs Colo.	5,563.2	416.4	5,146.8	5.2	49.4	96.4	265.4	915.1	3,880.2	351.5
Denver, Colo.	5,591.3	513.4	5,077.9	6.9	39.7	141.6	325.3	986.9	3,562.0	528.9
El Paso, Texas	6,623.4	802.0	5,821.4	6.2	42.4	168.9	584.5	659.4	4,555.5	606.5
Eugene-Springfield, Ore.	7,233.4	403.8	6,829.6	3.9	41.1	135.7	223.1	1,391.3	4,959.5	478.8
Fort Collins-Loveland, Colo.	4,405.6	301.0	4,104.6	1.8	66.2	24.4	208.6	660.7	3,278.9	165.0
Fresno, Calif.	8,566.2	1,189.0	7,377.2	13.9	49.1	335.7	790.2	1,678.5	3,760.6	1,938.1
Honolulu, Hawaii	7,627.8	327.4	7,300.4	4.3	24.7	155.7	142.7	1,150.4	5,304.8	845.2
Houston, Texas	5,633.8	856.1	4,777.7	12.0	42.0	308.0	494.2	1,127.5	2,788.1	862.1
Kenosha, Wis.	3,585.5	278.6	3,307.0	3.6	31.7	77.7	165.6	681.7	2,392.8	232.5
Las Cruces, N.M.	5,685.0	570.8	5,114.2	7.6	56.2	87.8	419.2	1,360.0	3,421.5	332.7
Las Vegas, Nev.	7,408.6	1,085.9	6,322.7	12.2	66.5	394.4	612.8	1,550.9	3,852.0	919.9
Los Angeles-Long Beach, Calif.	6,141.8	1,422.6	4,719.2	18.3	34.6	569.7	800.1	1,052.3	2,554.3	1,112.7

Madison, Wis.	3,978.3	259.2	3,719.2	1.3	25.9	87.5	144.5	559.5	2,913.2	246.5
Medford-Ashland, Ore.	6,273.9	470.8	5,803.1	4.8	39.3	56.3	370.3	962.1	4,481.5	359.4
Minneapolis- St. Paul, Minn.	5,287.2	489.9	4,797.3	5.7	57.2	198.5	228.4	878.2	3,474.3	444.8
Nashville, Tenn.	7,262.3	1,088.2	6,174.1	12.0	60.8	273.5	742.0	1,168.1	4,133.6	872.4
Olympia, Wash.	4,530.8	296.9	4,233.9	2.1	54.6	48.9	191.3	978.9	2,960.8	294.2
Orlando, Fla.	7,123.5	1,007.0	6,116.5	5.7	47.9	246.6	708.8	1,513.0	4,027.2	576.3
Phoenix-Mesa, Ariz.	8,808.5	765.0	8,043.5	11.9	32.3	209.5	511.3	1,618.1	4,932.4	1,493.0
Portland, Ore.	6,738.1	726.9	6,011.3	3.7	52.7	196.3	474.1	1,066.8	4,004.6	939.8
Provo–Orem, Utah	4,551.1	146.9	4,404.3	0.7	25.9	15.1	105.2	568.9	3,635.7	199.6
Pueblo, Colo.	6,724.2	1,072.3	5,651.9	7.6	37.5	140.6	886.6	1,314.6	3,916.2	421.1
Reno, Nev.	5,926.8	574.2	5,352.6	7.1	46.4	182.4	338.3	1,087.1	3,836.6	428.8
Riverside-San Bernardino, Calif.	6,409.2	945.5	5,463.7	12.3	35.8	266.9	630.4	1,605.8	2,809.2	1,048.6
Salem, Ore.	7,695.3	298.5	7,396.8	5.8	40.5	146.8	135.4	1,214.8	5,482.4	699.6
Salt Lake City, Utah	7,200.3	411.4	6,788.9	4.1	51.5	100.6	255.3	921.0	5,357.4	510.5
San Antonio, Texas	6,697.4	484.3	6,213.1	10.9	54.3	173.6	245.6	1,179.1	4,386.3	647.7
San Diego, Calif.	5,030.5	794.5	4,236.0	7.5	27.4	222.7	536.9	976.4	2,375.1	884.5
San Francisco. Calif.	5,833.8	884.3	4,949.5	8.5	30.2	459.4	386.2	779.9	3,467.1	702.5
Spokane, Wash.	6,693.7	510.2	6,183.5	6.5	50.2	142.6	310.9	1,239.6	4,560.0	384.0
Tacoma, Wash.	7,237.4	873.2	6,364.2	8.2	59.6	216.3	589.1	1,293.1	4,315.2	755.9
Tucson, Ariz.	9,769.5	877.2	8,892.3	12.2	52.3	192.0	620.7	1,157.0	6,740.9	994.3
Western U.S.	6,082.7	770.4	5,312.3	9.0	38.6	241.5	481.3	1,111.1	3,435.0	766.1
U.S.A.	5,277.6	684.6	4,593.0	8.2	37.1	220.9	418.3	987.6	3,044.9	560.5

Table 4.1 These crime statistics show incidence of crime per 100,000 population. The data here cannot be directly compared to Figure 4.2, which shows raw crime totals for some communities. Source: Federal Bureau of Investigation. Statistics are for 1995, released October 13, 1996.

Number of offenses known to the police

City	Population	Crime Index total	Murder, non-negligent manslaughter	Forcible rape	Robbery	Aggravated assault	Burglary	Larceny, theft	Motor vehicle theft
Boulder City, Nev.	13,747	483	0	3	5	21	117	316	21
Bremerton, Wash.	43,015	2,230	3	55	46	89	414	1,451	172
Coos Bay, Ore.	17,625	1,561	0	6	15	15	235	1,193	97
Grand Junction, Colo.	32,548	3,868	3	17	38	172	527	2,964	147
Lake Havasu City, Ariz.	33,014	1,890	0	7	12	86	403	1,277	105
Missoula, Mont.	46,106	4,118	3	14	29	76	355	3,471	170
Oak Harbor, Wash.	19,014	629	0	15	10	16	42	529	17
Pocatello, Idaho	50,948	2,522	3	22	24	157	405	1,759	152
Prescott, Ariz.	31,452	2,295	2	13	25	115	311	1,733	96
San Jose, Calif.	822,845	36,096	38	387	1,209	5,015	5,477	19,745	4,225
Santa Ana, Calif.	292,289	15,190	72	66	1,234	1,141	2,182	7,396	3,099
Seattle, Wash.	529,526	55,507	41	260	2,213	2,390	7,689	35,970	6,944
Twin Falls, Idaho	32,403	2,963	2	9	15	119	555	2,120	143
West Covina, Calif.	103,817	5,502	10	24	361	253	780	2,980	1,094
Vancouver, Wash.	52,700	5,804	1	85	145	394	1,039	3,410	730

Table 4.2 These figures show the raw number of crimes per community listed. The numbers cannot be directly compared to the crime figures in Table 4.1. Source: Federal Bureau of Investigation. Data is for 1995. Released Oct. 13, 1996.

amount of time it takes to collect and analyze crime data means that the FBI report is at minimum nine months old—*if* you see the data the day it's released.

Demographics

To create your own economic and demographic profiles of target cities and counties, use the resources of two massive, university-related Web sites. You'll find more information than you can absorb in an evening on the Government Information Sharing Project, at Oregon State University, and the Social Sciences Data Center, at the University of Virginia. (See the end of this chapter for Web addresses.) If you're not satisfied with the summary stats you get from a chamber of commerce, or you want to know more about the socio-economic level and ethnic backgrounds of the people in the area you're researching, head to one of these sites.

Each of the sites contains multiple databases. The pages devoted to U.S.A. counties on the Oregon site, and the city and county data books on the Virginia site, are particularly useful. Many of the reports provide immediate insight into the population, housing, economy, education, and climate of an area. As a bonus, the sites have easy-to-use menu systems and the data are easy to print out. The Oregon State Web site's School District Data Book contains state and national comparison figures for a variety of education, economic, and demographic statistics. Despite the vast amount of data available here, it doesn't take a degree in market research to sort through it and capture the reports you need.

A third useful online research site is the University of Michigan's Documents Center; you'll find it linked to the Oregon database. It's a table of contents to many of the government statistics available on the Web. It contains links to government and university sites and its main menu is a good starting point for any statistical search.

Cost of living

For cost-of-living information, there are several places to look. First would be the Bureau of Labor Statistics Web site accessible via the university sites just discussed. The BLS compiles the U.S. Consumer Price Index which you can use to compare one area against another. Your second source of cost-of-living data is a non-online resource from Gale Research, Inc. The company compiles an *American Cost of Living Survey* for 443 cities. The report is available in the reference sections of major libraries.

Also available in many libraries, and through mail subscriptions, is a third source, the *Cost of Living Index,* published by the ACCRA, the American

Chamber of Commerce Researchers Association. The ACCRA report provides extensive comparative data for more than 300 urban areas in the U.S. Each quarterly report is divided into two sections. The first section shows cost-of-living indexes for six categories of expenses and one overall composite index that is useful to compare one city to another. Table 5.2 reproduces an ACCRA index for selected cities. If you want minute details of local costs, the second section of each ACCRA quarterly index compares the price of 59 different consumer products and services in 300 cities. For example, if you want to know how much it will cost for a haircut in Midland, Texas, or a head of lettuce in Fairbanks, Alaska, the report will tell you.

Home swapping groups

Once you've selected a target town, the way to discover the true flavor when you visit is to stay in a home, instead of a hotel. One way to do that is to exchange homes with a family in that town. A variety of small firms and organizations exist as clearing houses for people who are willing to leave the key under the mat for another family, in exchange for the chance to sample a new community from the other family's viewpoint. Living in an established home gives you a much more realistic, day-to-day view of a town than does staying in a motel. You have a chance to talk with neighbors, shop for groceries, and sample public services.

Many exchange organizations publish directories of homes available, and some provide listings and pictures on the Web. If you would be comfortable having someone take over your home temporarily, and you can find someone in the right town, this may be a workable option for you. Insurance, references, and cleaning services are details to check carefully. For the names of home exchange services, talk to a travel agent or consult the resources at the end of this chapter.

Making the trip

You can gather only so much intelligence from your den. Once you've done the homework, you'll have to hit the road. Visiting a potential new hometown gives you a chance to walk the streets, breathe the air, sample the food—in short, pretend you live there and see how it feels. Relocation decisions are often made with the heart as well as the head. What you may remember most from a visit is not the local cost of living, but how you felt as you sipped a drink while looking out over a deep blue lake at dusk.

But rather than just soak up atmosphere, you need to talk to locals, examine the housing market, and try to engage your left brain in an activity that's decidedly right-brain oriented. To prevent yourself from becoming too emotionally involved, focus on collecting specific information and making specific observations. Objective tasks help balance subjective reactions.

The more time you can spend in a community the better. As many towns display different personalities during the week compared to weekends, it's advantageous if your visit can include weekends *and* weekdays. Make every effort to take your children with you. Call ahead and make appointments, if necessary, to be sure you will be able to talk with people you want to meet. Take a notebook for recording information and a camera for taking pictures of city streets, homes, offices, and the countryside. Take this book and continue to gobble up as many details as you can.

Scooping up quantities of information was the modus operandi of Maryann and Fred Sabatini of Anaheim, who researched several towns before moving to Michigan. One of their trips was to Minneapolis—highly rated in a magazine survey, says Maryann. Having reviewed information they received in the mail from many Minneapolis organizations, the Sabatinis descended on the Twin Cities to find out as much as they could.

They drove all over, visiting potential employers, chambers of commerce, city offices, real estate companies. Each night they stayed in a different motel in a different part of town so they could sample the flavor of different neighborhoods. Every place they went they picked up reading material: phone books, newspapers, booklets, brochures, magazines. Before their visit was up, Maryann says, they had collected enough to fill a box the size of a desk filedrawer. They shipped everything back home for later study.

"We tried to look at everything objectively. We said, 'How dirty are the streets? How friendly are the people? What's on the news?' We watched the news at night to see if the crime there is just like where we came from."

They returned home favorably impressed. In addition to all their other materials, they had collected the names and addresses of potential employers, including all the temporary agencies in town. "We didn't want to move somewhere blind," says Maryann. "I think when you move somewhere that you've never lived, there's going to be an element of that, but . . . . We didn't want to make a big mistake."

Walking the streets

What else can you do when you visit your dream location? Figure 4.1 shows a checklist of things to consider, people and places to visit. One priority should be to talk with as many people as possible (besides motel employees, waiters, and chamber of commerce representatives). Attending a local meeting of a national club or organization you belong to is an excellent way to find out about a community and its people. If you're a Rotarian, Toastmaster, or

Checking out your potential hometown

Visit:
- ☐ New and preowned homes (compare prices)
- ☐ Potential employers in your field
- ☐ Shopping areas, malls
- ☐ Recreation areas—
    - ☐ Parks/playgrounds
    - ☐ Pools
    - ☐ Skating rinks
    - ☐ Camping/hiking areas
    - ☐ Lakes/rivers
- ☐ Major employers (particularly if one industry or company dominates the local economy)
- ☐ A veterinary clinic (if you have pets)
- ☐ Bookstores, libraries
- ☐ Universities, colleges
- ☐ Drive through downtown at rush hour
- ☐ Check out schools, talk with school officials
- ☐ Attend a church service
- ☐ Attend local meetings of clubs, professional organizations
- ☐ Listen to local TV and radio news
- ☐ Read the local newspapers

Talk to:
- ☐ Bankers
- ☐ School principals
- ☐ Newspaper editors
- ☐ People in your business/industry/profession
- ☐ Merchants other than those catering to tourists
- ☐ Residents in neighborhoods you visit

- ☐ In smaller towns, look for the necessities such as a hospital, hardware store, auto repair facilities, restaurants, and supermarket. Also check for niceties such as movie theatres, golf courses, tennis courts, bowling alley, etc.

Figure 4.1 Ways to check out a future hometown.

university woman you could share a meal with locals, ask questions about the community, and test the friendliness quotient. (It's not a good sign if you say you're from California and the first thing someone says is: "You know it rains an *awful* lot here.")

A few expatriates say that before they bought a home they talked to neighbors, to see what their new area was like. You can do that even before you start house hunting. In fact, strolling down a residential street in the early evening, or on a weekend, is an easy, low-risk way to meet people and take a reading on a town. (Bad sign number two: you get mugged.)

Other places to visit are the same places you visit now. In other words, if you're a mall junkie, or spend hours in the library, or enjoy the club scene, those are the places you should check out in prospective towns. Take your children to places they will be spending time, such as schools, parks, playgrounds, rinks, and shopping areas. Local schools may become increasingly important on your itinerary, the more favorably impressed you become with a community. Whether or not you have obtained local educational data, you can visit schools and district offices and ask lots of questions. In addition to finding out about academics, your exploratory visit is a great time to check out schools' drama programs, student newspapers, advanced placement courses, sports teams, or other specialized areas. In my case it was basketball.

At the time, my daughter, Angie, was the leading scorer on her high school team in Orange County. She had already begun to get letters of interest from university coaches. A good girls' high school basketball program was priority number one in selecting a high school in Las Vegas. And selection of a high school became priority number one in choosing an area of town to live in. Preliminary research turned up the names of the high school coaches with the best records in town, so Angie and I were off on a basketball tour.

We talked with high school principals and coaches. No one turned us down when we called for appointments, and we received pleasant receptions. The coaches, after they learned about my daughter's record, became more interested in her than she seemed to be in them. At one school someone told us about a highly touted women's coach who had just moved to the district from out of state.

The visits also let us ask questions about the surrounding neighborhoods and the precise residential areas served by the schools. The friendly greetings we received helped to reinforce our favorable impression of Las Vegas.

Whether your interest is in sports, science, or some other area, you can do as we did and you should come out with a variety of useful info. Even if you get rude treatment somewhere, that's useful too. Better to find out before you move.

The public information director of one state's education department suggests asking principals to give you the names and numbers of three parents you can call to ask about the school. Even if the principal gives you the names of PTA board members, you'll still have more information that you otherwise would. And when you're talking to parents about the school, who says you can't ask about local weather conditions, politics, or anything else you're curious about? If you visit schools in rapidly growing areas, be aware that school boundaries may change. Ask about it. When you are ready to buy a home, call the district or county superintendent of schools and give them the address of the property. Ask what school boundaries are now, and if they are expected to change.

Seasonal searching

The time of year you visit a future hometown may unduly influence you. Many people plan their exploratory visits for summer—usually a pleasant time to visit the Northwest, but not the Southwest. If you visit Tucson or Lake Havasu, Ariz., for example, in the middle of summer you could be shocked by the heat, even in the evening. Conversely, if you visit the Puget Sound area in July and see nary a cloud, you may think that stories of gray months without sign of sun in Seattle are exaggerated. If you're considering a location where the weather is drastically different from what you're used to, spend a week there when the weather is likely to be its most severe. Las Vegas in August. Durango, Colo., in February.

The majority of expats interviewed cruised several states and took vacations on wheels, wondering if the next name on the map would be *the* idyllic town. Experience generally is the best teacher in checking out prospective communities.

You might develop a routine for quickly scanning a town's possibilities. When you find a place that's initially appealing, you can then implement a full investigation using suggestions from Figure 4.1. The Hessons, formerly of La Palma in Orange County, who explored the west in their motorhome, finally narrowed their search to two communities: Kalispell, Mont., and Sandpoint, Idaho. After their initial exploration via motorhome, they returned by train, then rented a car. They checked out both towns, meeting with real estate agents in both areas. They settled on Sandpoint, near the Canadian border in the northern finger of the state. At 5,000 people, it was closer to the Hessons' idea of a small town (Kalispell in northwest Montana has 12,000 people) and, says Pattie, Idaho's property taxes were more favorable.

Resources

Weather information

National Climatic Data Center
151 Patton Ave.
Asheville, N.C. 28801
(704) 271-4800

Publications:

> *Climatic Averages and Extremes for U.S. Cities No. 6-3 Comparative Climatic Data, Nationwide*

> For the following booklets, specify the state(s)

> *Climatography of the United States No. 20*
> Includes climatic summaries for selected cities.

> *Climates of the States No. 60*
> Includes city data and a narrative describing state weather patterns.

> *Climatography of the United States No. 81*
> Monthly normals for temperature, precipitation, and heating and cooling degree days.

School information

SchoolMatch *http://www.schoolmatch.com/*

National Association of Independent Schools
http://www.schools.com/index.html

Arizona Dept. of Education *http://www.ade.state.az.us/reportcards*

Crime statistics

U.S. Dept. of Justice
Bureau of Justice Statistics
http://www.ojp.usdoj.gov/bjs
Contains thousands of statistics on crime with particular attention to victim studies.

Federal Bureau of Investigation *http://www.fbi.gov*
Produces annual Uniform Crime Report with detailed information on crimes known to the police, reported by city and state. The reports are available online but the printed version is easier to use. Check your library.

Demographics

Social Sciences Data Center, University of Virginia
http://www.lib.virginia.edu/socsci/index.html.

Government Information Sharing Project, Oregon State University
http://govinfo.kerr.orst.edu

University of Michigan Documents Center
http://www.lib.umich.edu/libhome/documents.center/stats.html

FedWorld Information Network *http://www.fedworld.gov*
   Useful site when you're looking for federal government data but don't know which agency or Web site to query.

U.S. Census data
   For a non-online source of demographic information, try the reference section of your local college or public library. Designated libraries have government sections where you can spend hours poring over mounds of studies. Reports from the U.S. Census Bureau, for example, provide demographic information for every area of the country. Reports divide the country into small areas or geographic *tracts*. For each tract, averages are available for monthly housing costs, income, marital status, family size, and other demographics. Data you can't find in your library can be requested from the Census Bureau or the U.S. Government Printing Office.

Cost-of-living data
   The quarterly ACCRA *Cost of Living Index* is available in many libraries and chamber of commerce offices. It's also available though the mail. One issue is $60, an annual subscription is $120. Write to: ACCRA, 4232 King St., Alexandria, VA 22302.

   Gale Research *http://www.thomson.com/gale/gale.html*

Home swapping

Home Exchange Vacationing
Bill and Mary Barbour
Rutledge Hill Press, 1996
   The authors, veterans of 80 home swaps, give you all the details you need in this how-to. It contains listings of home-exchange directories.

International Home Exchange Network *http://www.homexchange.com*

Home Exchange Clubs, Web directory

http://www.aitec.edu.au/~bwechner/documents/travel
/lists/homeexchangeclubs.html

Environment/Health

National Resources Defense Council

To find out the incidence of premature death due to air pollution in many cities throughout the U.S. visit *http://www.nrdc.org*—the site of the National Resources Defense Council.

Med Access *http://www.medaccess.com*

Here you'll find one of the largest and most highly-rated sites on the Web. Operated by MedAccess Corporation, the site contains thousands of pages of tables, articles, and charts. Health Care Locator pages within the site let you investigate the background of physicians, locate hospitals, find nursing homes, and search out speciality treatment facilities. On other pages you can review the number of people who die each year in each state as a result of automobile crashes, homicide, and other causes.

One portion of the site—accessible at *http:/www.medaccess.com/ environ/env/_db.htm*—lets you search city and state databases for information about air pollution, water pollution, and mortality rates. States are ranked on tables showing 17 different causes of death. You can learn which state leads the nation in deaths caused by circulatory diseases, respiratory diseases, and 15 other causes (including injuries). For example, according to the tables, based on information from the Center for Disease Control, New Mexico has one of the highest death rates for diseases of the digestive and musculoskeletal systems, but has one of the lowest death rates for cancer and diseases of the circulatory system.

5

What to expect when you move: Culture shock and a collection of trade-offs

But it's a dry heat.

It's a Southwest cliché, common on t-shirts and the knee-jerk response in Phoenix, Las Vegas, and other desert towns when tourists ask if it's always more than 100 degrees.

Cliché or not, it's true. Many Southwest desert towns can be blast-oven hot in summer, but with single-digit humidity, the temperature is tolerable—at least to most residents.

Welcome to the world of compromise and trade-offs. For every disappointing facet of a new location, every inconvenience or strange way of doing things, you'll probably find a *quid pro quo*. Sometimes the trade-offs are obvious, sometimes you have to look for them. Missoula, Mont., an energetic university town with a growing job base and vast recreational activities, calls you to Big Sky Country. But the big sky is as cloudy as Seattle's and there are only five months out of the year when the average low temperature is above freezing. Quiet Baker City in eastern Oregon has low housing costs, more sun than Missoula, and no such thing as rush hour. But for big-city shopping you have to travel almost as far as the pioneers who passed through Baker City on the Oregon Trail in the 1840s.

Life: pluses and minuses

Vern and Pattie Hesson, whose motorhome trips finally landed them in northern Idaho, enjoy the relative isolation. They have deer, moose, wild turkeys, and even an occasional bear on their unspoiled, verdant property. "Things you just don't see in the concrete city," says Pattie. True, they have to walk a half mile to pick up their newspaper and the mail, but it seems like a fair trade to them.

Wherever you move you'll find pluses and minuses, rewards and challenges. Whether your vision of an ideal existence is the mountains of western Montana, the wind-blown Pacific coast of Washington or the arid, high plains of New Mexico, it's guaranteed that things will be different from California. Life in a small town, or even a small city, will bring changes—not all of them welcome.

One of the best ways to make your great escape a success is to have realistic expectations and be prepared for surprises. Leaving urban California can bring positive life changes to you and your family, but it will not solve all your problems. Obviously, the purpose of the research discussed in preceding chapters is to help you gain a reasonably accurate picture of life in your destination city. But even with the research, you could be drawn into what psychologist Wayne Dyer calls idealizing about the future to the detriment of present moments. It's the belief that just as soon as some expected event happens—a pay raise, marriage, divorce, vacation, relocation—everything in your life will be perfect. When the expected event takes place, and life is not magically transformed into the dream world it was supposed to be, people are typically disappointed, says Dyer. They start idealizing about some new future event that will deliver them from the trials of everyday life.

Yet everyday life is all we have—one day after another. You waste those days when you spend too much time, which is to say any time, idealizing about the future or worrying about the past. Your relocation can be a dream come true, but so much depends on your expectations and your attitude. If a new job or transfer brings you to a small community, you could take pleasure in the open spaces, the slower pace of life, the ease of getting around. Or you could lament that you'd transplanted yourself smack into podunkville. Paradise and podunkville have much in common.

Consider Moni and Floyd Smith. Approaching retirement, they moved from San Bernardino to Deming, N.M., in early 1997. According to Moni, the town of 12,000 lacks tourist attractions. "No high mountains for skiing, no lakes for boating or fishing," she says. The big events in town are the annual duck races, the outhouse races, and a chili cook-off. "Mostly retired folks are moving here," she says.

But the small-town atmosphere appeals to them. "Deming has lots of desert, distant mountains, palm trees, and serenity." At 4,500 feet elevation, in the southwest corner of the state, Deming has clear air. "Absolutely no smog, ever," says Moni. Deming gets only about eight inches of rain per year, she reports, and the local drinking water is so good that it's bottled and sold. Locals are friendly toward retirees, and Deming has the best Mexican food Moni says she's ever tasted.

If you're looking for things to be perfect when you move, look again. What you'll see are advantages and disadvantages. Reviewing these trade-offs will help you develop a balanced perspective on life beyond the bend in the road.

When we moved to Nevada, we had mixed expectations. Unlike many people who relocate to areas where they have spent vacations, we looked at Las Vegas as relatively new territory. We didn't have pleasant holiday memories to influence our thinking. In fact, we had few memories of Vegas at all. Neither Anne nor I are interested in gaming, so we had never even considered so much as a weekend in Las Vegas. A couple of business trips between us were our only exposure to Las Vegas in 20 years. Like most people, we didn't know if southern Nevada had anything to offer beyond the Vegas "strip." We hoped life there would be better; we knew it would be different. And different it was. We moved from the nation's most populous state to one of the least populous. Moving from an established area to a boom town brought new experiences daily, hourly. Our personal and business lives were filled with trade-offs.

In the first weeks, I felt out of place, almost disoriented. It was not just from the obvious differences—in where I lived, where I worked—but from many little incongruities. Minor changes served as a constant reminder that I was in unfamiliar territory. When I dialed 411 to get directory assistance, nothing happened. (In Nevada you have to dial 555-1212.) Some of the stores and restaurant chains I was used to in California didn't exist in Nevada. The utilities and other institutions in the state and town were unfamiliar. Even some of the language was daunting: *Trop, RJ, Spaghetti Bowl, Brian Head*. I had to learn the local jargon to discover that these shorthand terms referred to: Tropicana Avenue, the *Review Journal* newspaper, the busiest freeway intersection in town, and a popular skiing area in Utah. Even the weather was a greater change than I'd expected. Winter brings icy winds and freezing temperatures to southern Nevada.

Climate

Few aspects of a move out of state receive more attention than the weather. All California expatriates had to consider the climate as they checked out other states. Ignoring pollution (if you don't breathe often, you don't notice it), most urban areas of California are blessed with moderate weather. August and early September heat can be stifling, but for the rest of the year seasons seem to blend one into another with only mild climatic variations. For this reason, excesses of rain, snow, humidity, or heat can be bugaboos for would-be expatriates. Astoria, Ore., would be great, if it didn't rain so much. Boulder, Colo., would be wonderful, if it just didn't snow. Yuma, Ariz., would be heaven without the heat. In fact, all these places, and others, would not have the desirable characteristics they have if they did not also have their weather. (See Table 5.1.)

"We like the changes of the seasons," is a common sentiment among California expatriates from Olympia, Wash., to Ogden, Utah. In many other states you can trade urban California's weather for four separate seasons. Winter in the Colorado Rockies, for example, is distinctly dissimilar from anything found anywhere in urban California. Should you move to Denver, or another city where you can expect the roads to be cleared regularly, your inconveniences in the mountains may be minimal. Not so if you live in a small town or travel to the countryside. People who move from California to the Rockies are often unprepared for driving conditions, particularly navigating unpaved roads in the winter, says Robert Tongsing.

Originally from Colorado, he and his wife moved to Orange County in 1984 and returned to the Rocky Mountain State ten years later. So Tongsing knows about both environments. He says living in the mountains can be a romantic idea, but when winter comes you must be prepared. The four-wheel drive vehicles so popular on California freeways are better suited to snow-clogged dirt roads in Colorado.

Of course winter precipitation can also be liquid. Puget Sound rain, for example, is a most common topic in newspaper and magazine articles about the California exodus. Dick White, of Bothell, Wash., who moved there from Orange County with his wife Sheila, says the weather is not as wet as they expected. "You're told it rains here all the time," says Dick. "But that's not true. Often it's a light rain and you don't even need an umbrella."

But while the Whites don't have to shovel much snow, they say they do need to pressure clean the outside of their home to remove mold and mildew. When summer arrived last year, says Sheila, they also had to clean off their new redwood deck and their outdoor furniture which were both green with mold.

Mold and mildew are not concerns in desert communities. It's so dry in Las Vegas, for example, that towels and wash cloths are bone dry a couple of hours after you take a shower. That kind of dryness does have its own costs— on furniture, the wood trim on your house, and your skin. Wood furniture needs to be regularly oiled to keep it from cracking. The dry desert air and the summer's heat, coupled with below-freezing winters, mean that you frequently have to paint or seal wood doors and trim on your house. And in the first few months we were in Nevada I probably used more hand lotion than I had in years in California. (After a while your skin seems to get used to the lack of humidity.) On the plus side, the dry weather contributed (I presume) to the lack of fleas in Las Vegas. (If the lower taxes or abundant

Climate for selected cities

| | | Temp.(F) | | | | Sunny Days: | | | Rain |
| | | Jan. | | July | | Clear | Partly Cloudy | Cloudy | (inches) |
		Max.	Min.	Max.	Min.				
Alaska:	Anchorage	21	8	65	52	61	64	240	15.91
	Juneau	29	19	64	48	43	40	282	54.31
Arizona:	Flagstaff	42	15	82	51	162	102	101	22.80
	Phoenix	66	41	106	81	211	85	70	7.66
	Tucson	64	39	99	74	194	90	81	12.00
	Yuma	69	44	107	81	242	71	52	3.17
California:	L.A. Civic Center	68	49	84	65	186	106	73	14.77
	San Diego	66	49	76	66	147	117	101	9.90
	San Francisco	56	42	72	54	160	101	104	19.70
Colorado:	Colorado Springs	41	16	84	57	129	165	71	16.24
	Denver	43	16	88	59	115	129	120	15.40
	Grand Junction	36	15	94	64	137	107	122	8.64
	Pueblo	45	14	93	61	150	66	65	11.19
Florida:	Orlando	71	49	92	73	90	147	128	48.11
	Tampa	70	50	90	75	102	143	120	43.92
Hawaii:	Honolulu	80	66	88	74	90	180	95	22.02
Idaho:	Boise	36	22	90	58	120	90	154	12.11
	Lewiston	40	28	89	59	91	78	196	12.43
	Pocatello	32	14	88	53	106	99	161	12.14
Illinois:	Peoria	30	13	82	61	95	98	173	36.25
Indiana:	Fort Wayne	30	15	85	63	78	102	185	34.75

State	City	Jan max	Jan min	July max	July min	Clear	Partly cloudy	Cloudy	Rainfall
Minnesota:	Minneapolis - St.Paul	21	3	84	63	96	101	168	28.32
Montana:	Helena	30	10	85	53	82	104	179	11.60
	Missoula	30	15	83	50	75	83	208	13.46
Nevada:	Las Vegas	57	34	106	76	211	82	72	4.13
	Reno	45	21	92	51	159	93	113	7.53
New Mexico:	Albuquerque	47	22	92	64	168	110	87	8.88
	Roswell	54	25	95	67	168	113	84	12.58
North Carolina:	Charlotte	49	30	89	70	111	103	151	43.09
Oregon:	Eugene	46	35	82	53	75	82	208	49.37
	Pendleton	40	27	88	58	101	91	173	12.02
	Portland	45	34	80	57	68	74	223	36.30
Tennessee:	Nashville	46	27	90	69	102	106	156	47.30
Texas:	Austin	59	39	95	74	116	114	135	31.88
	El Paso	56	29	96	68	193	99	73	8.81
	San Antonio	61	38	95	75	106	118	141	30.98
Utah:	Salt Lake City	36	19	92	64	125	101	139	16.18
Washington:	Seattle	46	36	74	56	71	93	201	38.00
	Spokane	33	21	83	54	86	87	192	16.49
Wyoming:	Cheyenne	38	15	82	55	106	127	132	14.40

Table 5.1 Table shows the mean daily maximum and minimum temperatures, averaged for January and July. The number of sunny or cloudy days per year are shown. (Definitions: Clear, a day which averages 0 to 3/10 of the sky covered by clouds. Partly cloudy, when 4/10 to 7/10 of the sky is covered by clouds. Cloudy, when 8/10 to 10/10 of the sky is covered by clouds.) Temperatures and numbers of days are rounded. Rainfall shown is annual averages. From *Climatic Averages and Extremes for U.S. Cities*, National Climatic Data Center, U.S. Department of Commerce.

entertainment aren't enough to entice you, move to Las Vegas because you'll never have to spend money on flea collars for your dog or cat!)

Humidity aside, the quality of the air is usually a positive trade-off when you leave urban California. Smog, or whatever you choose to call it, does not have to be a fact of life. "The high degree of pollution in most seasons of the year was emphatically a factor in our decision to leave," says former Walnut Creek resident Julien Wagenet who, with his wife Marian, moved to Santa Fe, N.M., in 1989. "The condition [smog] frequently is not apparent to many California residents; they become accustomed to 'hazy days.' But pollution is dramatically apparent when you return to California from a cleaner environment.

"In New Mexico we sit on our deck at night and watch the Milky Way. We see many stars you never see in California, except in the mountains," says Wagenet. "We can watch the traffic lights in Los Alamos change—more than 20 miles away. And in the winter we can see snow on the mountains in Colorado more than 120 miles to the north. It's a most unusual day in New Mexico that clean air is not the norm."

Even significant climatic differences—such as the difficulty of breathing air you can't see—may not be daunting if you maintain a positive attitude about your move. For that matter, any trade-off, welcome or otherwise, will diminish your enthusiasm for a new hometown only if you let it. Case in point: A Las Vegan, originally from Illinois, has a marvelous outlook on the 100+ degree summers. She compares them—favorably—to winters in the Midwest. In Las Vegas it's the *summer* season when you don't spend much time outdoors. But when you do venture out you don't have to wear layers of clothing and the roads are never blocked by snowdrifts.

Public services

Whatever the weather, one universal concession to smaller towns is the inferior condition of freeways and roads compared to California. Many expatriates say that when they moved out of state they gained an increased admiration for California freeway engineers. City freeways, surface streets, and county highways in many states almost make you wish for the old California freeways—until you remember the other trade-off: traffic. The best engineering in the world can't make I-5 any faster when it's choked with too many cars. Conversely, even poorly designed highways in other states are a pleasure to drive when you're not sharing the road with several hundred thousand other cars.

Nevertheless, pot holes, dirt roads, and seemingly endless construction zones—that in California could cause the recall of the governor—are tolerated in many cities and towns in other states. It's surprising to see dirt and gravel roads in one of the high-rent districts in the middle of Las Vegas. Dirt roads are uncommon in Vegas to be sure, but they do exist, particularly in outlying, growing areas of town. But then municipal services in general are different in Nevada and other states.

When you move to a smaller town in a smaller state, resources may be more limited. So may services. Again, there are trade-offs. When we moved to Las Vegas, we were delighted to find that trash was collected twice a week and that the disposal company also picked up recyclables if you sorted them into the bins they provided. Silver State Disposal is also not as picky about what they pick up compared to our old California refuse collection service. On the other hand, we were told cable TV service was not available where we lived. At the time, the northwest portion of town was sparsely settled and the cable company had not run lines out to our tract. After a couple of months, however, cable did arrive. We were pleased with the service and variety of stations that were available, including selections our California cable company did not offer.

Municipal and other government services in smaller states may not be quite what you are used to either, but sometimes that's a pleasant surprise. The smaller the state and the smaller the community, the less bureaucratic the government and the more accessible the elected representatives. The political system in Nevada is refreshing, and unlike anything in California (except, of course, that there are Republicans and Democrats in both places). The legislature works only part time, as is the case in Oregon and other small states. In Nevada, legislators meet in Carson City for sessions only every other year. And then for only a few months; Nevadans don't give their legislators time to pass too many laws. Members of the State Assembly and Senate are not full-time politicians. Even lieutenant governor is a part-time position.

As a result of this system, and the fact the entire state has about the same population as Santa Clara or San Bernardino counties, Nevada politicians aren't supercilious celebrities with entourages. Los Angeles County supervisors probably have more perks and bigger staffs than the governor of Nevada. Compared to dealing with state government in Nevada, Sacramento reminds me of the federal government.

My first exposure to Nevada-style politicians was a barbecue, sponsored by a business-communicators organization. It was a candidates' night and several State Assembly and Senate members were invited. Being new in town I knew none of the office holders and only a few of the organization members, so I volunteered to grill hamburgers outside. This gave me a chance to talk with nearly everyone as I served them, but I couldn't pick out the politicians from the common folk without help. One of the association members had to tell me that several of the people I'd been talking to—who were wearing worn jeans and sport shirts—were state senators. They had no aides around them; they drank beer, ate hamburgers, and talked about sports.

Here's another example of how Nevada politicians are different: Community Psychiatric Centers, a publicly held company (now called Traditional Hospitals Corp.) which employed about 10,000 people in 1995, relocated its headquarters to Las Vegas from Southern California. The corporation's chairman, Richard Conte, says when the firm relocated, he thought it would be helpful if he could talk to Nevada Governor Bob Miller about the corporate building project. Conte's experiences trying to contact California politicians didn't provide much encouragement, but he called the governor's office anyway to explain what he wanted.

"The secretary said she would have to check with him, and I said I'd be happy to come up to Carson City any time in the next month or two. I'd just like to have about five minutes of his time," said Conte. "About 15 minutes later, he's on the telephone. And I'm saying, 'Governor I know you're a busy man; I don't mean to take up much of your time . . .' And he's saying, 'No, no, you guys moved here and we're glad to have you. If there's anything I can do for you, shoot.' I explained to him what I wanted and he said, 'Why don't I come by your office? I'm going to be in Las Vegas on Thursday, how's three o'clock?'"

Conte contrasts the governor's visit to his office with repeated, unsuccessful attempts to even speak on the phone to his Orange County supervisor—at a time when his company was the fourth or fifth largest in the county. It was not until news of his pending corporate relocation reached the California newspapers that someone in the supervisor's office called him. A supervisor's assistant called him, he says, "to see if there was anything they could do to keep us from moving." Too little, too late.

Culture: Quality vs. accessibility

Another set of trade-offs involves cultural and entertainment opportunities. Compare what you may have enjoyed in California to what you might find in a typical small town. The deficiency is obvious. There's no San Francisco Symphony, no Dorothy Chandler Pavilion, no Los Angeles County Museum of Art, and no Balboa Park brimming with museums and theatres. You find no Orange County Performing Arts Center, no San Francisco Ballet, no San Jose Tech Museum, no Laguna Beach Pageant of the Masters. But ask yourself, isn't a trip to the symphony or museum a once-a-year occasion? These outings are limited, not because you don't enjoy them, but because accomplishing them is a challenge. They involve time and money. Long freeway drives, parking hassles, and high prices combine to keep people at home.

In a smaller town, in another state, you won't have the Golden State's vaunted cultural institutions, but you will have access—indeed convenient, relatively inexpensive access—to whatever your community does offer. Fort Collins, Colo., has community theatre, says Scott Gordon, formerly of Southern California. "You're not going to get *Phantom of the Opera* like you would in L.A.," he says, "but here [live theatre] is one-third the price it is in California and it takes 15 minutes to get there."

Many small towns offer cultural and entertainment opportunities. Ashland, Ore., and Cedar City, Utah, for example, have nationally recognized Shakespeare festivals. The best collections of Western and Southwestern art anywhere reside in galleries and museums throughout the West: Great Falls, Mont., has the Charles M. Russell Museum. Taos, N.M., had, at last count, 57 art galleries. Cody, Wyo., is home to the Buffalo Bill Historical Center, one of the largest museums dedicated to the culture, history, and crafts of the American West. Santa Fe has opera; Elko, Nev., is home to an annual Cowboy Poetry Gathering; Superior, Ariz., has the Boyce Thompson Southwestern Arboretum. The Museum of Art in Maryhill, Wash., features Rodin sculptures. You can attend a Bach festival in Mount Angel, Ore., or the Lionel Hampton Jazz Festival in Moscow, Idaho. Wherever you go, you'll also find state historical and natural history museums, local symphonies, bands, and theatre companies. You may even be able to catch performances of national touring companies performing Broadway plays.

Even with its beautiful beaches and famed state and national parks, California does not have a monopoly on outdoor recreation. Other states boast beautiful rivers, lakes, mountains, and sea shores. What the other states lack is 32 million residents competing for the resources. The best weekend getaways in the Golden State are no secrets. You share the trails, campsites, motels, restaurants, and highways with your fellow Californians.

Andy Schneider, who moved his family to Coeur d'Alene, Idaho, in late 1995, was tired of having to drive for hours just to share national parks and other scenic areas with crowds. "It's beautiful up here," the former Westminster resident says of the open spaces of north Idaho. "We have lakes and there's nobody on them. It's God's country."

Community involvement vs. privacy

Another difference between urban California and elsewhere is community spirit. Many people move to smaller towns seeking a sense of belonging, a way to connect with others, and a way to make a difference in their communities. Possibilities for such involvement are plentiful and the smaller the community, the greater your potential impact. The trade-off is privacy.

The smaller the community, the less privacy you can expect. If you've always lived in a metropolis, the difference may be striking. "In a city you're a perpetual stranger," says McKown of Wyoming. Not so in a small town.

Loss of privacy may sound threatening, but it simply means you will see people you know more frequently than you are used to. For escapees from urban California, that constitutes a tremendous change. Many urban Californians live in one community, work in another, and often shop and dine in still other communities. How often do you run into someone you know? In a smaller city it's an everyday occurrence. How often you stop to talk with people and how long you linger is up to you. It can slow your pace, if you want it to.

For my wife and me, it was new and refreshing to regularly see people we knew in the aisles of stores, in restaurants, in the cars next to us at stop signals. At the time we moved to Las Vegas, the population was about 750,000, a big city to some, a smaller town to us. The size difference between Southern California and Las Vegas was emphasized to us because we bought a house in a small development in the sparsely settled northwest. In one direction was town, in the other, hundreds of miles of empty desert. It gave us opportunities to get to know neighbors.

Everyone has his or her ideal sized community. I'm still not sure what mine is, but I know what it's not. My first job out of college found me working for a weekly newspaper in a farm town of 10,000 people. As an outsider I was not privy to the local gossip, but I heard enough to know that when our paper came out every Thursday most of the news in town had already been chewed and digested. In a town that size, everyone's comings and goings are grist for the local rumor mill. I prefer larger towns, but not because they don't foster gossip. Cities have gossip too; it's just confined to blocks or neighborhoods. Larger communities are preferable because of what they can offer: broader news coverage from the local media, greater shopping and entertainment possibilities, more job opportunities, the resources of a college or university, and expanded choices of services for everything from banking to health care.

A small city that's growing has additional benefits for newcomers. The more people moving into an area from out of state, the less you will stand out. As we met our neighbors in Las Vegas, we found people from Indiana, Colorado, California, Arizona, and yes, even a family from Nevada. If a growing percentage of the population is from somewhere else, they are less likely to disparage your origins—even if you are from California. Having a national or regional mix of population brings in new ideas to a community and keeps it from becoming too provincial. A growing population usually reveals a healthy local economy along with other favorable attributes that attract new residents.

The hazards of growth, of course, can be a limited amount of housing, at least until supply meets demand, and overburdened public services, including schools. Too much, or haphazard, growth can also lead to clogged roads, pollution, strip malls, and urban sprawl—the very things you want to be rid of. In addition, overdependence on one rapidly expanding industry or employer can be portentous.

Big fish, small pond

Salaries are significantly different in California compared to just about anywhere you move to in the West. You may not have to accept a lower salary when you move, but many expatriates did. Table 6.1 shows that California has the highest per capita income of any Western state even though its economy in the '90s has not been as strong as other states'. In most towns you will find that salaries are lower than in California—but generally so is the cost of living. Table 5.2 shows that the cost of living, for example, in Pocatello, Idaho, Cheyenne, Wyo., or College Station, Texas, is dramatically lower than San Francisco or Los Angeles. The extent to which you can balance your income with a lower cost of living may dictate your satisfaction with this trade-off.

Although you may not match your California salary at a similar job in another state, a move may give you a different form of business advantage. The demands and pressures of business in California's large metro areas are as exacting as they are anywhere in the world. You're exposed to stiff competition; you learn to make quick decisions; you work hard just to keep up. The local media, the up-and-down economy, a sprawling market, and other factors complicate and accelerate your life.

When you move to a smaller community, with a slower pace and fewer business demands, you may find it easier to excel. You may not be smarter than your competition, but your seasoning in the California pressure cooker may make you move faster and think more quickly than locals. Gordon, of Fort Collins, Colo., confirms that the pace of business outside California is easier, slower. "In sales, people here are more open and receptive to see you. In California, people are getting pounded by 50 sales people per hour and they blow you off."

Small business owner Jim Frisch, who moved to Brookings, Ore., from Southern California in 1993, characterizes local business the same way. "They're very laid back up here. A California business person who has any ability at all will do well in Oregon."

Using your urban California business advantages successfully requires restraint. You may find an, "I don't care how you did it in California" attitude. Chapter 14 explores the topic in more detail.

ACCRA Cost of Living Index

State	Urban area	100% Composite index	16% Grocery items	28% Housing	8% Utilities	10% Trans- portation	5% Health care	33% Misc. goods and services
Alaska	Anchorage	125.7	125.6	134.1	105.0	110.3	171.8	119.5
Arizona	Flagstaff	112.8	106.7	132.5	94.4	118.0	109.9	102.7
	Lake Havasu City	100.8	108.3	88.2	114.1	103.5	116.2	101.0
	Phoenix	102.5	105.2	97.5	106.6	113.7	115.0	99.2
	Scottsdale	105.3	105.9	115.2	106.6	119.0	114.1	91.1
	Tucson	98.1	107.1	92.9	104.5	100.4	114.0	93.2
California	Fresno	103.8	104.2	98.7	112.5	108.8	106.6	104.0
	Los Angeles - Long Beach	117.1	114.2	126.8	115.6	105.5	124.7	112.3
	San Diego	119.4	111.8	148.5	101.1	122.5	117.0	102.5
	San Francisco*	167.5	120.7	288.1	102.4	129.0	175.4	112.8
	San Mateo County*	150.6	111.2	246.1	102.4	120.2	148.2	109.1
Colorado	Colorado Springs	103.5	96.1	121.1	70.3	98.9	127.6	97.1
	Denver	104.4	95.8	118.1	81.1	111.8	123.9	97.1
	Fort Collins	104.6	105.2	118.2	68.5	104.2	117.0	99.4
	Grand Junction	98.8	98.3	101.3	77.7	109.1	101.3	98.9
	Pueblo	92.2	103.2	82.7	76.8	94.1	114.1	94.1
Florida	Orlando	98.8	98.4	92.4	104.6	99.7	115.4	99.9
	Tampa	99.2	100.7	93.0	117.9	98.0	111.8	97.1
Hawaii	Honolulu*	174.2	157.5	284.1	149.2	134.3	134.4	113.3
Idaho	Boise	102.2	93.4	112.2	67.6	102.0	114.0	104.3
	Pocatello	92.9	104.8	82.6	80.3	95.7	93.8	97.9
	Twin Falls	97.3	100.9	99.2	76.3	102.7	86.3	99.5
Minnesota	Minneapolis	100.4	98.5	95.2	101.6	115.1	124.5	97.1
Montana	Great Falls	104.6	103.8	120.0	70.8	102.8	106.2	100.4
	Missoula	101.5	104.9	104.0	80.9	106.6	108.4	100.2
Nevada	Las Vegas	103.3	106.7	106.6	75.8	112.4	120.3	99.9
	Reno - Sparks	115.1	105.8	132.2	91.1	112.4	129.1	109.2
	Carson City*	103.9	103.3	103.6	91.3	109.2	127.3	101.9
New Mexico	Albuquerque	101.8	100.2	104.6	98.2	98.7	106.2	101.0

	Las Cruces	99.5	98.4	102.9	93.7	96.9	96.5	99.8
	Santa Fe	112.7	105.2	132.9	91.2	113.8	106.5	105.2
New York	New York (Manhattan)	238.1	147.4	479.6	175.2	121.3	199.6	131.2
North Carolina	Charlotte	99.5	96.0	99.9	103.8	96.3	103.1	99.9
	Raleigh - Durham	100.3	96.7	107.0	105.9	93.9	102.7	96.4
Oregon	Eugene	111.4	91.1	148.4	73.7	102.8	116.1	100.4
	Portland	109.2	100.9	125.0	89.2	108.8	119.4	103.2
	Klamath Falls	95.5	100.9	90.5	79.6	109.3	93.7	97.7
	Bend*	104.6	87.0	117.5	89.4	106.5	111.4	104.1
Tennessee	Nashville - Franklin	94.3	100.9	91.3	91.3	95.4	94.4	94.3
Texas	Austin	101.1	91.8	105.6	84.2	102.0	113.7	103.3
	Bryan - College Station	90.2	89.0	82.3	106.1	87.5	98.4	92.6
	El Paso	97.2	105.8	87.4	84.7	110.0	89.5	102.2
	Houston	94.3	94.4	81.8	98.9	107.0	102.7	98.7
Utah	Provo - Orem	102.8	98.0	111.5	79.6	107.2	115.9	99.8
	Salt Lake City	103.8	105.8	114.0	76.8	109.4	113.2	97.8
	Cedar City	93.6	103.4	83.8	73.5	110.0	99.4	96.6
	St George	102.1	106.2	105.4	86.3	106.4	94.8	101.3
Washington	Bellingham	106.5	104.0	115.9	84.4	98.1	125.3	103.4
	Seattle	114.8	106.9	126.3	78.6	112.7	148.0	112.5
	Spokane	104.5	102.4	118.6	61.2	94.1	120.8	103.9
	Tacoma	104.0	106.0	102.6	79.0	102.0	132.6	105.3
Wisconsin	Oshkosh	100.6	103.7	101.5	86.2	101.2	103.2	101.1
	Madison	111.8	99.0	127.0	92.2	104.8	110.6	111.7
Wyoming	Cheyenne	94.5	103.0	92.4	65.7	96.6	94.2	98.7
	Laramie	95.6	102.5	97.5	79.3	95.9	106.2	92.7

*First quarter 1996 data.

Table 5.2 The average for all participating areas, both metropolitan and nonmetropolitan, equals 100. Each participant's index is read as a percentage of the average for all places. For example, the cost of living index for San Diego is 119.4, or 19.4 percent higher than the national average. The cost of living in Pocatello, Idaho (with an index number of 92.9), is 7.1 percent below the national average. The index does not measure inflation, nor does it include state or local taxes. The index is weighted by the ACCRA to reflect a mid-management standard of living. For instance, home ownership costs are more heavily weighted than they would be if the index were structured to reflect a clerical worker standard of living. Except as noted, all data are as of the fourth quarter of 1996. Reprinted with permission. The ACCRA Cost of Living Index is a copyrighted publication of the American Chamber of Commerce Researchers Association. Subscription and reprint information is available by contacting the ACCRA at 703/998-3540.

Realistic expectations

The true attitude of locals in a town you're checking out may not be obvious the first time you visit. And if you have exaggerated notions of how your life will change when you move to a small town, you may be in for a surprise. Certainly that was the case with John and Debi Mann.

In 1988, the Manns had a mid-six-figure income, a live-in housekeeper, and membership in a country club. John was a stock market trader and his Southern California life was good.

"I had all the trappings of the lifestyle I enjoy," says John, "but we were looking for something more."

One evening at a movie they saw a glimpse of what life could be like. "The leading character in this movie lived in a small town," says John. "As he walks through town everyone says 'hello' to him. He's in a restaurant and everyone says 'hi.' It's a friendly place with beautiful countryside.

"Debi turned to me and said, 'Why can't we live in a town like that?'

"I loved California," says John. "I loved Malibu, the restaurants. But what I didn't love was the Bloods and the Crips and the guy who tried to run me off the freeway."

Debi did some research and discovered Coeur d'Alene, Idaho, a promising small town in a recreation/resort area. They visited the town, staying at the Coeur d'Alene Resort, an elegant lakeside hotel and marina on Lake Coeur d'Alene. The attentive service they received impressed them, and after talking with a real estate agent, they decided they had found what they were looking for.

When they arrived with their household goods, they received a decidedly cool reception. Was this the same town that seemed so friendly when they were visitors?

"When we first came up here all the service people we talked to were nice. The hotel people, the waitresses, and the real estate people all treated us wonderfully. We marveled at how nice everyone was," says John. "Well of course they were nice to us. They're supposed to be nice; they're paid to be nice in order to get a bigger tip or keep their jobs. Where was the light switch for that one? It just didn't click with us until later. I look back at that now and I think, how naive."

The locals' collective image of the Manns was influenced in part by stories that the couple was planning to build a 7,800 sq. ft. home on a hill overlooking Hayden Lake, near Coeur d'Alene. John says his original house plans called for just over 4,000 feet of space. But after a local architect added mother-in-law quarters, and modified the plans to fit the property the Manns had bought, the house (including basement) had grown to 7,800 sq. ft. "People talk about a house that big," he says.

When he moved to Idaho, John continued to invest and trade in the stock market. He set up his own office in a trailer on their hill-top property. Due to the condition of the market, and the fact he severed some important business ties when he moved, his business did not go well. In addition, he began to hate the isolation of working alone.

So when his market trading faded, John took a job as branch manager of a bank. (Before trading his own stock investments, he'd been a mortgage banker.) Despite his hard work to try to catch up on changes in the banking business, John says he struggled and didn't always do a good job. One important responsibility was selling mortgage loans. But when he called on people in real estate he discovered, "I was just the rich Californian who took over the branch, so no one wanted anything to do with me."

Within three months he left the bank—quitting, he says, before he could be fired.

Socially, things were not much better. Although he had only a limited social life with neighbors in California, he thought things would be better in Coeur d'Alene. "I came up here envisioning block parties, where families took turns cooking for each other. The Smiths would come over to our house and later other couples would come over. We'd have a wonderful time, then two weeks later we'd be invited to their homes.

"That didn't happen. The ingrained Idahoans never warmly accepted us . . . We'll never be invited to the *in* parties."

The Manns also failed to connect with other parents—many from California—at the private school their children attended. "Maybe we weren't their kind of people," John says.

In spite of such setbacks, the Manns stuck it out. John put his energy into work. He started his own custom embroidery business from scratch and while the family lived off their savings, he nurtured the business along. Seven years later, he had built a million-dollar company.

Among the things they've learned over the years is that people tend to categorize others. He says he tries hard not to do that. He even avoids asking people he meets socially what they do for a living. Although Coeur d'Alene is not what the Manns initially expected, these California expatriates have come to love their adopted community and state.

Mann considers himself an Idahoan now, although when asked where he's from, he'll sometimes offer an honest-yet-safe answer: "South of Lewiston."

Making a decision

Finding your dream town is a balancing act. How much emphasis should you put on climate, the cost of living, or other factors? And what about size? Big cities have more resources, but can be impersonal. Small towns can have characteristics of an extended family—and that implies pluses and minuses too. You have many options and trade-offs to consider, but don't be overwhelmed. You can spend too much time gathering and analyzing information. Said one former Californian, "If you question it too much, or ask opinions of too many people, you're never going to move."

Resources

Books by Wayne Dyer

The Sky's the Limit
Pocket Books, 1993

You'll See It When You Believe It
Avon, 1990

Your Erroneous Zones
Harper Collins, 1993

6

Finding a job out of state

Imagine peace and quiet, crisp clean air and a place where you can think clearly again. Imagine a place where friends and neighbors welcome your family and business with sincerity and a helping hand. Imagine one of nature's most inspiring landscapes, ever-changing through the seasons.

Can you imagine moving there? This description from the Wallace and Kellogg, Idaho, Chamber of Commerce sounds inviting. But finding an idyllic new hometown (and developing reasonable expectations) is only part of your task. You also have to figure a way to make a living in your new desert-mountain-ocean hideaway. There are only a few ways to do it. Short of winning the lottery you have five choices:

(1) Obtain a transfer within your company
(2) Get a new job in your field
(3) Get a job in a different field
(4) Start your own business
(5) Take your present business or profession with you

The first two options are examined in this chapter. Options three, four, and five are in Chapter 7. These chapters are designed to get you started in your job/business planning, and they refer you to other sources of information. The techniques are applicable to several forms of out-of-state employment searches, so it's best to read all sections of both chapters. For working couples, the five strategies can be combined to give you the greatest number of possibilities.

Employment searching skills

Computers and the Internet can automate many of your job searching tasks. But when you're looking for work today—especially outside your state—it's best to couple the high-tech techniques with the traditional ones. This look

at out-of-state job searching begins, therefore, with a review of the basics—
skills that will help you no matter which of the five strategies you select.

Résumé writing

Bad advice about résumés is plentiful. Pick up four current books on job
hunting (as I did as an experiment) and you might find this mélange of advice
on résumés:

- Don't use one. It gives employers reasons to reject you.
- Print yours on parchment paper using colored ink.
- Have your photo printed at the top of the page.
- Put your age, gender, marital status, and the number of children you
have at the beginning.
- Never make your résumé longer than one page.

This advice—all of it bad—accounts for at least some of the volume of
poor résumés circulating through offices today. Although your résumé may
give a potential employer something not to like about you, résumés are still
a foundation of job hunting. That's one reason why thousands of résumés
are circulated daily on the Web. Before you write or revise your résumé, however, start with a preliminary exercise: write up a personal inventory. The
purpose is to develop raw material you can use to (1) analyze your job possibilities, (2) write one or more résumés, and (3) write cover letters. For this
exercise, forget for a moment that you are working on your résumé. Simply
jot down a brief, personal history in outline form. Then go back and fill in
the details.

In essence, this is a solitary brainstorming session. Start anywhere and write
down everything. Remember that quarterly sales award you earned? Those
Dale Carnegie classes you took? Keep writing until you have down on paper
everything you've done that might translate into a job skill.

Here are subjects you should cover:

Employment

- Jobs held (full and part-time)
- All work-related accomplishments, awards, recognitions
- What you learned, such as: specific job skills, how to deal effectively with
people, written communication, etc.
- Specialized job skills: computer programs you use, machines you can
operate, licenses and professional certifications

Education

- High school, job training, college, graduate school

- Academic awards, school clubs and organizations, athletics
- Professional training programs and seminars attended
- On-the-job training you've received

Military service
- Training received, jobs held, states/countries visited

Organizations
- Your activities, duties, offices in:
  Community groups/service clubs
  Professional/fraternal clubs
  Church organizations
  Youth groups

Other activities
- Countries/states you've lived/traveled in
- Languages you speak
- Hobbies or other outside activities and the skills involved (e.g. computing—programming, electronics)

While not all the information in your inventory will be included in your résumés, this activity has multiple benefits. One benefit is that it helps you identify experiences that might translate into advantages for new employers. Keep in mind some of the key business skills that employers look for: speaking, writing, managing a budget, supervising, and just plain getting along with others. Many of your experiences may demonstrate those skills, even if they're not in the same field you're trying to enter. Your personal inventory also helps you create different versions of your résumé, which you direct to different types of employers. Also, examining your background and accomplishments can serve as a personal pat on the back for all the things you have already done in your life.

Unless you have experience and education limited to one narrow field, and you plan to stay in that field, you should write multiple résumés to highlight different skills and accomplishments. Customize your résumés to appeal to different employers. Here are the general building blocks of a good résumé:

Heading List your name, address, phone numbers, and e-mail address. Employers are prohibited by law from asking questions about your age and marital status, and there's no reason to provide this information. Your gender, height, and weight are also irrelevant for all but a few job classifications.

You may list your health as excellent, but there's generally no reason to do that either.

Summary The summary section should be brief, but packed with accomplishments and whatever you're proudest of. You might call this your "Summary of Accomplishments." If someone only looks at your résumé for 20 seconds—as is often the case—what do you want him to know about you? You can customize résumés by changing the summary to attract the attention of different employers.

Bulleted items or a list of short statements is best. Keep in mind this is a summary. Some people write their job goals or objectives where the summary should be. Objectives are acceptable, but remember your résumé is sales literature and you must show a potential employer—in a few seconds— what you've got to offer. Why waste the space at the top of your résumé with a generic statement such as: "Seeking a responsible position in a forward-looking company that will allow me to utilize my (fill in the blank) skills to their highest level while contributing to the company's growth." It's better to start your résumé with your accomplishments.

Experience The two most common ways of displaying skills and experience in a résumé are: functionally or chronologically. In the functional résumé, you explain your skills, abilities, and accomplishments at some length, then provide a list of your employers and the dates of employment at the end. The chronological résumé (which is used more often) describes the jobs you've held and is arranged in reverse time order (i.e. latest first).

Either format is acceptable provided you not only emphasize your abilities but also show how they translate into accomplishments. Be sure to use a variety of verbs to demonstrate what you *did*. For example, instead of saying, "Responsible for the design of displays in all store departments," say that you "supervised the design," or you "created the designs," or simply that you "*designed* all store displays." Lead with the verb. Instead of saying your "duties included the organization of new work units," say you "created and organized dynamic new employee production groups."

Cite specific information rather than generalities. Say you increased sales by 29 percent in seven months; that's much stronger than saying you, "helped bring about a significant boost in sales."

Education List the colleges you attended, and degrees you received. If you did not receive a degree, identify your major, or course of study. Your grade-point average in high school or college is extraneous if you've been out of school a few years. In fact, it's generally not worth mentioning in any case unless it's exceptional.

Should you be worried that you're a little too old (or too young) for a position, omit the date you graduated from college. Your employment dates give the reader clues to your age, but college dates can be more revealing.

Other information If you belong to any professional or trade associations, list them and any offices you have held. Depending upon your field, membership in civic groups and clubs may be beneficial; it shows your interest in serving your community. If you've published articles, in trade publications for example, mention that fact.

Hobbies, other outside activities, or information about family members, should be included only if they have a direct bearing on the requirements of a job you're applying for. Otherwise, omit this information.

Using a cover letter

As important as your résumé is, it shouldn't have to stand alone. Never send out a résumé by itself; always send a cover letter. While your résumé must satisfy many long-standing business requirements, your cover letter can be your own creation from start to finish. The letter focuses the reader on your strongest qualifications and tells her why she should talk with you. The language you use should be friendly yet businesslike. Talk directly to the reader and use personal pronouns, particularly "you." Avoid using "I" too much in your letters. (*Never* use it on your résumé.)

Writing about yourself is challenging. You want to demonstrate your valuable qualities and experience but without bragging. One way is to focus on specific details of your accomplishments, rather than using superlatives about yourself or your work. *Never* refer to yourself in the third person (he, she) in your letter or résumé.

Use your cover letter to explain why you may be qualified for a particular job—even if your résumé shows little direct experience in that area. Your letter may include personal-inventory material that's relevant, but not appropriate for your résumé. With a letter you may be better able to explain what you learned in other jobs that will make you a valuable employee. You can talk about your positive attitude, interest in working with people, and your sense of humor, all important attributes that are difficult to communicate in a résumé.

Unlike résumés, your cover letter should probably be no longer than one page—but don't be afraid to fill the page. A letter that says, "Here is my résumé. I hope to hear from you soon," is useless. Remember, the number-one purpose of your résumé and cover letter is to obtain an interview. Your résumé is not an application, or a simple recitation of your work history; it's a sales document and an interview is the product you're selling. Your goal is to get in the door.

Finally, to make your résumé as professional and effective as possible, pay attention to these details:

• Triple check for spelling and grammar mistakes, typos, and other oversights. Even one on a résumé can give the impression that you're careless or lack grammar skills.

• Print your résumé on good-quality bond paper, using a laser printer in an easy-to-read font. Serif type, such as the type you're reading now, is considered easier to read than sans-serif. Although word processing and desktop publishing software permit you to use multiple typefaces, limit yourself to a maximum of three. Résumés that use too many typefaces look like ads for the circus.

• No matter what you've been told, two-page résumés are acceptable. The length is less important than what you have to say. If your résumé is well written, if it shows you have just the skills, background, and attitude that potential employers are looking for, do you think they're going to stop reading at the bottom of the first page?

Interviewing techniques

Hundreds of books, articles, seminars, and classes are available on successful interviewing methods. Here are a few considerations to get you started:

Be prepared Gather and study as much information about the company as you can before the interview. First, this will help you decide if you really want to work for the firm, government agency, etc. Second, it may prompt questions to ask. Third, knowing something about a firm gives you a chance to demonstrate your preparation and interest in the company. Let the interviewer know that you've researched the company. If possible, use your knowledge of the company to show how you could fit into the organizational structure or help the company accomplish its objectives. Read a potential employer's annual report, sales literature, Web page. Read magazine and newspaper articles about the firm. At the very least, look up the company's profile in a directory such as those published by Dun and Bradstreet.

Dress appropriately This does not necessarily mean that you wear a dark business suit. If possible, visit the offices before your interview to see how people are dressed. If they're all dressed like bankers, then wear the dark suit. But if you're applying at an ad agency, small high-tech firm, or municipal department, where the dress is more casual, tailor what you wear to match your surroundings. The key is to look like you belong there. Good personal grooming is essential as well.

Know your answers to stock questions Many interviewers, even the less conventional ones, still tend to ask stock questions that you can anticipate. There are books with lists of these questions, but with a little imagination you can come up with your own list of expected questions for your industry or profession. Here are some samples: What would you like to be doing in five years? What is your biggest strength? Weakness? Why did you select this company? Are you looking for a career here? What did you like best about your previous job? Why did you leave your last employer?

Ask questions By asking intelligent questions, you can show your interest in the position and your knowledge of your field. Don't ask first about salary or benefits; it sounds as if that's all you're interested in. Remember, salaries in cities and towns outside California likely will be lower than what you may have been used to. Be prepared to discuss your expectations and, if necessary, explain why you are willing to accept a lower salary than you are making in California. Leave questions about relocation expenses until second interviews. You need to get the employer interested in hiring you first.

As you ask questions during an interview, you can gather information about salaries, about the company, and how well you might fit in. The answers you receive will give you an idea of the candidness of the interviewer and the company.

Listen Many of us are not good listeners. We frequently focus too much attention on what *we're* planning to say, and not enough on what someone is saying to us. Under the pressure of an interview, you may tend to concentrate on what you're going to say next. Here's a thought that may help you listen more carefully: Usually interviewers will tell you not only the requirements of the job but also some of the skills or traits they're looking for. In other words, if you listen carefully the interviewer will—indirectly—tell you what you need to say to attract his interest. Careful listening also will tell you if this is the kind of organization you want to join.

Review your strengths Before going into an interview, review your qualifications for the job, and decide what points you want to make about yourself. At some point in the interview you will be asked to explain your experience or skills. Think about the best way to present yourself.

Practice One advantage of interviews, as we'll see later, is that even if you don't get the job, you get experience interviewing. If you haven't looked for a new job for several years, and consequently don't have any current experience in interviewing, practice the techniques before your first interview. Have your spouse or a friend ask you the stock questions. Make a list of the points you want to discuss, and practice talking about yourself. (Remember, some organizations may schedule you for multiple interviews the same day. Be prepared to repeat yourself.)

Be yourself The advice to prepare and practice does not mean that you need to create a slick public relations version of yourself for interviews. In addition to looking for business qualifications, interviewers in smaller firms in smaller towns are going to be looking for someone who will fit in, not someone from a big city who knows all the answers. Strike a balance; be professional, but don't hide your personality.

The training director for a Southern California firm provided a perfect example of the importance of being yourself. She said her department was interviewing for a new training coordinator, and had narrowed the candidates down to two people. The first one, the training director said, was perfect. She had the right qualifications, the right experience, and she answered all questions with precision. She even faxed a thank-you note within two hours after her interview. The second candidate's background was not quite as impressive as the first's, but she was personable and both people who interviewed her agreed that her personality would mesh well with everyone in the office. Who got the job? The second candidate. The interviewers said they just didn't think "Ms. Perfect" would be right for them. (The interviewers apparently were correct. When "Ms. Perfect" found out she did not get the job, she called the company and angrily criticized the people who made the decision.)

Networking

To find a job or start a business out of state, networking is not an option. It's a necessity. Effective networking is a combination of good interpersonal skills and simply getting your face and name in front of as many people as possible, as often as possible. The people who are best at business networking are not the glad-handing, back-slapping comics, but the serious individuals who get involved in organizations and demonstrate a genuine concern for others. They're people who don't adopt a persona when they meet others; they act like themselves.

The more contacts you develop, the more your job leads multiply. Don't just join an organization, volunteer when you can. Don't just attend meetings, circulate, talk to people, be a speaker or workshop leader. If you're not a natural extrovert you may need to push yourself to build your contacts. Try to meet a certain number of new people every time you attend a meeting. Ask people you already know to introduce you to others. Good networking skills are important to expand your contacts in California *and* to get your name known in your target city. Networking is discussed in more detail later in the chapter.

Computer savvy

Computer knowledge will help your job hunting in many ways. E-mail is a convenient way to keep in touch with people, with a minimum amount of time expended. The World Wide Web has become a valuable source of jobs and referrals. Public and private databases make research a snap and save you hours over the old methods of sorting through dusty business directories and files. Your computer and a laser printer make it possible for you to write, design, and print top quality, professional résumés. Your correspondence, even if you do it at home, can be sharply professional-looking and spelling- and grammar-checked. All of these things make computer knowledge a strong business asset, not to mention the advantage your high-tech knowledge will give you as a potential employee.

Courtesy

It shouldn't come as a surprise that not everyone uses the golden rule in business today. But just as the flock of poor résumés flying around corporate America will make yours stand out, courtesy and thoughtfulness can make the difference as you search for a job. A thank-you note after a job interview can emphasize your interest in the company and demonstrate your professionalism. (Just don't fax it two hours after your interview.)

When someone sends you material you requested, send him a thank-you note. When you get a referral from someone who says you can use his name, drop him a note or call him briefly to express your appreciation; tell him that you followed up on his suggestion. Follow-ups serve several purposes. You never know when you might need additional information from someone. If he remembers you from your thank-you note, you're likely to get continuing and enthusiastic help. If you let people know that you used their names as a reference, they will be prepared if the person to whom you gave their names calls to check you out. But the best reason for being courteous is that it can become a habit.

(1) Obtain a transfer

In addition to job-hunting skills, you need a strategy to accomplish your goals. One strategy is to be transferred. It's the easiest way to insure a job when you move out of state. Or, if your company joins the hundreds that have relocated to another Western state, you might have an opportunity to move with your firm. According to the Employee Relocation Council, a trade group, hundreds of thousands of people receive job transfers every year. Many of these transfers involve California companies. (See Appendix B.)

The trick, of course, is to be transferred to a desirable location. If a job transfer is a possibility, use the information-gathering suggestions in Chapters 3 and 4 to collect data on the cities where you could be relocated. Even if your company has out-of-state facilities only in places like Wenatchee, Wash., or Pahrump, Nev., don't despair; do the research. You could find out that strange-sounding places such as Wenatchee and Pahrump have many of the things you're looking for in a new community.

If you are offered a transfer to another site, you can expect to get help from your employer in moving, finding a new home, and other necessities. The amount of assistance companies give transferring employees varies. "No matter what anyone tells you, the amount of money and assistance you get in relocating is based on your title [with the company] and how much you make," says a relocation specialist from a large Southern California aerospace firm. A brief review of some California firms' relocation policies seems to confirm this. Company policies vary, of course, and employee relocation assistance also depends on how far you're going to move and whether or not you own your home in California.

The "standard" relocation policy, according to the ERC, includes these elements:
- Shipping of household goods,
- Temporary living expenses in the new location,
- Real estate sales assistance,
- House-hunting trips (usually including expenses for a spouse and some-times children),
- Home-purchase closing costs,
- Miscellaneous expenses (often without itemization required).

According to the ERC, companies that provide real estate sales assistance frequently do it through an outside firm that contracts to buy your home, either immediately or after you have tried to sell it for a specified period. Most employers will not provide closing costs for the purchase of a home if you don't already own one.

Some corporations don't bother with detailed, tiered relocation policies; they just give employees a specific sum of money. Often, lower-level employees will just get a lump-sum payment. That payment may be based on many factors, such as the cost of a rental truck, plus expenses for doing a self-move. (One company that relocated to Nevada offered hourly employees $5,000 to make the move.)

Other services you may receive from your employer, if you are transferred, include help locating schools for your children, and job-search assistance for your spouse. The ERC says that about half of all corporations that transfer employees provide some type of employment help for spouses. The majority of companies that provide help do so by paying outside placement or counseling agencies. Specific services for spouses may include the costs of résumé preparation and printing, job hunting trips, and required licenses or exams.

Before you agree to a move, or perhaps before you ask about a job transfer, review your company's relocation policies. Your situation may dictate that you negotiate with your employer for the best relocation package you can get. Lest you think that only big shots receive all the help, the ERC says that the average transferee makes between $45,000 and $60,000, and is between 36 and 40 years old.

An alternative to getting a transfer is the possibility of telecommuting. The term refers to people who work at home and communicate with their companies by phone, fax, and modem. While the concept of telecommuting has received wide media exposure, the number of people who are full-time telecommuters is smaller than you may think. Some surveys that purport to show the number of telecommuters at more than 8 million include people who may work at home *some days*. It's actually rare for people to never go into the office. Discounting people who stay at home part time, William Barrett, in the July/August 1990 issue of *Worth* magazine, estimated that there may be only about 2 million telecommuters in the country. If you think you could become one of those 2 million, don't propose the idea to your boss right away. First, prepare a telecommuting proposal that shows the benefits to your organization *and to your boss*. If you're on good terms with your boss, present your proposal orally and see what happens.

Two-income families

Partners in two-income families need to plan job-hunting strategies together. If one of you can obtain a transfer, is the other one willing to move and look for a job in the new location? If neither of you have a possibility for relocation, then what? You could both search for jobs out of state and move when one of you lands something. Some couples take turns, alternately moving to advance his or her career. But if your purpose is to move out of California, rather than move up the career ladder, how is that going to influence your plans? One good job offer—for you or your spouse—could be your ticket out of state. So why not double your chances? Pick your target states or towns and start two networking campaigns.

If one or both of you is able to take your job with you, that can simplify your decision. For example, when Lee Taylor and his wife, Billi Cusick, moved from Mountain View to a mountain home outside of Telluride, Colo., in 1993, both were able to take their work with them. He is a software technical writer and Web site developer. She is a pediatric physical therapist who conducts specialized training programs for other therapists. Regardless of your work/job interests, discussing your options first will help you find a job-hunting strategy you can work on together.

(2) Get a new job in your field

The growth of the World Wide Web has substantially expanded possibilities for job searching out of state. Many of the job- and information-searching capabilities on the Internet and Web have only begun to be tapped by job seekers. Nevertheless, Fred Jandt, co-author of *Using the Internet and the World Wide Web in Your Job Search,* says there are already as many as one million jobs available on the Web today. While online communications may be your best resource in hunting for a job outside California, remember that your Web surfing and related activities have the same goal as mailing out a résumé: getting an interview.

Use all possibilities open to you, including the more conventional forms of job searching—networking, cold calling, and studying the trades. First, we'll review these traditional methods of job hunting, then move on to the growing online possibilities.

Association help

In the early 1990s, I was president of the Orange County Chapter of the International Association of Business Communicators, an organization of people in public relations, marketing, and related fields. My name was listed in IABC directories and publications and, as a result, I was repeatedly contacted by communicators interested in relocating to California. I received phone calls and unsolicited résumés and cover letters from IABC members, primarily from the East and Midwest. I tried to be honest about the job market, which at the time was relatively poor. But I always gave everyone I talked to suggestions about local trade publications and other professional contacts they might not have considered.

During my term as president, before we moved to Nevada, my wife had a job opportunity in the Portland area. The job seemed so promising that I started thinking about finding a job for myself up there. One of the first things I did was call an IABC member in Portland I had met at a conference about six months earlier. He not only gave me the names and numbers of people I could talk with to set up interviews, but because he worked for a school district, he was able to give me advice on high schools in the area. He even volunteered to drive me around to show me different neighborhoods where we might want to live. Ultimately we decided not to move to Portland, but I will always remember the friendly help.

I have a theory that deep down, people want to be friendly and helpful to others. But they often need an excuse to do so. Belonging to the same trade or professional association can be that excuse. People who are normally interested in helping others may go out of their way to help a fellow association member. Even people who tend to be less than magnanimous usually will extend at least minimum courtesies to people who share a common bond with them.

Active membership in a professional or trade association is one of the best assets you can have in the business world, particularly when you are looking for a job. Belonging to a national or international club, association, or society can be a giant step toward effective networking locally. It also gives you a built-in system for connecting with colleagues in other states. If you're just starting a long-term plan to get out of California, joining an association is a great first step. A necessary second step is to volunteer to serve on a committee. Being active in your group lets you meet more people and lets more people get to see your name.

If you're a member of a business association, you have at least two ways to make contacts out of state. You can ask people in your local group if they know anyone in your target city. You also can attend a meeting of a local chapter (if available) in your potential hometown. At minimum, call the president of the chapter in your target city or region and introduce yourself. Tell him or her that you're a member in California and are interested in relocating. This is far more effective than sending an unsolicited résumé. The next action you take will depend upon the reception you receive.

Most organizations have directories or databases you can use to put together a list of out-of-state contacts. Your list could include people in your field who are the same level as you, and also senior-level members or company officers who might be in the market for a new employee with your skills. In addition, many local and national organizations sponsor job banks or publish employment newsletters. Often jobs listed through an association are filled without the listing ever reaching a newspaper or online site.

If you belong to a business association it usually means you're a professional interested in maintaining the standards in your field, remaining informed about industry trends, and enhancing your skills. These things are of interest to potential employers. Then again, some people join associations simply to receive the groups' job newsletters. And some people say they join associations so they can add the groups' names to their résumés.

Networking, cold calling

Networking extends well beyond formal associations and includes people you know, and people you don't know—yet. Without broadcasting to your present employer that you're planning to move, you can use all of your routine business contacts to hunt for leads and referrals to out-of-state companies. Your customers, clients, suppliers, friends, colleagues, former bosses, and casual business acquaintances can be sources of leads. Some people you talk with may be able to offer only encouragement, or tell you they're envious of your plans to leave. Keep trying. Use your imagination to locate people you can talk with in your target cities.

In his perennial best seller, *What Color Is Your Parachute?*, R. N. Bolles suggests using your college connections. This is one of many useful ideas you'll find in his book. If you have a directory of graduates from your college, look up people in your dream hometown. See if you can find people from the same academic department, or from your graduating class. Look for people who are working in your field. Call them up. Don't ask them for a job referral, just explain that you graduated from the same college they did, and that you're thinking about relocating to their town. You may be pleasantly surprised. What's the worst they can say? Other people to contact, if you can locate them in your destination city, are fraternity or sorority members, service club members, or simply people in your business or profession.

A common form of job hunting involves combining your networking contacts with cold calls and letters to set up interviews. Unless you know about a specific opening, it's easiest to obtain a brief interview by saying you're just gathering information. Explain that you are currently employed, but that you are thinking about relocating. This takes the pressure off the person you're going to see; she knows you're not asking for a job, (even if, indirectly, you really are). Trying to land information-only interviews this way, long distance, is more difficult, but not impossible.

Glenn Sweitzer a graphic designer, and his wife Sheri, moved from Burbank to Tennessee in 1993. Glenn cites quakes, violence, a poor job market, congestion, "and a lot of bad attitudes" as their reasons for leaving California. At the time, Glenn was a partner in a design agency, having previously worked as a designer for Walt Disney. The couple invested vacation time over several years checking out different states. In the towns they visited on vacation, Glenn set up interviews to check out the job market in his field. Here's what they did:

Their selection of places to visit was based on library research, a trip to visit a cousin of Sheri's in one case, and some dreaming about their ideal hometown.

Their method of job hunting was straightforward. In many cases they persuaded realtors to send them local phone books. Glenn then reviewed the phone books, looking for listings under "graphic design," "advertising," and related fields. He followed up with cold calls. Some calls he made before they left; others he made after they arrived in a prospective hometown.

When at a location, the couple drove around to find areas they liked. Then Glenn called nearby firms. Or, since design firms are often small, two-person shops, Glenn sometimes stopped in unannounced. This often gave him a good chance to chat with the owner.

The couple's travels took them to (picturesque, but not picture-perfect) Vermont, Colorado, Pennsylvania, Georgia, and finally the Nashville area. Sweitzer said that when he set up interviews he tried not to let people know he was from Los Angeles. In some cases, of course, it was unavoidable.

One of their trips took them to Atlanta, where his California connections didn't open doors for him. "I had set up about 10 job interviews before I went out there and not one of them panned out. Everybody had a different excuse: 'we're too busy' or 'the place just burned down.' It was frustrating. I couldn't even get in the door. They knew we were coming from L.A.; I didn't think it would be that big of a deal . . ."

In spite of the reception, Glenn and Sheri liked Atlanta. They returned to California determined to move, and put their house on the market. When it didn't sell, they took it off the market and waited.

At the recommendation of a relative, they next tried Nashville. Sweitzer got an entirely different welcome. "The second day we were here, we knew this was it. I made cold calls and set up three job interviews. Everyone was so friendly. They would say: 'We may have something coming up, but why don't you call so-and-so and say I sent you.' I met so many people that way. . . . It just started snowballing."

The Sweitzers moved to Franklin, Tenn., but Glenn decided to keep working for the Southern California agency for a while. After about eight months, however, he knew he would have to go to work for someone else in Tennessee or start his own business. The decision "fell into my lap," says Sweitzer. He was coaching a men's softball team and one of the players was president of a local record company. The company became the first client of Sweitzer's new design firm and represented 90 percent of his business the first year.

Like Sweitzer, you will get different reactions from people in different places. But if you're persistent you may find your Nashville. Keep interviewing, polish your skills, and see what happens.

Using conventional resources

As many expatriates have learned, a phone book can be a handy guide to finding potential employers and temporary agencies in a distant city. While it's not recommended that you move on the basis of obtaining temp work, it's a good entry into the local job market if your spouse has a job offer or transfer, and you therefore have one steady income.

Other useful publications include newspapers, trade magazines, and business journals. Most medium-to-large areas have weekly business newspapers. Often these papers give you a more in-depth look at the business community than the business section of the local daily newspaper (which is usually devoted to stock quotations, national stories, and some local reporting). Local business weeklies often run lists of top companies in different fields. For example, the *Las Vegas Business Press* has run lists of the top ad agencies, construction firms, and banking companies in town. The listings usually include the size of companies, number of employees, and contact names. When you're reading trade and local papers look for news of companies moving into town, expanding, or offering new products. Each of these events may create a company need (a job opening) that you can fill.

States' commerce departments and city and regional chambers of commerce usually have statistics on local economic conditions and per capita income (see Table 6.1), lists of major employers, and a variety of other helpful business data. Much of the information is more useful if you're thinking about starting your own business, but try these sources anyway.

You also can call on companies without notice. Obviously it's better if you can arrange a meeting ahead of time, but if you're driving around looking for your heavenly place to live, and you spot a company that you think employs people with your skills, stop in. Even if you don't get to speak with anyone beyond the receptionist, you might be able to get contact names, make an appointment for later, pick up company literature, and see what the working environment is like.

One ex-Californian suggests getting a post office box or other local address in a town that you are thinking of moving to. That way you can put a local address on your sales letters and résumé. You might also add a local phone number on your résumé, says Keith Robinson, director of professional services at the San Jose office of the outplacement firm, Lee, Hecht, Harrison, Inc. He explains how a California client, whose parents lived in Tampa, Fla., used their address and phone number on her résumé. The client used her parents' Tampa retirement home address and installed an answering machine on their phone to take her messages when she was trying to find a job in the Tampa area. If you use this strategy, says Robinson, even though your

Per capita income by state

Alaska	$24,182
Arizona	20,421
California	23,699
Colorado	23,449
Florida	22,916
Hawaii	24,738
Idaho	19,264
Illinois	24,763
Minnesota	23,118
Montana	18,482
Nevada	25,013
New Mexico	18,055
New York	26,782
North Carolina	20,604
Oregon	21,736
Tennessee	20,376
Texas	20,654
Utah	18,223
Washington	23,639
Wisconsin	21,839
Wyoming	21,321

Table 6.1 Source: U.S. Bureau of Economic Analysis, Survey of Current Business, May 1996 issue. U.S. Bureau of the Census, *Statistical Abstract of the United States;* 1996 (116th edition). Data for 1995.

résumé shows your last or present job in California, you can explain that you are in the process of relocating. This doesn't put you in a good position to ask for relocation costs, he says, but you might be able to negotiate a hiring bonus because you're paying your own moving expenses. Robinson cautions that relocation cost negotiations "really, really vary," depending on many factors. In some cases, he says, if you're relocating to your ideal destination and get a good job offer, any help you get at all with moving expenses should be considered gravy. Robinson also stresses the need to spend time—weeks if necessary—networking in your target city.

In all of your cold calling, networking, and interviewing, remember to do one thing: ask for referrals. Ask if the person you're talking with can refer you to someone else who might help you. Even potential employers may refer you to other companies. It's an axiom in sales to ask for referrals. You're selling yourself; do the same.

Of the conventional ways of finding a job, using classified ads is the only topic not yet mentioned. Employment experts and head hunters urge you not to rely on ads as your chief source of leads. The idea is to find a job opening before it gets to the classifieds. Many thousands of jobs, however, are advertised the traditional way, so don't overlook this source.

Remember the value of cover letters and never send out a naked résumé in response to an ad. Use the letter to draw attention to your background and the experience you have that matches the requirements in the ad. If an ad asks you for a salary history don't necessarily comply. While not complying could mean an employer would not consider your résumé, your past salary could peg you either too high or too low. If you have earned national awards or other recognition, have an impressive-sounding job title, or have worked for a well-known company, stress these attributes to get an employer to respond.

Job hunting on the Web

Online resources for employment are even more vast than the Web sources of information on states and cities. While conventional job-hunting techniques are important, the Web lets you

- network with colleagues and potential employers,
- dig up background information on attractive-looking companies,
- submit your resume,
- read job-hunting advice, and
- scan the classifieds

—all while sitting at your computer. Thousands of job and employment related sites are awaiting.

"If I were relocating, I'd go first to the newsgroups for that city," says *Job Search* author Jandt, also a Cal State University - San Bernardino professor.

Newsgroups, discussed in Chapter 3 and defined in Appendix A, can be more than sources of information on your projected destinations. They can be a way to find job openings, gather information on local job markets, and obtain answers to questions about finding work in a distant city. You can gather a variety of relevant information through city and regional newsgroups, but there are also many newsgroups devoted strictly to jobs, résumés, new business opportunities, and related topics. Some newsgroups deal with jobs and employment within a state as their simple names indicate: *AZ.jobs, CO.jobs.* These obviously cover employment in Arizona and Colorado respectively. Other state newsgroups are *UT.jobs, NV.jobs,* and *NM.jobs.* City job newsgroups are also available such as *Portland.jobs.offered* and *Seattle.jobs.offered.* Use these specialized groups to hunt for jobs.

As mentioned earlier, you need time to become familiar with newsgroup postings before you use a particular newsgroup. In addition to job listings, you'll find a generous helping of business opportunities—many of which seem to fall into the get-rich-quick category—and a variety of résumés. Reviewing résumés is excellent preparation for revising your own. Reading dozens of résumés—good and bad—gives you an idea of what human resource development people go through daily. You quickly learn that the cute ideas designed to attract attention do only that and are not professional.

Another main area for Web job research is sites dedicated to résumés and classified ads. These sites attract thousands of individuals looking for jobs, and employers looking for people. Many also contain job-hunting and career advice. To get an idea of how these sites work, review a few of the most popular ones. As mentioned earlier, the Web is constantly changing. The job- and business-related sites discussed here may be different by the time you access them. Some sites may be expanded, others discontinued. Regardless, using search engines and directories of links you'll be able to locate new, similar job-related Web pages.

Jandt recommends three sites for people looking for work out of state: *Online Career Center, Monster Board,* and *Intellimatch.* The first site, abbreviated OCC, lets you search for jobs three ways. The quickest is to scroll through a list of cities and select the ones you're interested in. Page through the site and you can find listings for jobs in Albuquerque or Provo, Utah, for example. You may also look for jobs using a keyword search or OCC's search agent. The agent scans all posted jobs using key words and phrases you provide. After you've reviewed the results of the search, the agent will remember your job criteria; when you log on to OCC again, it can retrieve any new job postings that match. Many of the listings—like those on other sites—allow job seekers to mail, fax, or e-mail their résumés. To post your résumé on OCC, you can send it electronically or submit a paper copy through the (U.S.) mail.

The second site, the *Monster Board,* has colorful cartoon graphics to match its unconventional name. The name might refer to its monstrously large database of jobs. (It's in the tens of thousands. You'll see the exact number of jobs as soon as you sign on.) The *Monster Board*'s job search agent is called

Jobba-the-Hunt. You give Jobba a job profile and it searches for listings and posts them to your *Monster Board* "in" box. The *Monster Board* also lets you post your résumé, read career advice articles, do research on companies, and conduct keyword searches.

There's a potential drawback to using keywords when looking for job ads. For example, if you're looking for a job managing microwave communications, and you use those two words for your search, you might get back listings for jobs repairing microwave ovens or writing business letters. Actually you're not too likely to find jobs for appliance repair people on the *Monster Board* because the majority of its listings are in high-tech fields. This is one of the disadvantages of Web job searching if you're not employed in high technology. As the Web becomes a more common tool for human resources people in all fields, job listings will become more diversified. Some Web job listings, however, particularly those that come from daily newspapers, do cover a broad range of employment opportunities.

Intellimatch, similar to the other sites in some ways, has a special service that earns Jandt's strong recommendation. When you post a résumé with *Intellimatch* you can specify two levels of confidentiality. You can block your employer from being able to see that your résumé has been posted, or you can simply have your name and all contact information omitted. You create your résumé online by answering a series of questions about employment history, education, etc. *Intellimatch* asks you to create a password that allows you to access and revise your résumé as necessary.

Another job/résumé site you should know about is *E-Span.* This site asks you a series of questions that it uses to hunt down job possibilities. You're asked about your education, the number of years of experience you have, and the level of employment you're looking for, i.e. entry level, management, etc. You then tell *E-Span* where to look for jobs, and you provide key words that describe your field. (As an experiment, I listed "marketing," and asked for a managerial job in Colorado. *E-Span* found four matching jobs including a marketing manager job in Denver, and a job as director of corporate communications in Boulder.) *E-Span* also searches for job postings in newsgroups.

After you have posted your résumé with one or more of these boards, it becomes immediately available to recruiters and HRD people at companies around the country. Some employers scan the electronic résumés as they do the paper versions. Other companies download entire résumé databases at a time, then use keyword searches of their own to find job candidates. For example, if Hewlett-Packard were looking for a mechanical design engineer, those are the words it would use to search though thousands of résumés at once. To get your résumé plucked from cyberspace, Jandt recommends that you use precise industry titles to describe the jobs you've held and the work you've done.

Employers and job search firms who use electronic searching may also look for people in their geographical area first—to avoid the trouble and expense of relocating new employees. This could be an incentive for you to obtain a local address in your target town to use in your electronic résumé.

You may find yourself communicating with potential employers by e-mail. It's easy for an employer to ask a few questions via e-mail before she calls you for an interview. Remember that your correspondence, although transmitted via computer, is nonetheless the equivalent of a business letter. In general, e-mail, both internal and external, tends to be more informal than printed business letters or memos. This is not necessarily bad; much business writing today is stuffy and difficult to understand. Don't be tempted, however, to use the slang and abstract abbreviations that you use when you send e-mail to friends within your office.

Beyond the few job Web sites mentioned here is an abundance of other employment information and listings of classifieds. One of the largest collections of ads is on *Career Path*. This site is a collection of classified job ads from many of the largest newspapers in the country, including the *Seattle Times, Orlando Sentinel, Denver Post,* and others. You can search these by location, category, and key words. If you're looking for a city not listed in *Career Path*, find the Web site of the individual newspaper you're looking for. Many online daily newspapers carry classified ads. You can search for a sales job in the *Anchorage Daily News* online classifieds, or scan for an accounting position in the *Billings* (Montana) *Gazette.*

Another good site to see is *Yahoo!* The popular search engine contains a wealth of business and employment information arranged in a logical pattern. From *Yahoo*'s category list, select "business"; then select "employment." You'll find links to dozens of other useful job sites, background information and links to employers all over the country, access to business-related newsgroups, and other information. Of course the *Yahoo* search engine is also handy for finding specific sites not listed in the index—such as out-of-town business publications, recruiting firms, or associations.

Some states and cities also have job information sites. Most of these are accessed from or linked to a state or city's main home page. One example, *Arizona Careers Online,* maintains a database of more than 10,000 jobs and 30,000 résumés. The site also has a list of major employers in the Phoenix and Tucson areas, plus links to colleges and universities, Arizona city home pages, and other sites. The online *Job Seekers Guide to Utah* is a veritable do-it-yourself kit for finding employment in the Beehive State. Among the many useful chapters are those on education and training opportunities in Utah, fundamentals of contacting employers, and tips on interviewing and salary negotiation. Of particular interest to Californians are the questions and answers about living in Utah and profiles of the job market and industries in Utah. The information-packed Utah site also has lists of job hot lines and data on school districts, labor organizations, career centers, and newspapers.

Finally, once you have identified potential employers in your target city, look up the companies' home pages. Not only will you find out detailed information about the firms, but many companies post job openings on their Web sites. Job listings on company sites are often more detailed that those elsewhere. See the next section for Web site addresses.

The next chapter explores further employment-search techniques as it reviews the remaining three strategies for making a living out of state.

Resources

Books

What Color is Your Parachute?
Richard Nelson Bolles
Ten Speed Press, 1997

Using the Internet and the World Wide Web in Your Job Search
2nd. ed.
Fred E. Jandt and Mary B. Nemnich
JIST Works, Inc., 1996
  Contains advice on understanding and using the Internet, job searching, electronic résumés, and much more. Includes examples of dozens of Web sites and online résumés.

Directories

To find information on companies, visit the business-reference section of your library and look for these directories:

Moody's Industrial Manual
Standard and Poors Register of Corporations
Thomas Register of American Manufacturing
Dun and Bradstreet's Million Dollar Directory

Web Sites
Online Career Center *http://www.occ.com*

Monster Board *http://www.monster.com*

Intellimatch *http://www.intellimatch.com*

E-Span *http://www.espan.com/*

Career Path *http://www.careerpath.com*

Yahoo! *http://www.yahoo.com/Business_and_Economy/Employment/Jobs*

Arizona Careers Online *http://www.diversecity.com/aztuc/jobs.html*

Job Seekers Guide to Utah *http://udesb.state.ut.us/lmi/jsguide*

Career Mosaic *http://www.careermosaic.com*
This site, similar to the others discussed in the text, features links to local online job fairs and includes extensive career guidance resources.

Best Jobs in the USA Today *http://www.bestjobsusa.com/alt_index.html*
Site contains the Résumé Pavilion for posting your résumé, plus a collection of career books.

MedSearch America *http://www.medsearch.com*
Employment site devoted to careers in health and medicine.

Virtual Job Fair *http://www.vjf.com/pub/rsubmit.html*
This site allows you to post your résumé with the database, and also send it off via e-mail in response to job ads. Your listed résumé may be confidential.

USA Jobs *http://www.usajobs.opm.gov*
To find government jobs, look to this site operated by the U.S. Office of Personnel Management. Contains listings for all categories of employment.

America's Brightest *http://www.americasbrightest.com*
You can subscribe to the online services of this consulting company. The site has a variety of experts on call to answer your questions about careers and small business.

State agencies
For a listing of state business agencies, see the end of Chapter 7.

7

Changing careers, starting a business

Mark Dorio was a lifelong employee at a corporation he loved: Xerox. For many years he worked for the high technology company by day, and went to college in the evening. He received his bachelor's degree and went on to earn a master's degree from UCLA. In spite of a job and a company that he praises to this day, he resigned from Xerox. He quit after 24 years to leave California and teach math at a community college in Carson City, Nev. The rigors of L.A. freeway commuting, high housing costs in the San Fernando Valley, and doubts about the quality of schools for his children were factors that prompted him to seek a change. He decided to change jobs so he could move to a small, more peaceful community; he and his family have lived in Nevada since 1990. "We love Carson City," he says.

Obtaining a job transfer, or finding a new job in your field, are traditional ways of seeking out-of-state employment. Dorio and thousands of other expatriates took different paths. This chapter reviews the final three ways (numbered 3, 4, and 5) to find work out of state: change job fields; start your own business; take your job with you.

(3) Find a job in another field

Dorio's successful transition from corporate California, to Carson City in the shadow of the Sierra Nevadas, demonstrates several strategies and techniques necessary to find work in a different field, in a different state. Many of the job-hunting techniques and suggestions in the previous chapter, particularly the online resources, apply to finding a job in a different business or occupation. But moving to another state *and* changing business roles often requires additional preparation.

If one of your driving forces is to relocate to a tiny community, your job opportunities will be more limited. Expanding the types of jobs you apply for can increase your chances of landing something. Take a look back at your personal inventory. Make sure you are not limiting yourself artificially. Are you a bank accountant or an accountant? Are you an office supply marketing manager or a marketing manager? Not everyone can transplant his or her speciality into every industry—but you can stretch. For example, if you're a field sales representative for a company that sells cleaning supplies to hotels, you could sell other products to hotels. Or you could sell cleaning supplies to factories or offices.

What experiences and skills do you find on your inventory that might translate into a different type of job? Have you worked part time or as a volunteer in a field that you might pursue as a career? Is your education in a field other than the one in which you're now working? Do you have experience as an officer in an association? If so, that could demonstrate your abilities as an administrator or organizer. Have you raised funds for charities, or done any other nonprofessional selling that you enjoyed?

You may have several areas of interest or experience in your background that you can translate into a job. If you don't, or if you want to multiply your job possibilities further, consider more training. Ironically, your best opportunities for developing additional job skills through education may be in California. The state's community colleges, for example, are one of the few true bargains for taxpayers. For nominal fees you can receive training in dozens of fields, from nursing to accounting to court reporting to cooking. Private trade schools, continuing education programs through colleges and school districts, and classes or seminars through your employer, are all available to you in California. Depending on the college and the state, classes in another state may be more expensive. You may have to pay nonresident fees.

Adding an extra skill or level of education to your résumé may delay your escape schedule, but it can be valuable for your future. Before you enroll in any course, study the job market in your target state or region to see what skills are in demand. Some skills, such as nursing and teaching, will be an asset in many states. Other skills may or may not help you find a job in a smaller community. Contact state and local chambers, business schools at universities, and trade associations to find out about the demand for certain skills in the geographic area you've selected. For example, the *Job Seekers Guide to Utah* (on the Web) lists the top 50 occupations in demand in Utah and the top 30 fastest growing jobs in Utah. Similar information is available from agencies in other states.

To find a job in a different field out of state, you should do many of the things you would do if you wanted to switch careers in California. The information-only interviews mentioned earlier can be a valuable way to learn about the requirements of a new career. Talk with people in California first. Then, if you decide you want to seriously pursue a new career, make appointments with people in that field in your destination city or cities.

Stick with it

Preparation, practice, and perseverance were the keys to Dorio's career transition. But his first choice for getting out of Los Angeles would have been a transfer within Xerox. He says he hoped for a transfer to Rochester, N.Y., so he could work at Xerox headquarters, but when he realized his chances were fairly slim, he developed other options. "My goal was to either be an instructor in fundamental Xerography at the [Xerox Corporation's] Leesburg Center in Virginia, or to be a math instructor at a community college." Dorio pursued both goals simultaneously.

After getting his master's degree in math, he started teaching part time in 1983 at Los Angeles Valley College in Van Nuys near where he lived. The work supplemented his Xerox salary, gave him experience in teaching college, and ultimately helped him relocate. When he and his wife, Lindsay, decided they wanted to leave Los Angeles, they were living in "a wreck of a rental home" in the San Fernando Valley community of Sherman Oaks. Dorio was spending an hour or more commuting to Xerox.

He found instructor job openings posted at Valley College, so he started applying to schools in small communities around the West. Oregon was one of his first targets, and his first interview was in Klamath Falls. After the interview Dorio called the college to find out how he did. "Usually they don't tell you . . . but the person I talked to said I came in 20th out of 40 or more. I couldn't believe it," says Dorio. "That was pretty bad."

But he was not discouraged. "It was my first interview and as time went on I got better and better."

Dorio says he gained from his experiences, improved his job hunting techniques, and learned new jargon. For instance, he had to discover the collegiate meaning for the term "references." "I didn't know that they wanted letters from people in education. I didn't take in letters, I just wrote down the names of Xerox people who I thought could be a reference for me."

As Dorio says, if you're not selected for a job, most employers will not tell you how you fared in the interviews. Nonetheless, he encourages job hunters to ask questions in order to obtain as much feedback as possible on their interview performances. Dorio continued to apply to community colleges in Oregon and in isolated small towns in Northern California. His experience as a part-time instructor, coupled with support from administrators at Valley College, helped him obtain interviews. With each interview he improved.

"That's what I would tell anyone who wants to follow this path. Go on interview after interview . . . you can feel yourself getting better and better. You get to know more of what [interviewers] are looking for."

In late 1989, after having applied at schools in several small Western towns, and having expressed interest to his employer in a job transfer to Virginia, Dorio interviewed for the Carson City job. He and his wife liked the community, so when the job was offered, he accepted. He says the only reason they are in Nevada now instead of Virginia is that he got the Carson City offer first.

"I felt that I had to make a choice. I was getting older. [He was 45.] I felt that this looked ideal. You know how corporations are. You could go to Leesburg, think it's wonderful, get an increase in pay . . . then two years later you hear that the corporation is going to divest itself of the whole facility and you're on the street."

Hunting up headhunters

Another possibility for obtaining an out-of-state job—either in or out of your industry—is employee-search firms. Judy Thompson, a San Diego executive recruiter with nearly 20 years experience, says search firms usually specialize in either a specific industry or in one type of occupation. Thompson, for example, is an occupational specialist. She finds accounting and finance people for companies in various industries. If you want to explore opportunities outside your present industry, look for headhunters—the slang term search firms—that work with people in your occupation or specialization.

The best way to approach a headhunter? Send a résumé and follow up with a call, or vice versa, says Thompson. If you can't get through to the recruiter, try to talk to an assistant. When you send your résumé to recruiters, Thompson says, your cover letter should specify not just that you're willing to relocate, but the specific city or area you're interested in. Thompson advises you to explain that you've studied the local job market. Tell the recruiter you're familiar with the cost of living, have done your homework, and are ready to move. Mention in your letter to the recruiter how you found his or her firm. Saying you received a referral from someone, or even that you found the firm in a directory, will gain more attention than an impersonal form letter.

Some search firms don't respond, even if you call them, says Thompson. And some recruiters don't have assistants you can talk with. The only way to find out these things is to call and ask if the firm is interested in working with you. "It's like following up with a company," she says. "If you send blind résumés and never follow up, you might be lucky and hear from them. If you make a concerted effort to talk to them, you're going to have more success."

When dealing on the phone and in writing with a headhunter, Thompson advises professionalism and courtesy. One of the most common mistakes people make, she says, is being rude on the telephone when her assistant calls to find out more information. The way you talk with search firm employees is an indication (to the firm) of how well you will do in an interview, if the firm decides to refer you.

Another mistake, she says, is complaining about your current or previous boss. You want a potential employer to know what you can do for him, not how eager you are to criticize your supervisors.

Thompson does not see an advantage in obtaining a local address and phone number for job-hunting purposes; it could be interpreted as deceptive. More important to a recruiter, she says, is your willingness to relocate to a specific area, and to make yourself available for interviews on short notice—even at your own expense. Make it clear that you and your spouse have researched the area and are eager to move.

Whether or not a potential employer will pay for relocation costs, says Thompson, depends upon the law of supply and demand for your particular skill. (Through networking or research, you may be able to find out how available your set of abilities are in your target community.) Salary and management levels are also factors in who pays relocation costs. Thompson suggests that you say you're flexible on relocation costs. Don't say immediately that you're willing to pay; but let the employer know it's negotiable.

To find headhunters, Thompson recommends two sources: the *Directory of Executive Recruiters*, available at libraries, and the *Recruiting and Search Report*, publishers of headhunter lists available through the mail. See the end of this chapter for details.

(4) Start your own business

Moving from the Golden State doesn't mean you have to find a job to make a living. Small business opportunities—without California government red tape—are available in every state. You still will need to learn local business regulations, but many state agencies are willing to help. State commerce departments, chambers of commerce, and other organizations, provide information on license and permit requirements, details on local business conditions, and even advice on the uncertainties of self employment. If you're interested in starting a business in the Phoenix area, for example, a call to the small business specialists at the Arizona Department of Commerce can yield enough information to begin a master's thesis on the Maricopa County economy.

Going into business for yourself in another state, in spite of a less regulated environment, may be more demanding than doing it in California. You have to learn a new marketplace in addition to a new enterprise. Moving from familiar surroundings brings changes, so for some people their work is the one constant in a move (even if they go to work for a different company). If you start your own business, you're changing just about everything in your life, not just your surroundings. That said, going to work for yourself can increase your freedom to do things your way. As with other activities mentioned throughout this book, planning pays dividends.

To start, ask yourself some serious questions. The U.S. Small Business Administration publishes a list of 31 questions asked most often by people getting into business. Adapting and modifying the SBA list yields a succinct collection of questions to think about:

1. What business should you choose?
2. How much money will you need to get started?
3. How can you obtain a loan, if necessary?
4. Will you hire employees?
5. Do you know your legal responsibilities toward employees?
6. Should you use only family members in the business?
7. Would a partner make it easier?
8. How can you determine a good location?
9. Should you buy or lease equipment and space?
10. What do you need to know about accounting and bookkeeping?
11. What do you need to know about marketing and advertising?
12. What is a business plan, and do you need one?

The answers to nearly all these questions will vary, depending upon your personality, your background, the decisions you make, and the information resources you explore. The answer to the last question, however, is constant. You do need a business plan. It is a how-to guide for business success, a guide you create for yourself. Most people have heard that a business plan is necessary to get a small business loan. That's true. But your business plan should be much more than a supplement to a loan application.

Several good books are available on how to create a business plan. Detailed advice on starting a business is beyond the scope of this book, but here is a summary. According to experts, your business plan should include:

Business goals Provide a description of your business, and explain clearly what your objectives are. You might include the opportunities you see in your business situation, and how you will take advantage of them.

Products and services Describe your products and services in detail, including any advantages you have over competing products.

Operations review Explain the equipment, facilities, people, and raw materials you will need to create your products, and how you anticipate acquiring all the elements.

Sales and marketing Determine the size of your market and its characteristics. How will you advertise your products/services? Will you sell directly to the public, or through distributors? What media will you use to promote your company and its products? What is your competitive position?

Financial plan Develop a projected balance sheet and cash-flow statement. The SBA recommends showing your expectations for 12 months ahead. Explain how much money you will need to capitalize the business, and what your sources of funds will be.

Other elements You may include background and qualifications about yourself and other principals, plus a persuasive discussion of how and why the company will succeed.

Your business plan can be complex. It serves as a sales document when you present it to bankers or potential investors. It also is your personal game plan to make your company work. It can be dozens of pages or longer. At a minimum, you need to consult reference books or online services to complete a business plan. If you have doubts about your qualifications to be the final expert on one or more aspects of the plan, such as marketing or financing, get help.

A variety of advice and printed resources are available from the SBA. It's better to get the help and start planning before you move, than to ask an SBA office in another state to rescue you. SBA offices may provide: computers and programs you can use to develop business plans and make financial projections, business start-up guides, audio and video tape programs, and general business reference books. For a low-interest loan, the SBA will refer you to a participating lender.

Small Business Development Centers are another valuable SBA program. Centers are found in every state, and are often co-sponsored by local government agencies or colleges. SBDC counselors are available to provide free advice and training to local entrepreneurs. For a list of addresses and phone numbers for all 900 centers in the country, visit the Web site of the SBDC Research Network, *http://www.smallbiz.suny.edu*. The site also contains links to many other useful small business sites.

The SBA has been on the hit list of Washington, D.C., budget cutters for years and it may not survive much longer. If it doesn't, some of its services probably will. Check federal government Web sites, the U.S. Government Printing Office, or even the office of your congressional representative for help.

Another place to check for help is SCORE, the Service Corps of Retired Executives, a volunteer, non-profit organization of retired business people. SCORE provides free counseling on a variety of business topics.

Local SCORE representatives often work out of chambers of commerce offices. You can solicit the opinions of an unbiased business expert either before you launch a new business, or when you run into trouble with an existing one.

If you are seriously considering starting a business, contact the department of commerce or related agency in your target state to find out the requirements for registering your company. The Colorado Department of Regulatory agencies, for example, offers a Colorado Business Start-Up Kit that explains the tax and business registration procedures. It also reviews a variety of decisions you will have to make, no matter where you start your company.

The Colorado kit begins by introducing you to the different forms of organization or legal structure you can choose from, lists advantages and disadvantages for each, and tells you where to register. You choice of organization includes:

- Sole proprietorship
- General partnership
- Corporation
- S corporation
- General and limited partnerships
- Limited liability company or partnerships (A new form of organization started in Wyoming and Colorado.)

Next in the Colorado kit is a discussion of your financial and legal responsibilities to your employees. It covers topics such as payroll taxes, workers compensation insurance, and the differences between employees and independent contractors. This section is filled with references to state and federal agencies where you can go for more information. Free payroll-tax classes are listed also. Information on Colorado sales and property taxes comes next. You learn, for example, that a retailer license, which permits you to collect and remit sales tax, costs $16 plus a one-time $50 deposit. (A similar permit in California may require a much larger deposit.)

Other resources and information in the Colorado kit include:

- A listing of the state's Small Business Development Centers,
- Details on the state's computerized information network and job training programs offered through community colleges,
- A listing of all chambers of commerce in the state, and
- Separate chapters on legal liabilities, marketing, financial planning, and trademarks.

Most Western states have similar assistance available. They also have reasonable tax rates and low fees. Washington State's Department of

Community, Trade and Economic Development offers a 268-page book, the *Business Resource Directory for Financial and Technical Assistance.* It explains all services offered by counties, chambers, regional business development organizations, plus the state and federal governments. This book is invaluable if you're thinking of setting up shop in Washington. The Washington package for small business also includes a detailed guide to developing your business plan prepared by Washington State University - Pullman.

As you research your business plan or look for an ideal market for your new endeavor, don't forget two of the online demographic resources listed in Chapter 4—the Social Sciences Data Center at the University of Virginia and the Government Information Sharing Project site at Oregon State University. They are ideal sources of information to develop profiles of market areas and communities.

Another factor you may want to consider is the extent of unionization in your target area. See Table 7.1.

Buying a business or franchise

It's possible to go into business for yourself without starting from scratch: buy an existing business or buy a franchise. What you get when you buy a franchise varies depending on the company. Name recognition, advertising support, management training and advice, and supplies are among the elements that attract entrepreneurs to small franchises. According to the International Franchise Association, franchisers in service-related fields are expected to continue their rapid growth. Areas that are growing, according to the association, include home remodeling and repair, carpet cleaning, maintenance and cleaning services, copying and printing, and temporary help services. The association cautions that rapid growth by a franchiser does not guarantee success. A firm that grows too quickly may not be able to adequately support its franchisees.

Before you buy a business or franchise, do the same detailed planning you would if you were starting your own independent business, including studying your market to see if it can support the business. In addition, there are several precautions you should take when checking out franchising organizations. Franchisers that are regulated by the Federal Trade Commission are required to give you a detailed disclosure statement at least ten days before you commit yourself to a purchase. Review the disclosure materials before making any final decision. The company is required to give you the names, addresses, and telephone numbers of other franchise purchasers; this is vital information. You should contact many other owners to find out about the company and see if the promises made to you are accurate, based on the

Labor union membership by state
Percent of workers

Alaska*	23.1
Arizona	8.0
California	17.7
Colorado	9.9
Florida*	7.3
Hawaii	24.6
Idaho*	8.1
Illinois	20.2
Minnesota	20.3
Montana	15.8
Nevada	20.2
New Mexico	9.4
New York	27.7
North Carolina*	4.2
Oregon	20.1
Tennessee*	9.5
Texas*	6.5
Utah*	9.0
Washington	21.0
Wisconsin	17.7
Wyoming*	11.2

*Right to work state. (Union membership, as a condition of employment, is prohibited.)

Table 7.1 Reprinted with permission from a 1996 BNA Special Report, *Union Membership and Earnings Data Book: Compilations from the Current Population Survey (1996 edition)* published by The Bureau of National Affairs, Inc., Washington, D.C. 20037. Authored by Barry Hirsch and David Macpherson of Florida State University.

experience of others. You should also get an audited financial statement of the franchise company, an itemized list of all costs you will incur, and a list of the responsibilities you and the franchising company will have after you agree to a purchase.

Further, get a copy of the *FTC Franchise Rule* and become familiar with its requirements. The FTC recommends that when buying a franchise, you have an attorney review the contract and disclosure documents, and have an accountant review the company's financial disclosures.

Finally, fifteen states, including Washington and Oregon, require franchise companies to register their offerings with a state agency. Check out your potential franchiser with the state as well.

One good way to do your homework is to compare the disclosure documents provided by different franchise companies. For guidance, order a copy of the *Franchise Opportunities Handbook* from the U.S. Commerce Department. Other ways to explore franchising include attending one of the franchise fairs held frequently in various parts of California. Stroll up and down the aisles of booths and you can come away with enough franchise reading material to last you for weeks. Franchise magazines and Web sites also offer information, advice, and connections to franchisers all over the country.

According to studies by the SBA and the U.S. Commerce Department, franchisee-owned businesses have a significantly lower failure rate than other business start-ups. That does not mean, however, that a franchise is a guarantee of success.

An alternative to buying a franchise is buying an existing business. It can have many advantages, too. Much of the development work is already done for you. The business should have established customers, cash flow, equipment, supplies, and facilities. But this course of action requires the same diligence as the other options for becoming your own boss. Whether you're buying an existing business or franchise or starting a business from scratch, advice from an attorney and a CPA is money well spent.

When you buy a business, you're purchasing liabilities as well as assets— and not all the liabilities refer to figures on the balance sheet. Susan and Gene Gonzales learned this when they moved to Chehalis, Wash., from Orange County. Their primary goal was to leave the Los Angeles area and live in the small western Washington town where most of Susan's family lived. The birth of their first child was the impetus to leave in 1991.

"We came here for our children. We wanted to be in a great school district where academics were still important . . . and yet they'd still be raised in a small town," she says.

When they moved, the Gonzaleses took over a catering business housed in a turn-of-the-century, two-story building. The family lived upstairs. With no previous experience in catering, they wanted to do research first and try the business before they bought. They leased the business with an option to buy. After seven months of almost constant work, they knew catering was not for them. Working sometimes two and three events a day left them exhausted with little time to themselves. In addition, they found they were not getting ahead financially. They did not exercise their option to purchase, and although they struggled for a time—with Gene working at a variety of jobs—they were able to move on without a commitment to the business.

No matter how you decide to go into business for yourself, remember there are trade-offs, just like in choosing a new hometown. Experts recommend that you evaluate your motivations, background, family priorities, special skills, and qualifications for the business you're thinking about getting into *before* you make any long-lasting commitments. It's a time for introspection. For example, if you're planning to go to work for yourself because you want to get out of the 9 a.m. to 5 p.m. routine, you may find that running your own business means working 7 a.m. to 9 p.m. Trade-offs such as these are well known to people who already work for themselves.

(5) Take your business or profession with you

If you already work for yourself, and are comfortable with the trade-offs, you may be a candidate for moving and taking your job with you. Many ex-Californians have. Expatriates say the challenges include retaining a profitable client base, maintaining suppliers or finding acceptable new ones, and making up for a loss in productivity during the move. Advantages, of course, include the ability to move and live anywhere you wish, opportunities to obtain new clients and new business, lower business fees, less red tape, and, says Lee Taylor of Telluride, Colo., "the view outside my window."

Moving may be easiest for consultants, programmers, and others who do not need frequent face-to-face meetings with clients. Even so, transportation is a factor to consider. Taylor says his wife, who conducts training programs, flies out on business about once a month and has to drive to the Montrose airport, 60 miles north, because air service to Telluride is "inconsistent."

Taylor, also self-employed, says had he planned their move better, he would have quit his full-time job earlier and built up additional clients before he and his wife left California. He says it is more difficult to win clients from a remote location. An established reputation is particularly important, he says.

Michael McKown, the dog-magazine publisher in Wyoming, says he solved the problem of lost production time due to a move by producing two issues of his publication in the time it usually takes to do one. "I never worked quite so hard in my entire life," he says, "but it gave me one month of free time." When McKown lived in the Bay Area he used an Oregon printer to print and mail the magazine. The move to rural Wyoming did not change his procedures significantly; his contributors still send him stories, which he still typesets. But he switched printers, and now a print shop in his Wyoming hometown prints and mails the publication for him. It's a relationship that has worked out well for both parties, says McKown.

No matter what job you bring with you—to Alaska, Nevada, or elsewhere—you still need to check with state and local agencies to determine licensing and permit requirements. The *Guide to Establishing and Operating a Business,* published by the Arizona Department of Commerce, outlines the regulations you need to consider when planning a home-based business. Depending on the city and state, you may be surprised at the lack of red tape. McKown, for example, said when he checked with his city government, he found there was no business permit required. "Up here they just leave you alone," he says summarizing Wyoming government regulation in general.

Many Western communities welcome the self-employed. Writers, consultants, programmers, and others who use computers, telephones, faxes, and other forms of technology to connect with their clients and the rest of the world are often called *lone eagles.* The term seems to have originated in Colorado, but is now common throughout the Rocky Mountain region. A brochure from the Kellogg and Wallace chambers of commerce in north Idaho says "Silver Valley Idaho welcomes lone eagles." The brochure, quoted in the first paragraph of Chapter 6, beckons the self-employed with information on low average home prices, small class sizes in school, and "peace and quiet." The Boulder, Colo., chamber has started a program for self-employed people called the Lone Eagles Nest, offering a monthly forum for the self-employed to discuss common concerns.

Other resources for the self-employed include national SOHO (small office/home office) organizations, magazines, catalogs, and Web sites. *SoHo Central,* Web site of the Home Office Association of America, features details on types of businesses that are well-suited to home offices. Another possibility to check out in your target city is small-business incubators. These facilities are similar in some respects to the executive suites that are popular in California. But the incubators provide far more mothering than the typical executive suite landlord offers. Incubators are designed to help nurture small or start-up companies, so they offer office space with flexible leases and often below-market rates. Common or shared business services—such as telephone answering, bookkeeping, photocopying, faxing, and word processing—are available at many incubators. Many also provide technical assistance in specialized areas. For example, an incubator in Spokane, Wash., provides technical assistance in accounting, marketing, business planning, distribution, and production maximization. According to SOHO America, a trade group, there are more than 500 small business incubators in the United States. The facilities are run by colleges and universities, economic development agencies, local governments, and private businesses.

Learn before you leap

Some people move out of California without a job and wind up doing anything they can to get along. For some, that's enough. But giving yourself the time to develop a solid career plan, or taking time for additional training, can mean stability once you move. The resources section that follows can lead you to many possibilities and variations on the five job-hunting strategies.

A final possibility comes from San Jose outplacement consultant Keith Robinson. In his relocation scenario, the destination doesn't come first. He suggests you start your search by examining what you want to do: brainstorm, ask questions, take aptitude questionnaires. "Decide what you really want to do, what you have a *passion* for, first," he says. "Then decide where you will find opportunities to exercise that passion."

Resources

Headhunter lists

Directory of Executive Recruiters
Kennedy Publications
Templeton Road
Fitzwilliam, NH 03447
(603) 585-6544

Recruiting Search Report
P.O. Box 9433
Panama City Beach, FL 32417
(800) 634-4548
   You can order lists of recruiting firms organized by industry, job specialization, and location.

State agencies

Alaska Small Business Development Center
430 W. 7th Ave. Suite 110
Anchorage, AK 99501
(800)478-7232

Arizona Dept. of Commerce
Arizona Business Connection
3800 North Central Ave. Bldg. D
Phoenix, AZ 85012
(602) 280-1480 or (800) 542-5684
   Provides *Guide to Establishing and Operating a Business* and other materials. Ask to talk with the small-business advocate.

Colorado Office of Regulatory Reform
1560 Broadway Suite 1530
Denver, CO 80202
(303) 894-7839
    Ask for the *Colorado Business Start-Up Kit.*

Business Resource Center
Capitol District Bldg.
250 S. Hotel St. 4th Floor Ewa Wing
Honolulu, HI 96813
(808)586-2423
http://www.hawaii.gov/dbedt/brc.html

Idaho Department of Commerce
700 West State Street
P.O. Box 83720
Boise, ID 83720-0093
(208) 334-2470
http://www.idoc.state.id.us
Starting a Business in Idaho is available.

Montana Economic Development
1424 9th Ave.
P.O.Box 200505-0505
Helena, MT 59620-0505
(406)444-4109

Nevada Commission on Economic Development
Capitol Complex
Carson City, NV 89710
(800) 336-1600
http://www.state.nv.us/businessop/

New Mexico Small Business Development Center
P.O. Box 4187
Santa Fe, NM 87502-4187
(800) 281-7232

Small Business Development
255 Capitol St. N.E.
Portland, OR 97310-1327
(503) 986-2222
http://www/econ.state.or.us/aaresour.htm

Business Information and Referrals
Texas Dept. of Commerce
P.O. Box 12728
Austin, TX 78711

Texas Department of Commerce
Office of Community Assistance and Small Business
(800) 888-0511

Utah Department of Workforce Services
140 E. 300 South
Salt Lake City, UT 84111
(801) 531-3780
    (Online) Guide for Doing Business in Utah
    http://www.ce.ex.state.ut.us/NAV/library/bizutah/title.htm

Washington State Community, Trade and Economic Development
Business Assistance Center
919 Lakeridge Way S.W. Suite A
Olympia, WA 98504-2516
(360) 753-5632
    Offers the *Business Resource Directory.*

Wyoming Small Business Development
P.O. Box 3922
Laramie, WY 82071-3922
(800) 348-5194

Federal Agencies

Small Business Administration *http://www.SBAonline.sba.gov/*
    This site is packed with information and lets you search for topics.

    Selected Small Business Administration Publications:
        Evaluating Franchise Opportunities MP-26
        Checklist for Going Into Business MP-12
        The Business Plan for Home-Based Business MP-15
        How to Buy or Sell a Business MP-16
        Handbook for Small Business MP-31
        Resource Directory for Small Business Management
                (Free list of SBA publications)
    Order from:
                SBA Publications
                P.O. Box 46521
                Denver, CO 80201

SBA offices:

211 Main St.
San Francisco, CA 94105
(415) 744-6820

550 W. C Street Suite 550
San Diego, CA 92101-3500
(619) 557-7250 or (619) 557-7272 (SCORE)

SBA/SCORE Business Information Center
3600 Wilshire Blvd. Suite L100
Los Angeles, CA 90010
(213) 251-7253

Service Corps of Retired Executives
330 N. Brand Blvd. Suite 190
Glendale, CA 91203
(818) 552-3206

Small Business Development Research Centers Research Network
  http://www.smallbiz.suny.edu.

Federal Trade Commission:

Headquarters

6th & Pennsylvania Ave. N.W.
Washington, D.C. 20580
(202) 326-2222

California Regional Offices:

11000 Wilshire Blvd. Suite 13209
Los Angeles, CA 90024
(310) 575-7575

901 Market St. Suite 570
San Francisco, CA 94103
(415) 744-7920

FTC Booklets:

Consumer Guide to Buying a Franchise
FTC Franchise Rule
Best Sellers, a complete listing of FTC business publications

Other helpful small-business resources:

SOHO America *http://www.work.soho.org/soho/*

Home Office Association of America *http://www.hoaa.com/main.htm*

American Society of Association Executives *http://www.asaenet.org*
This trade association site lets you find links to professional and trade associations in your field.

National Business Incubation Association
20 E. Circle Dr., Ste. 190
Athens, OH 45701
(614) 593-4331

Small Business Book
Online versions of large newspapers often contain valuable information for small business people. For example, Arizona Central, the Web site for the *Arizona Republic* newspaper, features a small business "book" filled with articles and links to help you start a business: *http://www.azcentral.com.*

The Ernst & Young Business Plan Guide, 2nd ed.
Ernst & Young, Brian R. Ford, and Jay Bornstein
John Wiley & Sons, Inc., 1993

Idea Cafe *http://www.ideacafe.com*
A site packed with serious business advice and humorous diversions for the small business person. Includes a business directory with site reviews and links to marketing resources, opportunities to chat with other small business people, and much more.

Franchise Handbook
Published by Enterprise Magazines, the handbook is a quarterly compilation of advice columns, franchise stories, and listings of more than 1,700 franchise possibilities. You can order the book at *http://www.franchise1. com/franchise.html*

FranNetReview *http://frannet.com*
This site provides information and advice to help you decide if franchising for you.

Business SuperStore Review *http://www.smartbiz.com/sbs/store.htm*
You'll find a variety of career advice articles, links, books, newsletters, videos, and other products for entrepreneurs.

Income Opportunities Magazine *http://www.incomeops.com*

American Demographics

Looking for marketing statistics? Try *American Demographics* magazine. Once a year the magazine lists its top 100 best sources for marketing information. A recent top 100 included the U.S. Census Bureau; Donnelley Marketing; Nexis, an online national news retrieval service; and Leisure Trends, Inc. (The latter source studies what Americans do when they're not working.)

Small Business Sourcebook
Carol A. Schwartz, Ed., Gale Research

A research potpourri for the small business person, it includes information on associations, databases, libraries, periodicals, statistics, training opportunities, and more.

8

Selling your California home

In the midst of the sharpest real estate decline in the past 15 years, I managed to sell our Orange County home. In fact, before we moved to Nevada, I sold it five times in six months; I got plenty of practice.

The first four sales never quite made it to escrow, for reasons that had nothing to do with a typical home sale, even in a down market. The problem was, our hillside home was foundation-challenged. Ten years after the house was built, the cut-and-fill soil beneath the foundation moved. Just a little. The resulting damage was repaired years before we bought the house, and we never noticed any problems for the eight years we lived in it. When we wanted to sell, however, the law required us to tell interested buyers about our home's sordid past. That news scared people away faster than you can say landslide. As a result, we had to learn more about home selling than we ever wanted to. We learned that selling your home, particularly in a soft market, requires a combination of energy, know-how, creativity, and patience.

Since you probably don't have earth-settlement problems to contend with, and your housing market is likely better, your sale should be a breeze by comparison. Nonetheless, you can learn from our experiences. Focus on these fundamentals and you should be on the road to Colorado in no time. To sell your home, use these six ingredients for success:

1. Price your home reasonably.
2. Make your house not just attractive but memorable for those who view it.
3. Gain the widest possible exposure.
4. Be inventive in your use of promotions and incentives.
5. Be open and flexible when you negotiate.
6. Understand financing options.

Before we review each of these elements, a look at one of the first questions most people have when they decide to sell their homes:

On your own or with an agent?

Should you use an agent to sell your home? Most people do. In many cases, agents provide valuable help at every stage of the marketing and sales process. In exchange, agents earn a commission. In California the commission is typically 6 percent—3 percent to the seller's agent and 3 percent to the buyer's agent.

Be advised that even if you use an agent, you will improve your chances of a quick sale by doing a *sizable* amount of work yourself. If you're on a tight budget, or you just want to save the agency commission, you might be thinking about a FSBO—for sale by owner (pronounced "fizz-bow"). Before you make that decision, consider what a good agent can do for you. A good agent should:

• Price your home and develop suggestions for making it as attractive as possible.

• Create a marketing plan that sets out how the home will be advertised and promoted, then follow through.

• Place your home in the multiple listing service so other agents and buyers will see it.

• Help you control how your home is shown to both potential buyers and agents.

• Negotiate with potential buyers.

• Advise you throughout the escrow process, and help you recover if your home should fall out of escrow.

Before we bought our Orange County home, Anne and I sold our previous home in Los Angeles County ourselves. We combined Anne's years of experience in home lending as a bank executive and my background in marketing. I wrote and designed advertising flyers, conducted a direct mail campaign aimed at brokers, and worked with my wife on open houses. Anne handled the financing and negotiating. She provided borrowing advice to people who looked at our home, and she screened potential buyers to get a rough idea of whether or not they would qualify for financing. She even handed out loan applications (from the savings and loan where she worked).

Although we did not list our house in the Multiple Listing Service, we did send flyers and direct mail letters to real estate agencies offering to *cooperate with brokers*. This is real estate jargon; it means we would pay a 3 percent commission to an agent who brought us a buyer. As it turned out, we sold our home to someone who did not have an agent. One of the most important factors in our success, however, was economic conditions: it was a seller's market with home prices rising.

Probably the biggest drawback to not using an agent is that you reduce the number of potential buyers who will find out about your house through the Multiple Listing Service. Eight years after selling our house in Los Angeles

County, when we wanted to sell our Orange County home, prices were falling and buyers were less abundant. We opted for the help of an agent and gained wide exposure for our house.

If you want to sell your home yourself but still want the MLS, it's possible to obtain multiple listing—without paying full commission—in two ways: First, you can take advantage of companies such as Help-U-Sell. Such companies will list your home for a commission below what most agents charge. Second, you can negotiate with a full-service agent or broker to list your home for a reduced fee. Commissions in California are set by convention, not by law, so they're negotiable.

Considering your options, it's in your best interest to use an agent. This is especially true if you have never sold a home yourself before. Here's why: When you obtain a multiple listing you are inviting agents to bring buyers to your home. Most agents will not do that, however, unless they know that you are willing to cooperate with them.

That means that if you sell to a buyer with an agent, you'll pay the buyer's agent commission in addition to whatever reduced commission you may have been able to negotiate for an agent to list your house on the MLS. In this situation you will have run up almost a full agent fee without getting full service. Conversely, if you sell to a buyer who does not have an agent, he may expect you to reduce your price by all or part of the commission he knows you're saving. In today's California housing market, you'll give yourself the best chances for success by picking an experienced agent and working with him to create a complete marketing program. If an agent cuts a month or more off the time it takes to sell your house, he will save you money in house payments, insurance, utilities, and other costs you incur while your house just sits on the market.

Picking an agent

Before you select an agent, interview several. Ask them to explain how they will market your home. Find out how long they have been in business in California and what they consider their strengths. Compare what services agents promise you against the main elements of home sales described in the balance of this chapter. Ask the agents for a comparative market analysis (CMA) of your home. Ask them for recent references, then check them out. Be sure to select an agent you are comfortable with, because: (1) you will be working closely with that person, and (2) when it comes down to negotiating a sale, you want someone you can talk to.

Agents will ask you for an exclusive contract, usually for a period of six months. It's better to sign an agreement for only 90 days. If your home is not sold in that time, reevaluate your arrangement. It's easy to renew the contract if you're satisfied with the agent, or move on if you aren't. If the escrow period of your sale extends beyond your contract period, you still pay the commission, but you're also still entitled to your agent's assistance. When you sign with a real estate firm, you'll be given a disclosure form explaining that real estate agents may represent both buyers and sellers—but are usually paid by the sellers. (A small percentage of agents specialize in working solely with buyers; they're discussed in the next chapter.)

For that matter, what defines a real estate agent? The terms in real estate can be confusing. A real estate agent is someone who works with clients to sell and buy homes. A broker may do the same thing, but she also manages or owns an office. And she supervises one or more agents. Becoming a broker requires a person to pass a more difficult state licensing exam. A Realtor is an agent or broker who belongs to the National Association of Realtors.

The discussion that follows assumes you will be using an agent. But you'll need the same information if you're selling on your own. These steps are designed to attract the greatest number of potential buyers in the shortest time:

1. Price it reasonably

Before we sold our Orange County house in 1991, we reduced the price twice. We lost much of the inflation equity we'd built up, but we were glad to sell it. Our low—and going lower—price helped to attract buyers. Our strategy contrasts with that of asking a top price for a home, in hopes of making a big profit. If squeezing every dollar possible out of your house is your primary goal, be prepared to show your house for months. And the longer it's on the market, the less attractive it will seem to agents and buyers, who will know how long you've been trying to peddle it. (Days on market [DOM] is recorded with your house data on the MLS.) If you want to relocate as soon as possible, price your home competitively.

Of the ways to establish a price for your house, the most common is to obtain three or more CMAs from agents. To help determine a price, the agents will look at a list of homes, similar to yours, that have sold recently. The more similar these comparables or *comps* are to your home's floor plan, size, age, etc., the easier it is to peg your house's value. Starting with the comps, agents will add in for the value of a swimming pool, bonus room, and other upgrades to your home. They will subtract for the age or condition of your home if it is different from the comps.

To get a good idea how this works, ask an agent to show you the computer printouts of the comps. Using recent comps, looking at market conditions, and reviewing the price of similar homes for sale, you should be able to establish a reasonable price for your house. In addition to talking to agents, you can find price information yourself on the World Wide Web via the Multiple Listing Service or a variety of other sites listed in the next chapter. When you examine the asking prices of existing homes, either through the Web or newspaper classifieds, keep in mind that there's usually a difference between asking prices and what a home ultimately sells for.

Another way to price your house is to have it appraised by a professional appraiser. The appraiser will examine and photograph your home and measure all the rooms. If recent comps are not available in your area, the appraiser will use a time adjustment to establish the value of your home based on older sales. Essentially appraisers use comps about the same way agents do. And since an appraisal will cost $250-$350, you don't need one before you set your price. (Once you sell your house, your buyer's lending institution will order an appraisal.)

Your agent will tell you the average number of days that homes like yours are on the market before they sell. It's important to remember that this is only an average figure. If you work with your agent on promotion, you may help to reduce the time it takes to sell your home. But if you're facing an average DOM of several months, remember that a higher-than-market price may further extend the time needed for a sale.

Certainly you don't want to reduce your price substantially below the market. But inflating your price too much—to provide room to negotiate—could add weeks or months to your sales time. Be skeptical of an agent who tells you your home is worth much more than you think it is. Once in a while, an agent will try to get a listing by offering an inflated suggested price and trying to convince the owners that she can sell the house for that price. Many of the ex-Californians interviewed recommend reasonableness in pricing and negotiating rather than trying to get the highest possible price. "That last five thousand you want may make the difference between selling it and not selling it," says Robert Tongsing. (He sold his Southern California home in only one week before moving to Colorado.)

Southern California Inland Empire agent Marjorie Lewis recommends pricing your home just below common plateau prices, e.g. $249,000 rather than $250,000. First, the former price seems much lower than the latter. Second, says Lewis, an agent with Lois Lauer Real Estate, below-plateau prices will make your home show up on MLS computer searches when buyers are looking for homes *below* a certain price. For instance, if you price your home at $224,900, a computer search for all homes under $225,000 would put you on the list.

Table 8.1 contains a home-price-comparison index. This may be more relevant when you look for a house out of state, but the table provides a glimpse at relative California prices as well.

Home price index

The following home prices are based on an average 2,200 sq. ft., four-bedroom home with two and a half baths, a family room or equivalent, and a two-car garage. Homes and neighborhoods surveyed are typical for corporate middle-management transferees.

State	City	Average Sales Price	Index
Alaska	Anchorage	$206,275	100
	Fairbanks	176,725	86
	Juneau	223,937	109
Arizona	Glendale	133,676	65
	Mesa	142,875	69
	Phoenix	200,750	98
	Scottsdale	202,098	98
	Tempe	152,133	74
	Tucson	167,875	82
California	Brentwood	599,000	291
	Encinitas	265,500	129
	Fremont	389,833	189
	Fresno	162,062	79
	Hollywood Hills	315,725	153
	Irvine	253,333	123
	La Jolla	515,000	250
	Long Beach	317,500	154
	Mission Viejo	261,000	127
	Monterey Peninsula	396,000	192
	Oakland/Montclair	344,833	167
	Pasadena	421,500	205
	Pleasanton	348,243	169
	Sacramento	195,625	95
	San Diego	223,166	108
	San Fernando Valley	342,666	166
	San Francisco	583,325	283
	San Jose	387,488	188
	San Mateo	503,000	244
	San Rafael	382,500	186
	Santa Clarita	238,500	116
	Walnut Creek	321,833	156
	Yorba Linda	234,750	114
Colorado	Colorado Springs	164,375	80
	Denver	178,037	86
	Fort Collins	190,535	93
Florida	Orlando	147,500	72
	Tampa	144,225	70
Hawaii	Honolulu	430,000	209
Idaho	Boise	159,150	77
	Coeur d'Alene	143,710	70

State	City	Average Sales Price	Index
Illinois	Aurora	193,247	94
	Peoria	177,000	86
	Schaumburg	220,625	107
Indiana	Fort Wayne	141,665	69
Minnesota	Minneapolis	206,800	100
Montana	Billings	134,133	65
	Great Falls	177,167	86
Nevada	Las Vegas	152,475	74
	Reno/Sparks	166,713	81
New Mexico	Albuquerque	181,025	88
	Las Cruces	168,000	82
	Santa Fe	190,750	93
Oregon	Eugene	187,750	91
	Portland	204,100	99
	Salem	174,733	85
Texas	Austin	173,250	84
	Bryan-College Station	124,975	61
	El Paso	136,625	66
	San Antonio	127,500	62
Utah	Salt Lake City	176,356	86
Washington	Bellevue	275,125	134
	Seattle	228,000	111
	Spokane	168,987	82
	Tacoma	152,917	74
	Vancouver	182,250	89
	Tri-Cities	176,517	86
Wyoming	Cheyenne	171,975	84

Table 8.1 The home price comparison index was created by Coldwell Banker Corporation. It provides an index number that helps you quickly approximate how much your home might cost in another city.

For example, if you live in Long Beach, in a home with a market value of $317,500, approximately how much would it cost to replace it with a similar home in Las Cruces, N.M.?

Multiply the market value of your current home by the index number of a destination city, then divide that number by the index number of the market where your current home is located: $317,500 x 82 ÷ 154 = 169,058

To replace a $317,500 home in Long Beach with a comparably-sized property in Las Cruces, you could expect to pay approximately $169,058.

(All home price figures are based on existing market conditions in the fourth quarter of 1996.)

This information has been submitted by experienced local market specialists and represents a specific subject property. While striving for accuracy, Coldwell Banker Corporation assumes no liability for errors or omissions in this publication.

2. Make your house memorable

From the earlier discussion, you may think our Orange County house was an earth-slide disaster. In fact, our house was in good condition. Relatively. The original cut-and-fill slope had settled enough to crack interior walls, keep a few of the doors from closing tightly, and open a two-inch crack in the garage slab. The builder bought the home back, stabilized the ground, and repaired the damage. The home and lot were then monitored for several years before the property was put back on the market. Then we found it. The builders explained the house's history to us, and we took a chance. The home seemed to be in perfect shape; we didn't think about resale.

Before you sell your California home you will have to fill out a disclosure form that lists any soil settlement; code violations; drainage or grading problems; damage from earthquakes, fires, or floods; and defects or malfunctions in any part of the structure. If you have had significant earthquake damage, buyers may ask for an engineering report before they decide. Even a solid report from a county inspector or independent engineering firm may not be enough to cement a sale. Your potential buyers may get cold feet when they think about what *they* might have to face when the time comes for them to sell the house.

Incidentally, the disclosure form is typically given to potential buyers *after* they make an offer on your property. You need not disclose your skeletons to every lookie-loo who passes through.

Given the dubious history of our home, we worked hard to spruce it up and keep it tidy as the sales process dragged on. You should take a variety of steps to make your home look its best before you invite the public in for a tour. Many of the tasks are routine, others more complex. Let's begin with a look at major repairs and finish up with a review of the spit-and-polish chores.

Start with the roof. If it's shake or composition and in obvious need of repair or replacement, it's best to make the repairs. The deficiency, if not noticed by potential buyers, will be spotted by a home inspector or by the appraiser who evaluates the home for lending purposes. Therefore, solving significant roof problems becomes a matter of fixing it now or later. If you fix it now, you can tell potential buyers that you have a new roof or a recently improved roof. If you had leaks, that's another reason to have the repairs done right away. Roof repair or replacement work usually comes with a guarantee which you can show a buyer. Better still, if you're going to sell your home in the rainy season, roof repairs are a hedge against embarrassment or disaster.

Other conditions in your home may have you wondering about the advisability of making changes or repairs in advance. You could simply tell an interested buyer that you'll have the work done before escrow closes. Or you could say that you'll reduce the price by a certain amount. In many cases, however, it's better to spend the money in advance. Fix or replace an appliance; get the pool heater repaired; paint discolored ceilings. You want your home to be not just clean and attractive, but a place someone would love to move into. Cosmetic changes and functional repairs are often necessary to create that image. Further, when you offer a price allowance for an upgrade or repair, you often give away more than the cost of having the work done.

Obviously, you need to weigh the effect of not doing the work against the cost. Worn carpets are problematic. If your carpets are old, but relatively free of stains, tears, and worn spots, then just have them cleaned. Many people expect to replace carpeting when they move into a house anyway. If your carpet is worn out, however, and it detracts from the appeal of your home, then consider replacing some or all of it. Pick a medium-grade carpet in a neutral color and put it over a thick pad that feels spongy underfoot.

Don't remodel your kitchen or a bathroom; just patch cracks, caulk, and repaint if necessary. Actually, that goes for all rooms of the house. Neatly repair or replace peeling wallpaper, dripping faucets, loose handles and drawer pulls, split molding or baseboards, and non-functioning light fixtures.

The exterior of your home also deserves close attention. If the paint on your molding or trim is cracked, you can scrape and repaint it without repainting the whole house. Rusty metal, a broken gate, missing bricks in a walkway, broken sprinklers, creaking garage doors, spots of dead grass in the lawn—all of these things and more should be repaired or replaced. Look at the outside of your home as if you were a visitor. What catches your eye? A drooping basketball hoop on the garage roof? A tangle of weeds around the mailbox? These things not are costly to fix or replace; they just take time and elbow grease. The idea is to make the outside of your house attractive and inviting. When someone looks at your home you want them to imagine themselves living comfortably there.

Get your lawn in shape. Trim hedges and bushes that have gotten out of control, and plant plenty of flowers, front and back. Flowers are an easy way to make a dramatic change in your home's "curb appeal." One Las Vegas real estate agent swears that yellow flowers are the best, that they help make the sale. Try yellow and other colors; brighten up your yard. Do you have a junk or trash area in the back or side yard? Many people have a place where sits a worn-out barbecue, a partial roll of wire fencing, a half bag of fertilizer, pieces of broken cement, and other castoffs. Sound like your side yard? Get rid of that stuff. Haul it all away. Leave your yard clean and open, so some prospective home owner can imagine *his* junk pile there.

Your entryway and front door deserve your attention as well. Make a good first impression. Is the doorknob or hardware corroded or rusted? Is the paint or varnish on the door flaking? Is the door itself warped or split? The design of newer homes these days emphasizes entryways with porticoes and decorative, stained wood front doors. Don't neglect your entry. Try putting pots or tubs of flowers along your front walkway or on your porch.

Moving is a great opportunity to get rid of junk *inside* your home, too. Clean out clutter in rooms and storage areas and your house will look bigger. Clear off counters in the kitchen to highlight the open work surfaces. Remove clutter from bathroom counter tops, too. In short, make your house as attractive as it's been since you've lived in it.

Stay clean

When you're showing your house regularly, keeping it clean and fresh smelling is tiresome—but necessary. Dirty dishes and unmade beds are common in most homes, but don't let potential buyers see them in yours. You'll be a step ahead of the competition.

Here's where you can enlist the aid of your children. Once you've made a decision to move, don't isolate them from the work to be done. They can help you prepare your house for visitors by keeping their rooms relatively clean, and by doing small chores inside and outside your house.

One of the best ways to realize the importance of keeping your house clean and fresh is to go house hunting. You'll be astonished. In our last two house-hunting ventures, we saw an appalling array of conditions. In one kitchen, the dirt on the floor was as thick as you might expect it on a garden patio. In another house, stains streaked two walls in a corner where a generous amount of water had obviously flowed from the ceiling. We were told that the roof used to leak, but that it was fixed. Why weren't the walls fixed too? Garbage piled up in the utility room of another house left us with a poor impression. In more than one home, we saw scum and dirt in bathroom showers and stains in sinks caused by faucets that had obviously been left to drip for weeks or months.

One house in Las Vegas was well maintained and attractive, but a harsh toxic smell drove us out. California agent Lewis tells of showing clients one house that had a pile of dirty clothes on the dining room table. When she showed the home again two weeks later, the pile of laundry was still there. All of these conditions—and more—were found not in inexpensive, older homes, but in relatively new tract and custom homes. If you make a poor impression on a lookie-loo, you don't lose much. But if you make a poor impression on an agent, you won't see the agent—or the agent's clients—again.

To cinch a favorable impression, give your home a pleasant scent. Potpourri and air freshener are two ways to do it. In addition, when we were showing our Orange County home, buyers were often treated to the aroma of freshly baked chocolate-chip cookies. I kept a roll of prepared dough in the refrigerator. If I was going to be home when potential buyers were coming over, I'd rip off a piece of dough and shove it into the oven. The dough necessary for just a couple of cookies is sufficient to make your house smell like Betty Crocker or Mrs. Fields lives there.

Other hints you may receive from your agent are to turn your three-way light bulbs on high and to keep curtains open. Both steps make your house look as bright as possible. Some agents advise you to turn on soft music.

Are these light bulb, potpourri, and cookie dough techniques gimmicks? Of course. But even if home shoppers recognize the techniques, they are first captured by their effects. By that time, their senses are already telling them this is an inviting house.

3. Gain the widest exposure

Now that you've got your home looking (and smelling) like a showplace, get the news out to as many people as possible. Coordinate your efforts with your agent so the two of you work as a team. You may need to spend your own money on some of the activities, but it will be money well spent.

Agents' caravan

When new listings come out, agents get together and tour the homes they think will be attractive sellers. Local real estate boards organize the trips (usually called caravans because the agents show up en masse). With many homes to view on a typical caravan, agents don't spend much time at any one house. Your job is to make them linger at your home and soak up its advantages. Free food and drink is a good way to do it.

If your agent can get your home on a caravan, consider providing a buffet-style meal or snacks. When the agents know there will be free food at your place, they will be more likely to both stop by and stay. Each agent who records a favorable impression of your home might bring one, or two, or many potential buyers back for a look. Ask your agent how many caravanning agents to expect, and plan the food accordingly. Flyers about your home, strategically placed near the food, will help the agents focus on your home's most important attributes. Some agents recommend serving wine or champagne, but since many of the agents will be driving, it's a risk you shouldn't take.

Local caravan practices vary throughout California. In some areas, the real estate board provides transportation for the agents. In other areas, food is not just a good idea, but is expected. Some agents give away lottery tickets or hold a drawing for gift certificates to attract caravanners. (An aggressive agent may volunteer to pay for prizes or food to lure other agents. Ask about this when you're interviewing for an agent to list your home.)

Open houses

As many people know, open houses are more for the agents than for the home sellers. Open houses provide agents an opportunity to meet potential buyers. If the people who drop by are not impressed with the house on display, the agent will gladly show them many others. Nonetheless, an open house is a way to get people through your door. So when your agent suggests it, say yes. Neighbors often visit during an open house too. That's okay; they may have friends or relatives in the market for a home.

If you're going to sell your home yourself, open houses are a must. Ask people to sign a guest book, so you can call or write them later if they express interest in your home. In the guest book, ask them to write down how they heard about your open house. If you're running ads in more than one publication, this is a way to see which one pulls in the most lookers.

Chances are, you will not be the only one on your block selling a house. If you're going the FSBO route, you can piggyback on other open houses in the area. When someone else has an open house, you have an open house. Place your signs strategically so that when people are directed into your neighborhood by the other open house signs, they will also see yours. If the other open homes are advertised and listed, so much the better. Many of the serious buyers who look at the other homes will want to compare them to yours.

Writing your flyer

Usually your agent will write and design a flyer for your home. The flyer is sent to agents and handed out to people who tour your home. Not all agents are good at writing promotional literature, so check to see that your flyer contains these details (as applicable): size; price; number of rooms; den/library; size of garage; built-in appliances; pantry; air conditioning; view; lot size (if it's an advantage); fireplaces; pool or spa; garden, patio, deck; built-in storage; custom features (such as oak banisters, bookshelves, granite or Corian counter tops); space for an RV or boat. If you have mature trees, a completely fenced yard, or are close (but not too close) to schools and shopping, mention those items too.

Include any premiums you're offering, an assumable loan, or other advantages. Do you have new carpeting or a new roof? In addition, the flyer should include a brief subjective description of the house or its most attractive feature, emphasizing unique benefits for buyers. The flyer photos of your home should emphasize its advantages, such as a spacious family room or a beautiful view. Outside shots of your house should make it look attractive, if not dramatic. You obviously want to avoid a photo that highlights the crack in your driveway, or the less-than-spectacular home next door.

If you are a FSBO seller, you can mail your house flyers to local real estate offices along with a letter explaining that your home is in top condition, shows well, and that you will cooperate with brokers.

Advertising

Classified advertising and picture ads in real estate booklets or newspaper supplements are, like open houses, designed to attract buyers. Ads—particularly with a photo of your home—provide valuable exposure for you. When people are house hunting they tend to look at the pictures. If one strikes their fancy, they'll ask their agent to find the house. When you interview agents, tell them you expect them to advertise your house.

If your agent or broker does not advertise your home enough, or if you think the ads need to be supplemented, you can either offer to split the cost with the agent—which she may quickly agree to—or you can do it yourself. Don't compete with the ads your agent is already running; complement them. If your agent's ads are in a metro daily paper, put your ads in local dailies or weeklies. Then compare the results. The next question is, whose name and phone number should appear in the ads that you pay for? Your answer to that question will depend on the relationship you have with your agent. Let her know you're not trying to bypass her commission by advertising directly for buyers. You could agree to put her name on the ads, along with your name and your phone number. When we paid for advertising ourselves, we put our name and number in the ads. That way I was able to monitor the responses from different papers and give the callers a succinct, but description-rich, sales pitch.

Keep your house flyer or a fact sheet near the phone so you can answer questions from agents and potential buyers. Even though you've lived in your home for years, it's helpful to have an accurate list of the important features. You might take some details of your house for granted and forget to mention them. Be prepared; every caller could be your buyer,

Showing your home

The same need for preparation goes for showing your home. Some sellers are annoyed when agents call at the last minute—or show up unannounced. But it happens—sometimes frequently. The more serious you are about selling your home, the more you will take the interruptions in stride and be as gracious as you can. Naturally you can put a "by appointment only" sign out front and insist on advance notice. You can even refuse a lock box. But the more accessible your home is, the greater your chances of selling it. (Incidentally a lock box is exactly that, a small metal box to hold the key to your home. The box is secured somewhere on the front of your house. Authorized agents have the key or combination to the box so they can show your home when you're not there.)

If your house is on the market for a few months, and your patience with shoppers is getting thin, take a weekend off. Let your agent handle showings. Unwind with a visit to the beach or mountains with your family.

When you talk to potential buyers—either in person or on the phone—be prepared to answer a variety of questions. Some of them may not relate directly to your house. For instance: Where is the nearest bus stop, and does the bus take you downtown? Is the high school any good? How long does it take to drive to the airport? Other questions you may hear include: How difficult would it be to add on to the family room? Are there any kids in the neighborhood? What are your average utility costs in the summer? Winter? Several Orange County callers I talked with wanted to know what model our home was. I wasn't sure. When tracts are built, developers identify each model with a colorful name. As our home was more than 20 years old, the model names were no longer household words. A check with longtime residents gave me the answer.

When showing your home, don't leave valuables sitting around. Don't have checkbooks, credit cards, or bank statements sitting out. Even if you're going to be home when people come over, you should keep video cameras, small pieces of silver, guns, jewelry, and similar items out of sight. It's best to lock them up. Anything small could disappear. Don't make it easy for people who come over looking for souvenirs. It's also a good idea not to give visitors hints about your regular schedule. Don't tell them when you are likely to be out of the house. One of them might plan a return visit—through your back door or a side window.

Sell it on the Web

The World Wide Web will play an increasingly important part in home sales. Brokers and home builders across the country are now debating just how it will be used, and by whom. Portions of California were among the first areas in the country to be listed in public, World Wide Web MLS sites. Nearly the entire state is now represented on the Web. How and on what

Web sites your home will be listed is another question to discuss with potential agents. You can create your own *home page,* so to speak, advertising the advantages of your property. The key to your page's effectiveness will be how you link it to other Web sites—especially real estate sites—so that potential buyers can find it. (Specifics of home advertising on the Web are discussed in the next chapter.)

4. Be creative with premiums and incentives.

If the housing market where you live has become active—if homes are selling more quickly—you may not need to consider this next step. If your market is still sluggish, or if you want to take every step necessary for a prompt sale, consider using incentives and premiums.

Before you balk at the idea of giving something away to help sell your home, consider that the technique is used successfully in just about every field of business. Banks, furniture stores, restaurants, high-tech manufacturers, book publishers, automobile makers, and a host of other retail and business-to-business companies use premiums. Developers selling new homes use premiums too, such as carpet upgrades, landscaping, and other extras. Your reason for offering a premium is the same reason incentives are used in any business: to increase traffic and provide one more reason to buy. Few people selling homes use premiums, but that only means yours will attract that much more attention.

What should you offer? Some people have offered cruises. Others have offered one of their cars. The key is to give away something of perceived value that will attract attention. A new stereo or large-screen television might make an attractive offer. Avoid items that are too inexpensive, such as a portable CD player, standard size television, or even a microwave oven. These items could be an incentive for a savings account at a bank, not the purchase of a home. We offered a year's free gardening and maid service with our Orange County home. My marketing background told me that premiums or prizes linked directly to the product being sold are most effective. You could create your own package, for example, that included pool service and new outdoor furniture. If you give away merchandise, make it new; otherwise your premium may seem more like a hand-me-down you're leaving behind.

In exchange for—or along with—a premium, consider an incentive or bonus for the agent who brings you a buyer. Granted an agent who brings in a buyer will be entitled to the 3 percent commission. But agents get that no matter which home their clients buy. The incentive you offer an agent is often specified in the multiple listings. That way every agent who sees your listing finds out that she could earn an extra $1,000 if she steers a buyer to your place.

How high should the bonus be? That depends on the price of your house. Five hundred dollars may be a starting point. An additional 1 percent commission, for a limited time, would be an even stronger incentive.

Premiums should be spelled out in your ads and flyers; incentives should not be. A reputable agent will tell his customers you have offered an incentive, but he will likely tell them that after he's shown them your house. A home warranty for a year is a premium that more and more sellers offer. Your agent can give you the details. It's an attractive incentive for a small cost.

5. Be reasonable about negotiating

Once you have an offer on your home, you'll want to review it with your agent. If you've priced your house competitively, the offers you receive may also be reasonable. Of course speculators (who often are not serious home buyers) make offers too—usually lowball offers. Don't be disappointed if you receive one. Depending on how eager you feel, you can counter back and see what happens. Often low ballers will just move on.

Even with a reasonable asking price, it's possible you will not receive a full-price offer. Your incentives and the condition and location of your home have an influence on this of course. But even eager buyers often offer less than the asking price. If you do get a full-price offer, it may be coupled with conditions relating to financing, repairs, or length of escrow.

Sales conditions are common on other offers too. You may be asked to provide a carpet allowance, replace an appliance, or provide an inspection report. In these situations, you often have room to negotiate. For example, you could counter an offer that included a carpet allowance or other conditions by accepting all the conditions, but insisting upon your asking price— or close to it. (One home seller established a reasonable, market-based price of $325,000 for his home, then refused an offer of $320,000. That's the equivalent of saying you really don't want to sell.) Even if homes are selling in your area, you must be reasonable.

Perhaps the most significant contingency to an offer is the condition that the sale not go through until the buyer's home sells. Accepting such a sale involves risk. Your moving is then dependent upon conditions over which you have little or no control. Before accepting such a contingency you should gather information on your potential buyer's home. Is it priced to the market? (Your agent can pull comps of the buyer's house to determine how reasonable the price is.) Is the price negotiable? What is the house's condition? Does the buyer have an agent, and is the house listed? And perhaps most important, what is the condition of the real estate market where your potential buyer lives?

If you think such a contingency sale may be your best offer, you may want to tour the buyer's home and even make conditions of your own. For example, if the house is not listed, you should insist the buyer find an agent immediately. Examining contingent offers is a topic on which an experienced real estate agent can help you considerably. She should know the market and help you evaluate the pros and cons.

The marketing campaign we mounted for our Orange County home was successful—it generated five offers. But one look at our disclosure statements made the potential buyers disappear. Ultimately we sold our home through a trade. Accepting a trade for your home is not a normal offer, but it can work. A buyer who was interested in our house had his own home for sale. Rather than make his offer on our home contingent on the sale of his, he proposed a trade. His home was smaller and lower-priced than ours. He proposed to pay us the difference and transfer title on the two homes. We accepted, but only after we examined the buyer's home in detail. We discovered, for example, there was a massive above-ground pool in need of repair. In the end, our buyer got rid of his home and bought our home at a rock-bottom price.

The plus from our viewpoint was that the trade-in home was smaller and lower-priced and would be easier to sell. If you need to cash out your equity in order to come up with a down payment, a trade such as this may not help you—unless you're able to sell the trade-in home right away.

If you're planning to rent a home out of state, so you can live through a winter (or summer), then renting *your* current house may be a fall-back option if you're unable to sell it. Your broker or agent should be able to help you find suitable tenants and can continue to advise you on the condition of the California real estate market. You could even offer a lease-to-buy option

6. Understand financing options

You don't need to know as much about financing when you sell as when you buy. But the more you know, the better you'll be able to make decisions. Obviously you want to find a potential buyer who is qualified—someone who has a down payment and will be approved for a loan. Your agent can pre-qualify potential buyers for you, but here's the basic formula used by banks:

The payments for the principal, interest, taxes, and insurance on a house are combined into one figure, called PITI. (It's known by the individual letters, P-I-T-I; it's not pronounced *pity*.) Usually for a family to qualify for a loan, the PITI must not be more than 28-30 percent of its gross regular income. This figure is called the *housing ratio*. If there are homeowners association or condo dues related to the house, they become part of the PITI.

Loan approval is also based on a person's credit history, amount of time on his present job, and other factors. If you don't want to try to prequalify a buyer, you may simply let the lending institution do the job by making (preliminary) loan approval within seven days a condition of sale.

As the types of loans available today are of more concern to buyers than to sellers, they are discussed in the next chapter. You should, however, be prepared for buyers to ask if your loan is assumable. To find out, call your lending institution. No matter what your loan documents say, nearly every loan is assumable, *if the lender agrees.* The bank may, for instance, agree to an assumption, but raise the interest rate. It could be to your buyer's advantage to assume your loan, even with a higher rate than you're paying, because the fees for a loan assumption generally are lower than those for a new loan.

If your equity has eroded (due to falling housing values), your loan amount may be close to the asking price for your property. That could make your loan even more attractive. If assumable, it would require little down payment. Should you have little equity in your home, you could call your lender and tell them that you're moving out of state and are having difficulty making the payments. Tell them that you have a buyer who is interested in taking over your loan and moving into your house. In this circumstance it's important to the bank that the person assuming your loan *live* in the house, not turn it into a rental. If the lender agrees to consider an assumption, the institution will want to evaluate the prospective borrower, so a loan application may be sent to you to give to your potential buyer.

Banks usually lend up to 90 percent of a home's appraised value on a conventional loan. Many FHA loans require only a 3 percent down payment and most VA loans require no down payment. In other words, 100 percent of the home is financed. For a buyer seeking a conventional loan, the bigger the down payment—especially 20 percent or more—the better the chances of being approved.

If you're transferred

No matter how your house is financed, selling your home becomes easier, with fewer risks, if your employer transfers you out of state, or if you are offered a relocation and home buy-out package by a new employer. Having your employer assist in the sale/purchase of your home takes a burden off your mind, which is precisely the purpose. The company you work for wants you to focus on your new job, not real estate transactions.

According to the Employee Relocation Council, many companies provide home-sales assistance to transferees. The majority use an outside, third-party relocation firm to manage the transactions. The ERC says the cost of relocation averages about $45,000. House hunting trips, van lines charges, and interim living expenses are included in the cost, but the largest expense is commissions and fees for the sale of an employee's existing home and the purchase of a new one. By comparison, the ERC says, it costs only about $13,000 to relocate an employee who is renting.

As mentioned in Chapter 6, corporate relocation policies vary according to the rank and salary of the person hired or relocated. Many firms will guarantee the purchase of their transferee's home. Increasingly, however, cost conscious companies are emphasizing incentives for employees to sell their homes themselves. A buy-out or similar option is offered only as a last resort.

Assuming you qualify for, or can negotiate a buy-out package, you will still be involved in the sale of your home. In some instances, you may even put it on the market yourself. According to Kathy Walker, corporate accounts manager for Mason-McDuffie Relocation in the San Francisco Bay Area, a third-party buy-out should begin with the relocation company explaining the process to you. Typically you'll be given a list of appraisal firms and asked to arrange for two appraisals of your home. The relocation firm, says Walker, then will offer you a price for your home that's an average of the two appraisals. Walker says you will have enough time—45-60 days or longer—to market your home yourself to see if you can get a higher price. If not, you have the buy-out to fall back on.

The price you're offered for your home will be the main factor in whether or not you decide to try to sell it yourself. Walker says third-party relocation firms will tell appraisers not to be too optimistic in setting their estimate of your home's value. "We want you to give a fair estimate, but please don't over-estimate," is the advice Walker says the companies will give to appraisers. "So typically the offer that is made to the transferees is realistic, or leaning toward the conservative side," she says.

Under these circumstances, when you look for an agent to list your house, you will have to tell her the conditions of the listing. The relocation company will likely require your agent to sign an agreement that says you have the right to sell your home to the relocation company, at any time, with no commission going to the agent. Not all agents will accept a listing with a buy-out offer pending, but many do, says Walker.

No matter how you do it, selling your California home requires you to respond to myriad conditions. If your neighborhood has bank foreclosures for sale, make sure your house is spotless and in perfect repair. Foreclosed houses, although cheap, are often rundown. On the other hand, should your local market be bustling, be alert for other homes that sell. Stay actively involved in the marketing of your home, so you know what responses you're getting to ads and showings. If you are fortunate enough to live in an area where prices are rising, don't be greedy. Price your house for a quick sale—and a quick getaway.

Resources

International Real Estate Directory *http://www.ired.com*

For Sale by Owner Network *http://www.fsbo.net*

For Sale By Owner - California Edition
George Devine
Nolo Press, 1992

9

Buying a home out of state

FOR SALE

New custom four-bedroom, three-bath home with formal dining room, family room, master suite, view, lots of extras on one-acre lot. Close to schools and shopping. $187,900.

Does that sound like an ad for a house in your neighborhood? Or in your dreams?

Average home prices in most other states are low enough to make California house hunters reach for their checkbooks first and ask questions later. Even though prices have been rising at a robust pace in a number of Western cities and towns, compared to many places in California, homes are a bargain. This poses a problem for would-be escapees: Prices can be just too tempting.

Resisting the urge to buy the first big house you see is a challenge, says Dallas-Fort Worth real estate agent-turned Web publisher Becky Swann. "If you're coming from California to Texas, one of the biggest dangers is that you have such a distorted sense of (house) values that you're very likely to fall in love with the first home you're shown."

Adapting to significantly lower home prices may sound like a problem you'd be glad to deal with. But buying a home out of state is no easy job. Still, it can be exhilarating and, in the end, rewarding. To be successful, you should:

- Educate yourself on the market in your target towns.
- Consider your financing options.
- Select a good agent.
- Decide whether you want a new or resale home.
- Learn house-hunting idiosyncrasies—from septic tanks to private roads.

Shop carefully. This chapter and the next one examine each of these areas in order. So leave your inflated notions of real estate prices in California, where they belong, and get started.

To buy or rent

Moving to a less-populous, less-expensive area may be your first opportunity to buy a home. This may be one of your main reasons for moving. But whether you're looking for your first house, or are planning to sell your California home and buy out of state, you may want to wait and evaluate your options. You may want to experience a summer or winter before you buy. If so, renting for a year would give you the time. It also allows you time to decide the part of town in which you want to live. (If you have a limited amount of time for house hunting, you may not be able to decide which part of town will suit you best—particularly in larger towns and cities.)

Tax laws used to limit home sellers to two years before profits on home sales were subject to capital gains taxes. Federal legislation in mid-1997 eliminated this requirement, giving you as much time as you need to evaluate a new job, a new neighborhood, local schools, and other factors before buying a home.

Additional reasons for renting include gaining time in a new job to qualify for a home loan, or allowing you to move out of state even if you are unable to sell your California home.

One problem with the rent-first-then-buy strategy is that you may have to move twice in a relatively short time. Your second move, however, usually will be easier than the first, and you may be able to move some of your belongings yourself. Also, moving is inherently exciting, and moving twice in the same community gives you a chance to develop friends among two sets of neighbors.

Gathering information

No matter where you decide to move, you have a choice of resources for gathering information. If you have already contacted real estate agents, you may have received booklets filled with pictures and descriptions of homes for sale. You can also pick these up in supermarkets, visitors centers, and chambers of commerce offices during fact-finding trips to your destination cities.

These booklets, and the classified ads and real estate supplements in local newspapers, can be a good starting point to find out how low (or high) home prices are. You can also discover what types of homes are available in your price range. (Remember, the asking prices are not purchase prices.)

If the research stage of your escape plan will cover many months, you'll need to replenish your supply of real estate booklets occasionally to stay current on market conditions. This is especially true in high-growth and high-appreciation areas such as Salt Lake City, Albuquerque, and Tucson. Another way to keep abreast of local conditions is to read news stories in the business and real estate sections of out-of-town papers. Keep in mind that "news" stories in many newspaper real estate sections are often lightly edited press releases from local builders and real estate companies. Newspapers do, however, also run consumer-oriented real estate advice columns.

Independent library research also will yield information on real estate values out of town. News magazines regularly run articles and listings of home prices in different parts of the country. Also keep an eye on the business and real estate sections of your local paper for articles on how home prices in California compare to those of other Western states. As a starting point, refer to the home price comparisons in Tables 8.1 and 10.1.

Searching for real estate information and listings is another activity where the World Wide Web is valuable. Like the other topics already discussed, there is an abundance of material on the Web, and only some of it is useful. But some extremely so. Online real estate sources can be grouped into six categories: mega sites with links to a variety of resources; real estate associations; individual broker/agent sites; multiple listings; special purpose sites; and real estate newsgroups.

Mega sites

If you had to limit yourself to one jumping off point, the International Real Estate Directory, *http://www.ired.com*, would be it. Started in February 1995 with 45 links, the site has multiplied many times over under the eye of Swann, its editor and publisher. Today her listings are in the thousands and traffic to the site doubles every few months. If *ired.com* and the material it's linked to were to be printed as a directory, it would be larger than the collective New York City phone books. In spite of its magnitude, it's easy to use, and comes with Swann's unique rating system for the sites she lists.

From the main home page—which contains links to columns, calendars, classifieds, information on interest rates, and real estate news—select "for consumers" or the site index. You'll see a neat, alphabetized table of contents. From that simple list you can follow hyperlinks to a world of real estate listings, libraries of research material, page after page of information on movers, foreclosure sales, home builders, real estate associations, software, legal services, and much more. To find home listings, simply select the United-States-by-State link and then look for homes in your destination city. Swann's rating system, complete with colorful cartoon icons, ranks sites on a seven-point scale from "Top Ten" to "Don't Bother." She also includes search engines that let you either shop for a home or jump around in *ired.com* (rather than navigate through the directories). Swann's site is such an important part of real estate on the Web—for professionals and house hunters—that other sites tout their *ired.com* ratings.

Yahoo's "Business and Economy: Real Estate" section is also a good starting point. It lacks the detailed lists of *ired.com*, so you need to have a little better idea of what you're looking for. From the main page you can conduct a search or move through Yahoo's topics lists.

Homebuyer's Fair is a combination of how-to information, resources on mortgage financing, links to related sites, and a collection of calculators to help you determine moving and financing costs. One page, the salary calculator, helps you compare the salary you would need to make in a new city, to match the buying power of your present salary. Enter your salary, the name of the city where you live now, and finally, your destination city.

Realty Guide begins with eight categories, each leading to vast stores of information. Categories include real estate agents' resources (including links to everything from appraisers to roofing contractors), real estate software (for agents, investors, and homeowners), information and links on mortgage loans and home listings, and agent/broker sites organized by state. More than 2,000 real estate sites across the country are listed.

Real estate information also is available on America Online. Like many AOL features, the real estate services are constantly changing, to provide more options and a more visually attractive package. Many of AOL's resources are provided through outside sources. Some offerings simply take you to a Web site. Through key words "Real Estate" and "MLS" you'll find AOL's Real Estate Center. It offers articles, chat rooms, listings, and real-estate related software. CompuServe offers similar services, such as real estate forums, recommendations from a relocation firm, listings (go: classifieds), and an advice column.

Associations

If you have time and want to scavenge every bit of home buying/selling know-how on the Web, you can search through all the real estate association sites in *ired.com* or Yahoo Real Estate. Although many of these sites are not intended for consumers, a few are worth a visit. For example, try *http://www.nahb.com,* the site of the National Association of Home Builders. In addition to articles on real estate, you'll find information on building your own home, plus some esoteric topics, such as indoor air quality. The National Association of Exclusive Buyer's Agents also has a site which you can use to find a local buyer's agent.

The massive *http://www.realtor.com* site is the home of the National Association of Realtors. In the Find-a-Home section you'll see a map of the U.S. that allows you to tap into listings for literally hundreds of thousands of homes. The home page of the California Association of Realtors will be of interest to you when you're selling your home. It contains information on industry laws, policies, and practices in the state.

Broker/agent sites

Swann analogizes many real estate company sites to billboards or bus bench ads, because they are static displays with slogans and the obligatory agents' smiling mug shots. Many such sites receive her thumbs-down icon, her lowest rating. Only about 10 percent of agent sites are worthwhile, she says. For instance, one Web page that purports to be a real estate chat site contains snippets of conversations between agents, plus 13 identical mug shots of the host agent. Some agent/broker sites are more detailed than others and some contain useful links to local business and municipal information. Although time consuming, scoping out the sites of a variety of agents/brokers in your destination city will give you an idea of what homes are available and how much they cost.

Multiple listings

Ideally for consumers, the entire national MLS database should be accessible on the Web. Perhaps some day it will be. One of the reasons there is no one uniform national database, explains Swann, is that local realty boards don't all use the same data-processing systems. Reluctance of local boards to release their information to the Web is another reason, although Swann says that more are going online every day. While there is no single MLS site that covers the entire country, you can visit just a few sites and have access to nearly one million listings. As you'll notice, Web MLS listings differ from each other, and many do not include as much information on each home as you'll find on your agent's proprietary version of MLS.

Browsing for homes on MLS sites is simple. You enter your new home requirements, including price and location, and you receive a multi-page portfolio of homes. On some of the MLS listings you see one or more color photos of each home, plus a narrative and itemized list of features. Several of the databases let you specify the location by street or ZIP code, home size, number of bedrooms and bathrooms, size of garage, and other factors. One of the MLS sites, *CyberHomes,* contains partial listings from more than half the states. The site lets you zoom into maps showing street locations of the homes you select. You can find various Multiple Listing Service sites through *ired.com* and *Realtor.com,* or through search engines such as Yahoo.

Special purpose sites

To find out the purchase prices of homes (as opposed to the asking prices you see in ads), use one of a few specialized Web price information services. For a nominal fee per search, the *Home Sales Line* will give you purchase prices on individual homes or several homes on the same street. You can place your order online or via phone or fax for this service, which calls itself the Blue Book of homes. Price information is also available from the Case Shiller Weiss, Inc. site.

Another useful specialized site for real estate surfers is Hugh Chou's Mortgage Calculator. It lets you determine your payments based on your interest rate, amortization length, and loan amount. Online versions of some newspapers also carry real estate classified ads and some, particularly the *San Jose Mercury News,* have valuable consumer-oriented real estate columns.

Real estate newsgroups

Most of the housing-related newsgroups are maintained for real estate, insurance, construction, and lending professionals. Searching them is not a good use of your time. An exception is *news:misc.consumers.house.* This is your place to ask real estate and home-maintenance questions and scan comments from people buying and selling homes. On one visit to the newsgroup, 478 subjects were listed including questions and discussion on vinyl siding, smells from vent pipes, home inspections, cracks in garage floors, central vacuum systems, closing costs, and how to remove fungus from shingles.

Video tours

For years, large real estate chains have offered video tours of homes for sale. You sit in an office and preview homes on video tape. Some agents also mail videos to potential buyers. Several ex-Californians said they got their first look at out-of-state real estate this way. Recently, some home builders have taken the concept a step further and created tours of model homes that don't exist. When you visit a new home center, your tour is conducted on a computer screen. You see only three-dimensional graphic images of model homes. This saves the builder the cost of creating full-size copies of each model he offers. But as one newspaper critic said, virtual model homes will replace real model homes when virtual sex replaces real sex.

Considering the conventional and online research possibilities, you should be able to get a good idea of the prices and availability of homes in the town (or towns) you're considering. "People leaving California are a special case," says Swann. "They need lots of information." By learning how far your real estate dollars will go in another state, you can guard against paying too much or buying a larger or more opulent house than you need. With luck you may even be able to pick out some specific neighborhoods you want to investigate.

Finding an agent

After you've spent time researching real estate in your target town(s) and have an idea of local prices, you need to start looking for an agent. Agents offer a variety of help to buyers. They can be particularly valuable in sellers' markets. If online research does not appeal to you, that's another reason work with an agent. He or she can be your introduction to the multiple listings in your future hometown.

Housing markets are generally categorized as either a sellers' market or a buyers' market. In the latter, there are more homes on the market than there are buyers. Some homes remain unsold for many months. Prices may be stable or falling. As a buyer in such a market, time is on your side. You can make an offer below an asking price and if it's not accepted, you have plenty of other eager sellers from which to choose. The opposite situation is a sellers' market; prices are often rising and homes sell quickly. In a tight sellers' market you may even need to act right away on a home you like.

California was a buyers' market for much of the 1990s, but sales have been picking up in many areas. At the same time, many sellers' markets have heated up in desirable locations in Western and Southern states. In most Western sellers' markets, however, prices are still below urban California levels. For that reason, some Californians snap up homes at advertised prices without hesitation. This contributes to price increases and reduces availability of housing. Under such conditions, a street-smart agent who has your best interests in mind should be your guide. Prices will not seem cut-rate to him. He can tell you about the local market and help you find reasonable buys.

In fact, a savvy agent can be valuable no matter what the condition of the market. Moving to a new state means you will be subject to a variety of new laws and practices governing home sales. For example, in some states, attorneys rather than escrow companies conduct closings; in other states title companies are used. In Texas, when you buy a house you will not be able to take out a home-equity loan. The state's homestead law says home improvements are the only reason you can borrow against your equity. In some states you'll also find differences in home construction techniques and materials. These and other issues—some that may not even occur to you—are reasons for finding and using an experienced agent. And if a job change dictates that you must move quickly, an agent can be a lifesaver by prescreening homes to save you time.

Agents for buyers receive their commissions from sellers, so you normally will not have to pay directly for an agent's help in finding a home. But you may want to find out what the accepted commission rates are in your target town. In Arizona, for example, says Alice Held—a Scottsdale agent with more than 20 years experience—the going rate varies. In Phoenix the average rate is 6 percent, but in Tucson, it's 7.

You can search for an agent in your future hometown in one of several ways; none is foolproof. As mentioned earlier, contacting agents to send you relocation packages may lead to phone conversations or an exchange of letters or e-mail. This communication may be enough for you to form an impression of the agents and make a decision. Most people stop here, or pick an agent from an ad. At minimum, you should interview several agents before selecting one. Look for someone with experience in the town in which you're house hunting. If you're inexperienced at buying, or know that you will want to search several areas of town before you decide, tell the agent; see if he or she is willing to devote the time necessary. Determine also if the agent can answer basic questions about taxes, schools, and utility services.

Held suggests visiting open houses to talk with agents. You can talk with agents informally, without feeling any pressure to work with them. If you're unimpressed, look for the next open house sign. Rather than picking an agent yourself, you can call brokers and ask them to refer you to their most experienced agents. If you know people in your destination city, ask for referrals. To check out agents further, ask them for the names of recent clients you can contact.

Your best bet is to find an agent who specializes in relocation. As mentioned earlier, relocation specialists can provide valuable information on your new hometown beyond the real estate listings. Some relocation agents use the letters CRP after their names. CRP stands for the Certified Relocation Program of the Employee Relocation Council. To earn certification, an agent must pass an exam and regularly take continuing education classes on relocation subjects. Some agents use the term *certified relocation specialist,* which is a designation from a real estate company.

The vast majority of real estate agents list properties for sale and represent *both* sellers and buyers. Usually this arrangement does not prevent agents from providing valuable help to buyers. Since agents work both sides of transactions, however—and because of the commission structure in which the seller pays both agents—some buyers wonder about the allegiance of their agents. Exclusive buyers' agents provide the alternative. Few in number, buyers' agents work only for buyers and do not list homes. But, according to the National Association of Realtors, buyers' agents most commonly receive the typical selling broker's commission, taken from the proceeds of a sale.

An agent who works exclusively for buyers will not necessarily know any more about the local market, nor have any more experience, than an agent who works for both sellers and buyers. Therefore, apply the same standards to a buyer's agent that you apply to any agent. Many buyers agents belong to the National Association of Exclusive Buyer Agents, and are therefore expected to comply with a detailed list of professional practices. (See the association's Web site, listed at the end of this chapter, for a text.) NAEBA members are supposed to offer clients written contracts which spell out the details of their working relationship. Although fees for buyer agents are often paid by sellers, some buyers elect to pay their agents' commissions. Agents are sometimes paid by the hour. Obviously you should discuss the fee/commission arrangements prior to signing an agreement with any agent.

No matter what type of agent you use, Swann suggests you be sure he is interested in helping you learn the new market, rather than just pushing you into a quick purchase. Once you do find an agent you are comfortable with, tell him exactly what type of home you are looking for, what styles or layouts you do not want to consider, and, of course, your price range. The more information you give your agent, the better the agent can line up homes that match your requirements. A good agent should preview homes to find those that meet your criteria, then help you view them in an orderly a way.

Here are other areas where a qualified agent can help:

Loans Your agent should be knowledgeable about mortgage loans, but should not try to steer you to only one lender, regardless of your circumstances.

Schools Knowledge of school districts and school locations is just the beginning. A good relocation agent should be familiar with private and public schools and be able to advise you about the relative quality of schools, use of magnet schools in a district, and whether or not schools are on double sessions.

Pricing Your agent should know the market and be able to spot homes that are over- or under-priced. (Tell your agent the absolute limit to what you're willing to pay for a new home.)

Inspections Your agent is morally and legally bound to tell you of any defects she finds or suspects in any home you want to make an offer on. In addition, your agent should be able to refer you to professional home-inspection firms.

Negotiation and closing Negotiating is an area where a skillful buyer agent may be able to earn his or her commission. In an area that is more sellers' market than buyers', negotiation can be tricky. In addition, a thoughtful and experienced agent can see you through the intricacies of escrow and closing, reducing your stress level substantially.

Once you have an agent and are zeroing in on a neighborhood or two, financing is the next step. Where are you going to get the money?

Resources

Web sites:

International Real Estate Directory *http://www.ired.com*

Homebuyers Fair *http://www.homefair.com/home/*

Yahoo Real Estate *http://www.Yahoo.com/Business_and_Economy/Real_Estate*

Realty Guide *http://www.xmission.com/~realtor1*

CyberHomes Multiple Listing Service *http://www.cyberhomes.com*

National Association of Home Builders *http://www.nahb.com*

National Association of Exclusive Buyer Agents *http://www.naeba.org*
(800) 986-2322

National Association of Realtors *http://www.realtor.com*

California Association of Realtors *http://www.car.org*

Homes and Land Magazine *http://www.homes.com:8086/*
Find listings from around the country and shopping information in this electronic version of real estate brokers' printed advertising booklets.

The Mortgage Calculator *http://www.capecodconnection.com/mikrom/mort.htm*
Includes the mortgage calculator, links to other calculators, and information on software you can use to make further home buying computations yourself.

Other sources

Home Sales Line
The Blue Book of Homes
(800) 846-3377
http://www.insure.com/home/sales

Case Shiller Weiss, Inc.
(617) 354-1400
http://www.cswv.com
Residential real estate price information

Relo-Pro *http://www.relopro.com*

The site represents a network of relocation specialists, from a variety of companies. Fill out your name, address, and phone number plus the city you're interested in. An agent who specializes in relocation will contact you.

Real estate - homeowners Internet news group

news:misc.consumers.house

Buyer's Resource

(800) 359-4092

How to find an exclusive buyer agent

10

Home financing, inspecting, and sweating the details

The two main questions most people have about home financing are, "How much can I qualify to borrow?" and "Which type of loan should I choose?"

The real estate agent you select may not be an expert in mortgage lending—many are not. And you probably aren't either. Nonetheless, you can explore financing possibilities yourself—and answer these questions—before you're ready to make an offer. Visit financial institutions yourself. Talk with loan representatives.

This chapter concludes the discussion of home buying by explaining your mortgage options, reviewing further techniques for house hunting, and exploring the details of inspections and closings.

Applying for a loan

A previous chapter discussed the housing ratio, comparing loan payments to income. This ratio is the first of several factors lending institutions consider when you apply for a loan. Beyond setting your house payment (PITI) at no more than 28-30 percent of your gross income, lenders look at your debt ratio. For this figure, you add your PITI to any other regular payments you will be making for 10 months or longer. This figure should not exceed 36-40 percent of your gross income. For example, if you're making payments on a loan for new furniture, but it will be paid off in six months, you wouldn't include that in your debt ratio. But if you have two more years to go on your car loan, that monthly payment is included in your debt ratio. Minimum monthly payments on credit card balances also are included. Depending upon the lender, if you have considerable assets in the bank or if you are going to put more than 20 percent down, you could be approved with a slightly higher ratio.

If you are changing employers, or if you're starting or buying a business in your destination city, don't let that discourage you from applying for a loan. To examine your job security, lenders often look at how long you have been in the same business. For instance, if you were a mechanical engineer for one or two companies in California for 10 years and you move to Denver and accept a similar engineering job there, your longevity in the field will be in your favor. On the other hand, if you're an engineer in California, and plan to open a bagel shop in Denver, and you have never worked in a food or retail business before, your chances of qualifying for a loan as soon as you move are slim. If you are transferred by your employer, your continuing employment will be viewed as a plus.

Here are other factors that may affect your qualifying:

Two incomes If you are changing employment fields, but your spouse has a long, steady record in one industry and a full-time job in your destination city, his or her income will offset, to some extent, your career change.

Substantial savings If you have enough money in your savings to buy your home outright or make a larger than normal down payment, changing employment fields may not prohibit you from getting a loan. If you're willing to make a 30-50 percent down payment, and if the lender is reasonable, you should be able to qualify even if you're new to an area and are making a career change.

Spouse's employment history Some lending institutions may give you credit for your spouse's income, even if he or she does not have a job at the time you apply for a loan. For example, say you are transferred by your company or find a new job out of state. Your spouse has been employed in one field, perhaps with one company, for some time. She quits her job to move with you, and then starts looking for work. If she is looking for a job in her field in your new town, the bank may consider the average salary she could expect to earn. If your spouse's speciality is in demand in your target city, so much the better.

Existing business If you're buying a business that has a history of making money over a period of years, the lender will have something from which to gauge your potential income. If you're starting a business from scratch, and have no other income, your chances of getting an immediate loan are remote.

Continuing self-employment If you're self-employed, are staying in the same business, and expect the same relative income from the same clients, you may be able to qualify for a loan. You'll need to show at least two years' tax returns to substantiate your claims.

Credit history All of the above discussion assumes that you have a good credit record. If you don't—if your credit report shows a history of late payments or loans that were charged off—you'll need to repair your credit. If you're in doubt about what your credit record shows, obtain a copy of it. Major credit bureaus, such as Experion, TransUnion, and Equifax, are in the phone book. Each may charge a small fee for your report.

After taking all the above information into consideration, you may not be sure how large a loan you can qualify for. If so, apply for pre-approval and find out. There's virtually no disadvantage to applying for pre-approval. If you are approved, you are not obligated to borrow that amount, nor borrow from that lender.

Technically, banks (and other mortgage lenders) may offer pre-approval two ways. In the first option, you fill out an application and the bank reviews it without checking the accuracy of your information. (If you qualify, you'll be approved subject to verification.) In the second form of pre-approval, the bank verifies your information. If you're approved, you receive a letter or card that says you qualified for a loan up to a certain amount. This can help when you make an offer on a home, particularly in a sellers' market. The seller knows you are serious and that there will be no delays for loan approval. If you do not qualify, it's better to find that out before you make an offer on a home.

Federal law requires lenders to give you a written explanation if you are denied credit. You may then be able to take corrective steps to obtain a loan. You may find a mistake in your credit report. You may need to apply for a smaller loan. Or you may simply need to find another lender that is willing to consider your situation.

Once you determine how much money you can borrow, you'll know how much you can afford to spend on a home. But remember Becky Swann's advice: Just because you can afford the payments on a lavish home doesn't mean you should buy one.

Capital gains taxes are no longer the incentive they once were to plow all home sales profits back into another residence. Tax laws approved by Congress in 1997 provide couples with an exemption of $500,000 on profits from the sale of a primary residence. (For up-to-date advice on the tax consequences of buying and selling a home, you should consult your accountant or other professional financial advisor.)

In spite of Swann's cautions, if you're tempted to buy a big house, at least avoid the California strategy common in the mid-80s. At that time, home prices were rising steadily (as they are now in some Western cities). Buyers mortgaged themselves to the hilt, hoping price inflation would boost their equity. These gamblers never thought prices would drop. But prices did drop.

Types of loans and lenders

You should shop for a loan, not a lending institution, say the authors of *Kiplinger's Buying and Selling a Home.* Their advice is based on the concept that a low rate is all you're looking for since many lenders sell home loans to other institutions after they have made them anyway. That advice is appropriate provided (1) you deal with a reputable home-mortgage lender, and (2) you are not in a high-risk category. Home mortgages are typically made by savings and loans, banks, and mortgage companies. Credit unions in some states also make home loans, but you must be a member before you can borrow. If you are considered a high-risk applicant by traditional lenders, you may need to shop for a lender that specializes in difficult qualifications. Such lenders are sometimes called *B* or *C lenders* or *portfolio lenders.* The latter term means the institution will keep the loan in its portfolio rather than sell it on the secondary market as many other lenders do. Expect to pay a higher interest rate from B and C lenders.

Here are the common types of loans available:

ARMs Adjustable rate mortgages with attractively low rates receive much of the bank advertising and may be the type of loan for you, but there are factors to consider first. Your initial loan rate on an ARM is called a *teaser rate*—a low rate for only a short time. Find out how long that teaser rate will last. The period commonly is six months to one year. After that, the rate will change, almost always upward toward market rates. Your loan rate will be subject to change again, usually at the same interval, until it reaches a maximum or *cap.*

Changes in loan rates are linked to changes in a market indicator or index—such as the prime rate, one-year T-bill rates, or what's called the 11th District Cost of Funds rate (an industry average). Loan rates are typically *margined* or set at 2.25 percent to 3.25 percent above the index. As the index goes up (or down) your loan rate follows it. The specific market index that governs your rate will be specified on your loan agreement. Indices used by lenders are commonly published in the business section of newspapers, so you can keep your lender honest. Adjustable rate loans that will not change for three or five years are also available, almost always at a higher initial rate.

In addition to finding out how often your loan rate can be adjusted, and the index used, you need to know what the interest rate cap is. Two types of rate caps protect you during times of rising interest rates. Lifetime caps tell you the highest possible interest rate you could pay during the life of the loan. For example, many loans have *lifetime* caps of 6 percent, meaning that your loan rate cannot increase more than 6 percentage points, no matter how high interest rates in the country rise. Should your loan also have a *periodic* cap, that will limit how much your loan rate can increase during an individual adjustment interval.

Although it's easy to see the disadvantage in an adjustable rate loan—increased rates—ARMs have some benefits. With an ARM you will usually pay below-market rates for the initial period. Thus your payments will be lower at first, allowing you the chance to put that extra money into improvements such as window covering or landscaping. In addition, while most people focus on the possibilities for rate increases, rates on ARMs can go down if rates dip. Even if rates remain steady while you're making payments, your mortgage cost will likely be lower than if you had selected a fixed-rate loan. If you think you will be in your house for five years or less, a five-year-interval ARM may be your best choice.

Many ARMs used to be free of prepayment penalties, meaning you could pay off the loan early—such as when you sell the house—without an additional charge. But some people refinance ARMs about every two years, in an attempt to keep the interest rate down, so many banks have started charging penalties. The penalties on ARMs typically last only three years. (If you sell your home after the penalty period and pay off the loan, you pay no penalty.)

As mentioned in Chapter 9, most loans are assumable—if the lender agrees. Assumability built into the loan is more common with ARMs because the lender has greater control over the loan. It's also easier to qualify for an ARM. If you are moving and changing jobs, it's likely you will obtain an ARM.

Negative Amortization Loans Neg Am loans, as they're called, are a form of adjustable-rate loan with a few changes. Your start rate is often extremely low, but it usually rises within one to three months. Your monthly payment, however, remains constant for the entire year. Regardless of rate changes, your monthly payment is only adjusted annually and then the payment amount can only rise by 7.5 percent.

Payments do not necessarily keep pace with rate changes. So, during a time of rising interest rates, any additional interest assessed but not covered by your monthly payment, is added to your principal balance. You may pay off this additional interest at any time. If you don't, it's possible that your principal balance will increase rather than decrease. Every five years, the loan is reamortized over the number of years remaining. While a Neg Am loan is attractive for its initially low monthly payments, you must be prepared for the consequences.

Fixed-rate loans In exchange for the security of knowing your loan rate will not change, you usually pay a higher rate. Institutions are frequently stricter about enforcing their qualification guidelines for fixed rate loans, and the loans usually are made for amounts under $214,600.

FHA/VA The federal government insures these loans for qualified borrowers. FHA loans typically require 5 percent down or less; VA loans for veterans generally require no down payment. Both types of loans are available without prepayment penalties. Maximum loan amounts vary from state to state.

House hunting via shoe leather

With a loan-approval slip in hand—or at least an understanding of the loan process—you're ready to put your real estate research to work. No matter how many Web pages you've scanned, or how many booklets or videos your agent has sent you, you still have to visit houses. You can't discover the ambience of a family room from a Web site, or peek into kitchen cabinets through an advertising booklet. You have to drive neighborhoods and traipse through house after house until you find the one you're looking for. But before you and your spouse climb into your agent's car, you need to decide the areas of town you wish to explore.

How do you select a neighborhood? It's subjective. Spend a reasonable amount of time becoming familiar with various neighborhoods—either through several visits or an extended stay—in your future home city. Here are some items to consider:

- How geographically defined is the neighborhood?
- Notice the location of freeways or highways: close enough for convenience, but distant enough so the sound doesn't intrude?
- How close are parks, shopping centers, fire stations?
- What does the merchandise for sale in nearby markets and stores tell you about the socio-economic mix of the area?
- What is the condition of street surfaces? Are there sidewalks?
- Is it an area of mixed zoning and mixed land use?
- How far are homes set back from the street?
- How large are the lots?
- Is the area in a flood plain or other danger zone?
- Is landscaping well maintained?
- Are there boats, RVs, and trucks parked in driveways and streets?
- How close are restaurants?
- What is the average age of the homes?
- How long will it take you to get to work?

If possible, drive from your prospective neighborhoods to your office or work location during rush hour. (Depending on where you're moving, *rush hour* may be a relative term.) You usually get a different impression of a neighborhood depending on the time you visit. As time permits, drive through neighborhoods during the week and on a Saturday or Sunday. Real estate agents advise that it's best not to buy the most expensive home in a given neighborhood. Instead, buy in an area with homes that are priced higher than the one you've selected. This helps insure the value of your property. Established neighborhoods usually mean mature landscaping and little guesswork about the physical character of the area.

For example, different areas of Las Vegas were recommended to us by my wife's coworkers. We spent several weekends just exploring different parts of the city. By the time we got together with an agent, we knew we wanted to look in the sparsely settled northwest portion of town, and in Green Valley, an adjoining town to the southeast. Our agent, a Nevada native, associated Green Valley with the area's early industrial development. She urged us to avoid it. We had discovered several attractive neighborhoods there, however, so we insisted on looking at homes in both areas of Las Vegas.

When you settle on an area and start to tour homes, take notes, take your time, and take frequent breaks. Avoid seeing so many homes in a short time that you can't remember one from another. (Was it the house with the ugly fountain that had the big kitchen? No, that was the one with the orange carpet.) Discuss your shopping strategy with your agent ahead of time. If you don't have a deadline to move, decide how many homes you want to see each day, and how many days you can devote to your search. Sometimes your house hunting will be spread over a few weekends as you return to California in the meantime. If this is the case, coordinating your visits with your agent is important.

Sweating the details—country or city

When you find a home that pleases you aesthetically, and has the right number and size of rooms, don't jump to make an offer. Look at the house a little more closely. Poke into every room, closet, and storage area. Examine the attic or basement. Ask questions. With care, you can do this without being intrusive. Nonetheless, you must ask about obvious conditions such as cracks in floors or walls, stains on walls and ceilings, and conditions outside that may indicate problems with irrigation systems or grading. Flush toilets, run faucets, and notice the condition of kitchen appliances.

The older a house, the more likely it is to have been modified or altered. Halls or doorways that seem unconventional may be a clue to a room addition. Ask about home additions and whether or not they were inspected by the appropriate city or county building department.

The roof over your head should be another focus of attention. Shake roofs last about 20 years. Composition shingles come in 20- and 30-year versions. Cement tiles last much longer. Look at the roof closely. See if you can tell if the tiles are in neat rows or if some tiles are cracked or missing. The pitch of a roof is also important. My first home had a gradually sloping roof with a valley that regularly collected water, then leaked.

Other things to do:

Ask about association dues. Condominiums are not the only form of housing that come with homeowner dues. You could buy a single-family home and still be assessed for maintenance of common areas such as lakes, sports courts, streets, gated entries, and other private facilities or services.

Find out where you are. Many communities have outgrown their municipal boundaries. Areas that seem to be within city limits may actually be in unincorporated county areas. The City of Las Vegas, for example, includes less than half the population of the metropolitan area. Cities such as Denver and Portland cover several counties. Governmental jurisdictions influence everything from your tax rate to fire and police protection, building codes and more.

Take measurements. If your furniture includes a large entertainment center, many bookcases, a tall dining room breakfront, king size waterbed, or an arrangement that you don't want to break up, you may want to take measurements in selected rooms. Floor plans and home stat sheets don't always tell the full story.

Check the heating and air conditioning. A furnace's age, capacity, and condition are much more important in some locales than in urban California. Air conditioning may be extraneous. On the other hand, in Phoenix, Las Vegas, and other desert cities, central air is a necessity, not a luxury.

Talk to neighbors. When you're getting serious about a home, talk to neighbors. Introduce yourself and tell them you're thinking about buying in the neighborhood. That's what Scott Gordon did before he and his wife and children moved to Ft. Collins, Colo., from Orange County. He says he knocked on the doors of at least 10 neighbors, asking about schools and other concerns, before he and his wife bought their new home.

Obtain a copy of CC&Rs. When you're serious about a home, get a copy of the covenants, conditions, and restrictions for that area. This document contains a list of do's and don'ts for homeowners. It may impose limitations on such things as style of architecture, landscaping, home maintenance, parking, setbacks, use of satellite dishes, and even the color you can paint the exterior of your house. CC&Rs often impose more detailed standards than city or county codes and carry the force of law. In retirement communities, CC&Rs may also restrict to whom you may resell your home.

Get it in writing. If you're buying in an active adult (retirement) community, be sure to get a contract that spells out your rights to golf courses and other facilities, so that you don't face users fees or membership requirements later.

Rural concerns

Are you planning to move to the outskirts of a city or town? Or are you eying a truly rural location? In either case, you likely will have fewer municipal services and more do-it-yourself answers for civilized necessities. Here are four items to watch for when buying in the boonies:

Septic tanks Although their home in Southern California was on a sewer system, Gene and Susan Gonzales knew enough to order a septic tank inspection before they bought their home in Chehalis, Wash. When they reviewed their closing papers, however, they didn't notice that a bill for septic-tank inspection was missing.

"We moved in on Friday. By Monday the rice and corn that I put down the garbage disposal was coming up in the front yard," says Susan.

The Gonzaleses say they were misled about the condition of the septic system, and that an inspector was chased off the property just prior to closing. They considered suing, says Susan, but decided against it, opting instead to put the money they might have spent in legal fees into a new, expanded septic-tank system.

A professional inspection of a septic tank system is a must before you buy a home that is not connected to a sewer. Tanks need periodic pumping. If service is omitted, you could have the same problem as the Gonzaleses.

To examine a septic tank, an inspector first needs to find it. Just knowing where your septic tank and clean-out access are, is a plus. Be sure to obtain a map showing the location of the tank and the leach lines that fan out from it. If the lines spread out in the middle of your back yard, that could substantially increase the cost of putting in a pool.

Well water Your water supply may come from a small well and pump located on your property or on neighboring land. Before you buy a home that gets its water from a well, have the water tested. Even if locals tell you that they never need to test well water, do it anyway. Have the water certified for purity. Also check the flow in gallons per minute. And find out how big the reserve tank is and how long it takes to be refilled.

The location of all septic-tank leach fields (yours and your neighbors') should be identified to insure the lines don't contaminate your water supply. If you share the well with other residences, you should be given a copy of a community well agreement which details the parties' responsibilities for the maintenance cost. Also be sure there are recorded easements for access to the well. Proper inspection and testing of your well can insure you have a reliable supply of clean water in your new home.

Use of septic tanks and wells varies from one town to another. A knowledgeable real estate agent should be able to alert you to the possibilities. For example, Carson City, Nev., has a significant number of both, says local agent Victoria Williams.

Another factor to consider is connection fees. In Carson City, says Williams, residents are required to hook up to sewer and water when connection points are within 400 feet of their property. Single-family connection fees, she says, are more than $2,000 for sewers and about $3,000 for water.

Private roads I'd never lived on a private street before we moved to Las Vegas. I didn't realize the significance of it until our homeowners board had to consider raising money to seal the local roads. Living on a private road also means you may have to pay for snow removal in the wintertime.

State laws differ in how the costs of private road maintenance are assessed or divided. Some states require written road-maintenance agreements between parties that use the roads, other states do not. Private roads may also be an obstacle to your access. If you must drive on a private road to get to your property, be sure you have an easement that allows you permanent access. Your agent, title company, or real estate attorney should be able to advise you. Don't leave it to chance.

Propane tanks Many properties on the edge of towns, and in rural locales, have propane tanks rather than natural gas service. Tanks need to be inspected for integrity, connections, and distance from the house (as local regulations require). Also check the costs and frequency of delivery of propane.

Home inspections

As potentially daunting as a home purchase may be, you have four levels of defense against problems. First is your common sense, conscientiousness, and preparation. A deal that looks too good to be true, may be. Be skeptical, ask questions, and don't necessarily accept things at face value. Educate yourself by consulting the resources listed at the back of this and the two preceding chapters.

Your second line of defense is the sellers' disclosure. Many states have followed California's lead in requiring sellers to sign a detailed disclosure statement regarding defects and any known adverse conditions. In some states the form is not required by law, but disclosure is still a common practice. Such is the case in Arizona, says real estate agent Alice Held of Scottsdale. Even if the state you're buying in doesn't require such a disclosure, you may require it as a condition of your offer. Ask your real estate attorney or California real estate agent for the appropriate form.

Obtaining the advice of knowledgeable professionals is your third defensive strategy. Finding a skilled and trustworthy agent or broker is the first step. If you have legal questions, or if escrow companies are not used for closings in your destination state, you should seek the advice of a real estate attorney. Your escrow officer and title company also perform important functions to safeguard your interests.

Your fourth defense against unwelcome surprises is a home inspection. A satisfactory home inspection should be a condition of your offer. My introduction to home inspectors was during the first sale of our Orange County home. Our first prospective buyer accompanied the inspector on his rounds— as you should when you're buying. In addition to the obvious earth-settlement problem, seemingly no subsystem in our house escaped the inspectors' scornful remarks. *I* wouldn't have wanted to buy our home after hearing his derogatory assessment. I later learned that it's an inspector's job to point out as many problem areas—potential or actual—as possible. All inspectors are different, but a skeptical nitpicker may be just want you want when you're in the buyer's position. According to the American Society of Home Inspectors, the popularity of do-it-yourself home improvements has prompted many people to unknowingly make unsafe alterations. Skillful, experienced inspectors know what to look for.

If your target state licenses inspectors, be sure to hire one who is licensed. In some areas, anyone can advertise himself as an inspector. Ask your agent to recommend qualified inspection companies. If in doubt, check references, Better Business Bureau complaints, and other brokers who have worked with the inspection firms you're considering.

During the inspection, water, gas, and electricity should be turned on, and the inspector should check all appliances, floors, attics, windows, roof, ceilings, storm windows, plumbing, air conditioning, heating, electrical sockets, and fixtures. If there is evidence of a leaking roof, require a licensed roofer to inspect and certify it if repairs were already made. Even if you are buying a new home, you need an inspection. New homes are rarely defect-free, and an inspection report can support your request to the builder to fix deficiencies.

Even if the inspection shows no problems that would cause you to cancel your offer, it will likely turn up an assortment of major or minor flaws.

These are usually subject to negotiation prior to closing. For instance, the sellers agree to fix the cracked bathroom tile and you agree to overlook the broken garage door opener. Your agent can advise you.

Although most areas of the West have fewer incidences of infestation than California, a termite inspection is a wise precaution. In desert regions you can omit this step provided the home inspection shows no signs of termites. Termite inspection is frequently paid for by the buyer of the property, with an agreement that the seller pay for any corrective work necessary.

As our Orange County experience taught us, adverse conditions that you discover about your future home become your burden if you decide to overlook them and buy the house anyway. Even if you think you'll never move again, make resale possibilities part of your buying deliberations.

New homes, bargain homes

When you move, you'll probably have a choice of a new or preexisting home. Both types have advantages, depending upon your pocketbook and taste. The biggest advantage of a new home is that you can decorate (and landscape) it any way you wish. When Mark Dorio moved his family from California to Carson City, Nev., they bought a newly constructed home for a fraction of the price they would have paid in Sherman Oaks, and they decorated it just the way they wanted. Some people look at the clean white walls of a new home as an artist views a blank canvas. It's easier to decorate when you don't have to deal with the previous owner's taste in wallpaper and paint. In many new homes you are given a choice of carpet, kitchen and bathroom floor tile, and other decorator items. Many builders offer you a choice of kitchen appliances, the layout of closets, cable TV and stereo connections, patio covers, built-in shelves, and light fixtures. Buying a new home also means you can select your own window coverings and landscaping, although these items can substantially increase the total cost of your home. Existing houses usually come with curtains, drapes, lawns, and shrubs already in place.

Some builders construct homes only when they have buyers. That means you can select a new home from models, but then have to wait many months for your home to be built. New homes also tend to be built in outlying areas of town. That might mean a longer drive to work or shopping. On the other hand, newer parts of town may have wider streets, bright new shops and restaurants, and less congestion than older sections.

New homes should come with a warranty from the builder. You will do a walk-through of the home prior to closing and should make a *punch list* of flaws that need attention. Generally it's better to have the problems fixed *before* you close the deal, but after you move in you will continue to find imper-

fections. As you do, list them and present them to the builder's representative all at one time, rather than calling every time you find a crack somewhere. Walk-throughs prior to closing are standard for previously owned
homes too. The seller, his agent, and your agent should ideally be present
for your final inspection. Take your inspector's report with you and see that
all agreed-upon repairs have been made.

Some builders, particularly developers of large tracts, will not cooperate
with brokers. This means some agents may not be eager to show you new
housing projects. Builders sometimes sell their homes directly to the public through model home centers. Buying from a builder in this way is akin
to buying a new car in a showroom. Builders occasionally arrange with a bank
or other lender to provide loans at competitive rates for their buyers, but
you are also free to seek your own financing. An exclusive buyer agent is
less likely to steer you away from new tracts, particularly if you have agreed
to compensate the agent yourself.

Bargain homes

New homes don't usually come with bargain-basement prices. A new home
may be a bargain—compared to California prices—but not a bargain in the
local market. If the prices you find in your destination city still seem too high,
there are a few ways to find even lower prices. One way is to shop for older
homes.

In the fastest-growing areas, such as Salt Lake, Las Vegas, and Phoenix,
many builders are competing with each other. New tracts and developments
beckon from different parts of the city. Availability of low-priced new homes
puts downward pressure on the price of existing homes. For example, if someone can buy a brand new, three-bedroom, two-bath home for $125,000, why
would they consider an older home of similar size for more money? Of course
many other factors are involved, such as the quality, age, and location of the
existing homes. But all things being equal, sellers can't expect to get a premium price for an existing home when inexpensive new homes are available.
For another sample of home prices, see Table 10.1.

If you're not set on a new home, you may be able to find an existing house—
perhaps one only five or ten years old—for a reasonable price. Even if the price
of a five-year old home is the same as that of a new home, you may still save
money on landscaping, window coverings, and other extras that most existing
homes already have. If your target hometown is not booming with new construction, you may have to look elsewhere for bargains. Banks are a likely place.

When someone defaults on a home loan, the lending institution takes over
the house. Contrary to popular opinion, foreclosure is almost always a last resort.
Lenders will usually do whatever they can to help a borrower who may have

Median sales price of existing, single family homes

Albuquerque, N.M.	$122,300
Anchorage, Alaska	143,900
Austin, Texas	108,100
Billings, Mont.	97,800*
Bellingham, Wash.	144,000*
Boise, Idaho	101,200
Bryan/College Station, Texas	84,300
Carson City, Nev.	135,289
Cheyenne, Wyo.	90,900*
Charlotte, N.C.	116,800
Colorado Springs, Colo.	126,600
Denver, Colo.	133,400
Eugene/Springfield, Ore.	116,200
Flagstaff, Ariz.	130,000
Fort Collins, Colo.	143,000
Gardnerville, Minden, Nev.	145,000
Great Falls, Mont.	87,290*
Honolulu, Hawaii	335,000
Las Cruces, N.M.	98,541*
Las Vegas, Nev.	118,500
Los Angeles Area, Calif.	172,900
Madison, Wis.	122,200
Minneapolis/St. Paul, Minn.	113,900
Nashville, Tenn.	112,700
Orlando, Fla.	92,400
Phoenix, Ariz.	105,300
Portland, Ore.	141,500
Pueblo, Colo.	90,000*
Reno, Nev.	140,000
Richland/Kennewick/Pasco, Wash.	101,300
Salt Lake City, Utah	122,700
San Antonio, Texas	84,900
San Diego, Calif.	174,400
San Francisco Bay Area, Calif.	266,400
St. George, Utah	120,733
Santa Fe, N.M.	177,250
Seattle, Wash.	164,600
Spokane, Wash.	101,200
Tacoma, Wash.	125,400
Tampa/St. Petersburg/Clearwater, Fla.	81,300
Tucson, Ariz.	105,500
Twin Falls, Idaho	86,900*

*Average price, not median

Table 10.1 Reprinted with permission of the National Association of Realtors. Some prices courtesy local real estate boards. Prices are for 1996.

had some financial setbacks. Part of this, of course, (as my banker wife will attest) is based on a desire to be fair. But bankers are also practical and don't like to maintain and sell homes because it's expensive. When a bank forecloses, it must maintain a home and yard and in some cases provide upgrades to make a home salable. It must pay property taxes and utilities just like anyone else. In addition, the money a bank has tied up in residential real estate is not available for lending. For all of these reasons, banks like to sell the houses they own as quickly as possible—often at bargain prices.

California banks are more likely to have big inventories of homes for sale, but out-of-state banks have foreclosures too. To obtain a list of bank-owned properties, call the headquarters offices of banks and savings and loans in your target city and ask for the REO department. They will send you a list of all their REOs (bank jargon for real estate-owned). A bonus in buying an REO may be attractive financing—sometimes with a lower down payment— if the bank is eager to get the home off its books. Banks often will list REO property with regular brokers or cooperate with brokers. So you also can ask your agent about REOs.

Another potential source for home bargains is relocation companies. When a third-party firm buys a transferred employee's home as part of a relocation, the company wants to sell it quickly. Like banks, relocation companies want to keep expenses down by reducing their inventories of homes. Relocation homes for sale may be slightly larger (and thus more expensive) than the average home, but they often can be purchased at discount prices. If you're interested in a relocation property, ask your agent. Multiple listings usually identify homes as relocation properties. Keep in mind that the more healthy a local economy is, the less likely you will be to find companies with a backlog of REOs and relocation homes.

Closing the deal

Your agent may be most valuable when it's time to negotiate. In a sellers' market, there may not be as much maneuvering room: bargains will be harder to find. A few considerations:

Criticism Avoid criticizing a seller's home as a way of persuading him to accept a lower price. You're more likely to insult or anger the seller.

Days on the Market (DOM) The MLS printout of a home will tell you how long it has been for sale. The longer a home has been sitting, the more accommodating a seller is likely to be. Conversely, if a home has been listed for just a few days, a seller might accept a lower offer to get the transaction over quickly.

Prequalification for financing As already mentioned, if you're approved for a loan and can promise a quick close, make sure the sellers know that.

Closing costs, details

Your lending institution and your agent will help you determine what your new home will cost. Your lender will usually charge a loan fee expressed in *points.* Each point is equal to one percent of your loan amount. If you deal directly with a bank or other financial institution, rather than going through a loan broker, you may be able to shave a point or more from your costs. The final annual percentage rate (APR) that you are quoted will, by law, include the cost of all points. After you apply for a loan, your lender is required to give you a good-faith estimate of the costs you will incur. The costs will vary somewhat from state to state and may include a credit reporting fee, document fees, recording fees, title insurance premium, and escrow fees. The cost of inspections also may be your responsibility. You also will likely be asked to prepay a small amount of interest on your loan.

Usually there's no need to use an attorney in a real estate transaction. The escrow company acts as an unbiased third party to hold money and documents until all conditions in the escrow instructions are complied with. A title company issues a title insurance policy insuring that you and your lender have legal title to the property. But some states require that an attorney handle the functions of an escrow company. In this case, closing is often accomplished by all parties actually sitting around a table and exchanging documents and cashiers checks.

Be sure to get a title report from a reputable title insurance company insuring that you obtain legal title to the property. Your lender will require a title policy that insures that its lien is legal, but that policy will not necessarily cover you. You need an owner's title insurance policy. You'll know if the title is clear because a title insurance company will not issue a policy if there is a cloud over the title. Your title policy also will identify CC&Rs and easements executed against the property and exclude them from coverage. Obtain a copy of your title policy, and be sure you understand the exclusions. Ask your agent or your title company representative if in doubt.

Closing the deal on your new home out of state calls for a celebration. You mastered the intricacies of neg am loans and combed the Web until you were woozy. You found a sagacious agent, calculated your monthly payments, and had the septic tank inspected. You made an offer, settled on a price, and were careful not to spend more than you needed to. You're done. Now you can settle in.

No, wait! Now you have to pack.

Resources

Books

10 Steps to Home Ownership: A Workbook for First-time Buyers
Ilyce R. Glink
Times Books, 1996

Kiplinger's Buying and Selling A Home
Staff of *Changing Times Magazine*
Kiplinger Books, 1990

Sylvia Porter's A Home of Your Own
Sylvia Porter
Avon Books, 1989

Web Sites

Abele Owners' Network *http://www.owners.com*
Lets you list your property or search for FSBOs in all but two states and contains information resources for self-sellers.

American Society of Home Inspectors
85 W. Algonquin Road Suite 360
Arlington Heights, IL 60005
(847) 290-1919
http://www.mhv.net/~dfriedman/ashihome.htm

Real Estate Information Network *http://www.reinfonet.com/*
This general purpose site is California-based and lacks out-of-state home listings, but it does have detailed information on buying, selling, and financing.

How Much Home Can I Afford?
http://www.centerpointmortgage.com/howmuch.html
Site is sponsored by Centerpoint Mortgage of Laguna Hills.

HSH Associates, Financial Publishers
Financial Calculators *http://www.hsh.com/mort_calc.html*
Lets you calculate prices and payments (and more). Includes up-to-date rates for the common mortgage indices.

11

Ready for the Movers?

Don't start packing quite yet. There's more to do.

Like other aspects of your relocation, moving your belongings is an opportunity to evaluate, to take stock. It's a chance for you to reorganize yourself and your life, discover old treasures and memories, and get rid of unwanted baggage you've been lugging around for years. In other words, it's time to clean out your garage. And your closets. And any other place where junk is lurking.

Three good reasons for this are: (1) You'll feel smug as hell, (2) You may discover that lost sweater (first baseman's mitt, vase, etc.) that you've been looking for all these years, and (3) You'll save money on your move. Why pay the movers to haul your garbage?

If you haven't moved in five years or more, chances are you have lots of things to get rid of. As you map out a moving schedule, pull open a few cabinet doors, peek inside those boxes in the garage, and start thinking about what you're going to keep. More important, decide what you're going to throw away, give away, or sell at your getting-out-of-California garage sale.

How far in advance you plan your move depends upon the size of your household, the time of year you'll be moving, and whether you're going to move your possessions yourself. Eight weeks is not too far in advance to start planning. If you want to move during the summer months, eight weeks is the *minimum* amount of time to set aside.

Cleaning out

The optimum time to go through all your possessions is before you put your house on the market. That way you'll remove some of the clutter from your living or storage areas, making your house look more spacious and attractive. At minimum, you should be finished by the time the movers arrive.

How much you get rid of is up to you. I used to save everything—from newspaper articles I hoped someday to read, to bits of lumber too good to throw away but not precisely suited for any job. But before we left California, I went through our garage and threw out: an old bicycle, boxes of old letters, semi-functioning tools, magazines, chipped pottery, an old radio, bent lawn furniture, old board games, inflatable pool toys with holes in them, rolls of carpet remnants from a previous home, and boxes of other discards. If you have as much junk as we had, you might consider renting a trash bin. Most sanitation departments or independent refuse haulers rent large bins you can fill with trash and then have hauled away.

Give your whole house a going over. Think about aging furniture or appliances you're planning to replace. It may be cheaper and more convenient to get rid of some items before you go. For example, when we moved, we realized that our daughter in high school was younger than our washer and dryer, so we decided to replace them. (We threw the washer and dryer, but we kept our daughter.) We saved the cost of having to move the mechanical monstrosities, and when we arrived in our new home we bought a new washer/dryer pair that was delivered and installed for free. You can also consider donating items to charity, or passing them along to unsuspecting relatives.

If you're buying a house at your destination, a floor plan or diagram of the rooms will help you decide if all of your furniture will fit. You can use graph paper and little cutouts to do this figuring, but there's computer software that makes the job much easier. It even lets you experiment with colors for walls and floor coverings.

Once you're down to those possessions you're going to keep, it's a good idea to take pictures of your valuables and write up an inventory. Before moving, some people inventory everything they own. That sounds way too ambitious, but you might write up a list that includes your jewelry, antiques, works of art, electronic devices (from stereos to cameras), coin collections, and anything else you treasure. Some people set out all their valuables, then videotape or photograph them from different angles. Whichever way you do it, your photos and inventory list can be helpful in collecting damages if anything is lost or broken in transit.

Moving is time-consuming, but it's only a hassle if you're unprepared. Do your homework in selecting a moving company, then work with its representatives to prepare all your goods for shipment. You'll be ready to start a new phase of your life.

Working with movers

Summer is the busiest time for the moving industry. Nearly half of all interstate moves take place between June 1 and Sept. 30, according to the American Movers Conference, an Alexandria, Vir., trade association. If you will be moving during the summer, start calling movers eight weeks before you want to move and try to avoid moving the last week of each month. These are "real crunch periods," says a van lines spokesperson.

If an employer is going to pay for your move, that may determine which carrier you work with; companies that routinely move employees have contracts with movers. If you're being hired (or transferred) by a company that does not have a contract with a mover, you may be asked to obtain three estimates from different companies. If you're going to pay all or a part of the moving costs yourself, obtain at least three estimates.

You can find local numbers for the major national moving companies in the telephone book. When you make appointments for sales representatives, also called estimators, to come out to your house, plan for at least an hour's visit. If you live in an apartment or small house it may not take that long, but you want to allow yourself plenty of time to discuss costs, liability coverage, and other options.

Show the estimators *everything* in your house, garage, and yard that will be moved. Be sure to point out that cabinet stuffed with 33 rpm records, the dumbbells under your son's bed, and anything else that an estimator might miss. Company representatives may appear nosy. That's good. Their job is to figure out what your belongings weigh. Anything they overlook could mean an additional cost for you later. Be sure also to point out everything that will *not* be packed and shipped. Will the swing set in the back yard stay with your home? Are you leaving your second refrigerator behind? Make a list of those items that you are not taking with you so all the estimators will have the same information upon which to base your projected moving costs.

Most major moving companies provide both binding and non-binding estimates. The binding estimate is more like a price quote; it is the total base price you will pay if you choose that mover. Theoretically, the only way the binding estimate will vary is if you make any changes in what you are shipping. You can easily compare moving costs by obtaining binding estimates from several movers

Non-binding estimates are based on the sales representative's assessment of what your furniture and belongings weigh. It is strictly an *estimate* of your costs, which could vary. If you select a firm based on its non-binding estimate, the mover will weigh the van before driving to your home, then again after all your goods are loaded. The difference determines what you'll pay. Obviously, non-binding estimates will vary from one company to another, and are more difficult to compare. You won't know until moving day exactly what your shipment will cost. It could be substantially more than the estimate.

Incidentally, if you're the skeptical type, you should know that you are permitted to follow the moving van to the scales to watch the weigh-in.

Some experts say a binding estimate may result in slightly higher moving costs, compared to paying for the actual weight of your load. Nevertheless, a binding estimate is preferable. (You might choose a non-binding estimate if you are not certain before your move how much you will be taking with you.)

Regardless of which type of estimate you select, here are some factors that can increase your costs:

Walking distance If you're moving into or out of a flag-shaped lot with a narrow drive, or if you're in a condominium or apartment that is a long distance from the street, it may cost extra for your loading. If the moving crew has to walk more than 75 feet from the van to your front door, there will be an extra charge. For example, when Robert Tonsing and his wife Ann Imse moved to their mountain home in Colorado, the movers told them they would have to come up with more money than they expected before their goods would be unloaded. Their new home was at the end of a 150-foot driveway.

Stairs/elevators If movers have to use a flight of stairs or elevators to get to your front door, there may be an extra charge. But you are not charged extra simply because you have a two-story home.

Extra stops Be sure to tell the estimators if the van will have to pick up other items at other locations. When we moved to Nevada, I moved my office at the same time. The van had to make a stop at my office after our household goods were loaded. (The estimators had to visit my office as well.)

Pianos Some movers charge extra for moving unusually large items, such as pianos.

Your car If you have no other way of moving one of your cars, it can be loaded into the van along with your other possessions. Be sure to ask your estimator about it.

Storage Most people try to avoid having to put their belongings in storage, because it costs extra. Even if your employer is paying, try to avoid storage. It increases the likelihood of damage, because your goods receive more handling.

Shuttle Moving-van drivers are often exceptionally skillful at maneuvering their giant vehicles into small spaces. When my parents moved to Arizona, I was surprised to see the van sitting in the narrow alley behind their

Chatsworth condominium. If the driver cannot get his van near enough to your old or new residence, however, a smaller truck may be used shuttle your belongings between the van and your door. If you think this might be necessary, ask the estimators.

In fact, ask the estimators lots of questions about any unusual situations you anticipate, and anything you don't understand. Ask them if there are any other additional charges you could incur, and be sure to get the estimate in writing. If a company offers to give you an estimate over the phone, try another company. If the sales agent is not organized, or is not willing to answer questions now, imagine how you'll be treated later if you have a complaint or claim. In addition to judging a company on the basis of its sales agent and cost estimate, you should call your local Better Business Bureau to ask if any complaints have been filed against the company. You also can ask prospective movers for recent references. In addition, ask each company for its federally required Annual Performance Report. This report includes the number of damage claims the company received, and how often the company missed its delivery dates or incorrectly estimated the final cost of shipments.

One important factor to discuss with the movers is liability coverage. Most companies offer free limited liability protection. But this coverage pays only 60 cents per pound; you will want additional protection. Most movers offer different levels of coverage at varying costs. Your homeowner's insurance likely will not automatically cover your move; talk with your insurance agent to find out your options. Also, the policy covering your old home typically will be canceled when you move out, so talk to the agent handling the insurance on your new home. If you choose to obtain liability coverage from your mover, as many people do, understand the costs and the deductible amounts fully before you sign up.

Two other important elements of your contract with the movers are the pick-up and delivery dates and the method of payment. Both should be in writing. The farther you are moving, the greater the potential for delays. Your pick-up schedule becomes even more important if you are having the movers do the packing for you. You want the packing to be completed the day before the van arrives. Depending on the size of your load, your belongings will be placed on a van that also contains the belongings of one to four other families. Those loads may or may not be going to the same town you are. You can see the scheduling challenge this poses, but companies usually do their best to be on time.

If your employer is making direct payment for your move, you won't have to worry about paying the driver. But regardless of who is ultimately footing the bill, if you don't make prior arrangements with the mover, the driver will ask for payment at your new home, before the goods are unloaded. Don't expect to be able to pay by credit card or check, either. Cash, traveler's checks, or cashiers checks usually are required.

With a non-binding estimate, your costs could be higher than the original estimate, but according to current regulations, movers cannot require a delivery payment of more 10 percent above the estimated price. You're given 30 days to pay any balance. In other words, if your non-binding estimate was $3,000, and the total cost based on the weight turned out to be $3,700, you would have to pay $3,300 at the time of unloading and would owe a balance of $400.

Packing

Another option for your move is deciding who will pack your belongings. Ask the van lines' agents who visit you to give you estimates of the cost to pack everything. You'll need to evaluate these costs, along with the transportation charges, in order to select a mover. Once you find out how much it will cost to have the company pack everything in cartons for you, you can decide whether or not you want to do it yourself. If you plan to do the packing, you'll need dozens of sturdy cartons, packing material such as paper, and up to a week's time. The amount of time for self-packing varies, but it often takes longer than you expect.

You have a choice of places to find containers. Used cartons are sometimes free for the asking from grocery, drug, and discount stores. (Some people cruise behind strip shopping centers and raid the trash bins for boxes.) Or you can check classified ads. It's a good idea to get more boxes than you think you'll need. Once you add crumpled paper and other packing material to the boxes, you'll find they don't hold as much as you thought.

Of course you can buy boxes from truck rental firms, van lines, and mailing supply stores. Firms such as U-Haul International sell a variety of specially designed boxes and packing materials, including wardrobes, but the prices mount up. If you're on a tight budget, consider buying packing materials for your fragile and valuable items, and scavenging for the rest.

Having the movers do all the packing becomes more attractive, the larger your household. Movers have just the right cartons and packing materials to make the job go quickly. Professional movers can usually pack your belongings in a fraction of the time it would take you to do it. (This is especially true if you gaze at each item you wrap, pausing with the memories it brings to mind.)

To insure the best packing job, tell your estimator which of your possessions are the most fragile and expensive. Take time to review this with the person heading the packing crew as well. For your special items, ask the packing crew to leave the boxes unsealed so you can review the contents with the van driver. The purpose here is to let the driver inspect the quality of the packing for these extra fragile items, and let him see that they are in good condition before they're loaded. Schedule the packers to arrive a day or two before the van arrives. Again, this depends upon the size of your load.

Here are some special considerations in the packing of your belongings:

Crates If you have antiques or other large valuables that you think may get damaged in transit, you can have the packers, at extra cost, of course, make wooden crates for the items. I have a small, 180-year-old chest that's had the crate treatment twice. It's still in relatively good shape.

Clothing You'll need to pack a suitcase or two for your trip, but the majority of your clothes can be packed by the movers. Hung up in tall wardrobe cartons, your clothes on hangers should arrive in the same condition in which they were packed. Leave other clothes in dresser drawers.

Food Have as many potluck nights as you can so that the amount of food you take is minimal. Make sure lids on spice jars are tight and don't take open packages of cornstarch, flour, sugar, and similar foods; the risk of spills outweighs the value of the food. Pack no perishables for the moving van, even for what should be an overnight move.

Toxic materials Van lines won't carry paint, furniture stripper, lacquer, paint thinner, wood stain, cleaning fluid, pool chlorine, and similar materials. They'll also leave out aerosol cans such as hair spray, deodorant, and insecticide. Don't pack or transport these items yourself either. Drain gas and oil out of lawn mowers, chain saws, and other gas engines.

You may have to plan weeks ahead to get rid of most of your "toxic" materials. Some California cities, counties, and disposal districts have complex rules for disposal of toxics. Some have only annual or semi-annual pick ups. It's possible you'll have to cart the stuff away yourself to a toxics pick-up point or disposal site. California state law also limits the number of gallons of toxics you can carry in your car at one time, so if the disposal site is many miles away, set aside part of an afternoon.

Unpack-me-first boxes Some van lines have a time- and hassle-saving way for you to find important things like television cables, extension cords, shelf clips for bookshelves, and other necessities. All such items are placed in a small box with bright red markings all over it. The open-me-first box is ideal for everything from picture hooks to TV and stereo remote controls. If your mover doesn't have this service, do it yourself.

Special packing Grandfather clocks, computer components, and some other household items may have internal parts that need to be secured. Many record turntables, and some CD players, have screws you can tighten to secure moving parts for transit. Remove CDs and CD cartridges from players. Washing-machine tubs also need to be secured.

Take it yourself For cherished items that you could not replace, consider taking them with you rather than consigning them to the moving van. Let the movers handle your computer, but take backup disks or tapes with you. Small antiques, family heirlooms, expensive jewelry, a coin collection, 35mm or video cameras, are the types of things you might consider taking in your car. Some van lines also suggest taking with you your most treasured family pictures, slides, or videotapes.

In addition to valuables, there are several categories of items that you should take with you in your vehicle, if possible. These are items you will want access to as soon as you arrive. For example, a tool kit can become a desperate need. Good luck in finding it if it's packed among 47 cartons in the garage, each labeled only "garage."

Let the movers take the majority of your tools, but keep a small tool box with a few wrenches, screwdrivers, a hammer, pliers, and assorted nuts and bolts. A briefcase or small suitcase can become your traveling desk and file cabinet. In it you might have your checkbook, insurance policies, medical records and renewable prescriptions, address books, backup computer disks, final utility and other local bills, school records, business papers, and your extra set of glasses.

The third repository of moving essentials is your first aid kit. Carry all medicines that family members need. If you have room, also set aside kitchen items such as a can opener, sharp knife, serving spoons, and condiments you'll want the first night or two in your new home.

Watch the packers

If you opt for professional packers, you won't have to do the work, but it's a good idea to keep an eye on them. At least one member of your family should be at home at all times. When we moved from California, we were around when the packers wrapped everything in the house, but to our regret we left them alone in the garage. Many of our garden tools were piled into a huge box with little packing material. Then the packers added a bottle of algicide, a small container of lubricating oil, and an open box of laundry detergent. Fortunately the ensuing mess—which we didn't discover until weeks later—only stained our new garage floor. Other California escapees have had packers who wrapped up full waste baskets or even half-eaten food.

Some moving companies provide stickers you can use to label boxes or items. Atlas Van Lines, for example, provides stickers that say "Do not pack" and others that say "Do not load." You shouldn't need to put one of those on a ham sandwich. But the stickers can help you identify items you don't want packed because you're going to give them away or transport them yourself.

Don't stand over the packers as they box every item, but you may want to influence how some of your things are packed. For example, I have a pair of four-drawer, wooden, lateral file cabinets in my office. Filled with files, they're extremely heavy and tend to flex. I asked the packers to unload most of the drawers and pack the files in boxes. This, I think, saved my cabinets from cracking under their own weight, but it meant I spent hours resorting my files when we arrived. Again, a tradeoff.

After the packers have finished, it's a good idea to make a thorough check of cabinets, closets, and cubbyholes before they leave. Before my parents moved to Sun City they checked their garage cabinets as the van was being loaded and spotted several items the packers had overlooked.

When the van arrives, the driver will write up an inventory of your belongings. Review this carefully. He will then attach numbered stickers to every box and piece of furniture you own. The numbers will be recorded on the inventory lists. When that is complete, the movers will start loading the van. It's surprising how quickly your belongings will disappear into the truck.

If you have small children, make sure they don't get in the way of the movers, but don't exclude them either. They may be fascinated to watch the van being loaded, or they may have questions about what is happening. Giving them a task to do may help them feel they are contributing to the project.

Plants and pets can pose special challenges. Plants can be loaded into the van, but it's risky. Some plants will not last in the heat of a closed moving van for more than a day. Also, your plants may not survive the transition from the climate where you live to the weather in your new location.

Animals may become frightened and disoriented when all of your belongings are being moved out of the house. Your cat might run and hide down the street. Boarding your animals, or having a friend look after them, removes one more potential problem on moving day.

We moved to Nevada with a large dog and a small cat. The day before the movers arrived, we checked Duke and Duchess into a kennel. We picked them up on our way out of town. Some animals travel well, but to be safe, we had our vet prescribe tranquilizers for our pets.

Arriving and unpacking

Although Americans are transient—the AMC says one out of five families moves every year—most furniture is not made to be shipped. Glass-topped tables, delicate chairs, ornate floor lamps, framed pictures, and many other items are vulnerable. When you think about the complexity of trucking everything you own hundreds or thousands of miles, moving companies do a remarkable job. But they're not perfect. If you assume that something will be scratched, cracked, or chipped during your move, you won't be too disappointed if you discover a scratch down the leg of an end table or a scrape along one wall of your new house. Mistakes happen and they shouldn't spoil your enthusiasm for your new home. To minimize your disappointment, however, and to help establish claims for damages, here are some suggestions:

• If you see any damaged cartons or otherwise suspect damage inside a box, open it in the presence of the driver. This applies to boxes you have packed and to those packed by the movers. Be sure to label or mark boxes containing especially fragile items so you can unpack them while the movers are still there.

• Be prepared for hard work. The movers will do the lifting, but you and your family will have to inventory the items as they are unloaded, tell the movers where to put the furniture and boxes, then check everything carefully for damage.

• Have a family member or friend assigned to look over all furniture and the exterior of all cartons, after they're unloaded from the truck. Report any damage to the driver right away.

• Be sure to identify any damage in writing on the inventory sheets that you sign after your possessions are unloaded. File a damage claim promptly. (Call your moving company to confirm damage claim procedures.) Movers must acknowledge your claim within 30 days.

• If you find damaged items in boxes you unpack after the movers have gone, keep each item in its box to show the moving company's agent after you have made a claim.

If you do have a claim, it could be settled quickly. In many cases, settlement is done within 30 days. Expensive, complex claims may take longer. Collecting a claim for damaged goods you packed yourself could be challenging. An AMC spokesperson suggests that prior to your move, you ask the sales agent for a statement in writing what the movers' liability will be regarding self-packed goods.

If you can't resolve a dispute, one alternative to suing the company is arbitration. The AMC, through the American Arbitration Association, sponsors a Household Goods Dispute Settlement Program. You can get information on the program from your moving company or the AMC.

Depending, of course, upon the care given to your belongings, it's a good idea to tip the driver and his helpers after your possessions are loaded. (This may ensure that the van arrives promptly and is unloaded carefully, although the driver may have new helpers at your destination.)

Doing it yourself

Renting a truck or trailer and hauling all your goods yourself is less expensive than hiring a mover, in part because you do all the packing. It's easy to compare direct costs. Have one or two moving companies give you estimates, then contact a few truck-rental firms. To find out how much a truck will cost, you have to decide how big a vehicle you need. Here's a general guide to the truck sizes used by U-Haul International:

Your current home		Truck length
Bedrooms	Square footage	you need
1-2	up to 1,200	14 ft.
2-3	1,200 to 1,600	17 ft.
3-4	1,600 to 2,000	24 ft.
4 and up	2,000 and larger	26 ft.

Truck-rental rule number one: Make sure you have a confirmed reservation and reservation number for your truck. This requires calling or visiting a truck rental agency and giving them a deposit, either by cash or credit card. At least one of the major companies has an 800-number reservation line. If you visit your local rental outlet, it gives you a chance to check out the sizes of the trucks, buy boxes, and get as much free advice as you can on packing. A U-Haul spokesperson says you should make reservations three to four weeks in advance during the summer. Fridays and Saturdays are the busiest days for truck rental firms. If you arrange to pick up your truck on another day, you will be less likely to have to wait.

Truck rental rates are often based upon a flat fee for a one-way rental. You're allotted enough miles and days to reach your destination comfortably. When analyzing costs, consider the price of the gasoline. Also ask about the cost of additional accident coverage on the truck. Truck rental firms offer damage-waiver protection similar to car rental companies. Additional coverage may also be available. Check with your insurance agent to see what coverage you may already have—for vehicles and goods—before buying more. (It is unlikely that your auto insurance will provide full replacement coverage for your household goods while in transit.) Other extra-cost items include dollies, furniture pads (get plenty of these), cartons, and other packing materials.

When you pack your rental van, do what the professionals do: disassemble tables and other items to make them easier to load and less susceptible to damage. Legs and pedestals to dining and kitchen tables, for example, often can be unscrewed. Separately pack glass table-top inserts, removable glass cabinet doors, and mirrors. Original boxes for computers, stereo components, and other items are usually the safest way to pack these breakables. Most van lines and truck-rental firms have free booklets on packing household goods. U-Haul even has a video on packing you can borrow.

Hybrid do-it-yourself option

A third, relatively unknown moving option exists for those on a budget who don't want to worry about driving a big truck. A few companies offer a low-cost moving service in which a giant shipping container, or truck trailer, is parked at your house for you to load. When you're done, the van or container is picked up and delivered to your new front door—for you to unpack.

Fred and Maryann Sabatini discovered this economical method when they moved from Anaheim to Michigan. Maryann wanted to travel in the same vehicle with her husband and pets, rather than having one person drive their car, while the other drove a rental truck. She said the container method saved money they would have spent on gas in a rental truck, as well as the time and aggravation of driving the truck across country.

One hybrid mover is Lowest Price Movers. According to President Cindy Sutch, the company uses commercial trucking lines to move your goods. A truck trailer is parked in front of your home for you to load. When you're finished, your boxes and furniture are sealed off inside the truck. The balance of the space is used for dry commercial goods, often palletized loads. The company usually can deliver from California to any place in the United States within 7-8 days, says Sutch.

Another company, Mobile Mini, Inc., primarily a storage firm, will transport an 8-by-20-foot container from Southern California to some locations in Arizona and Texas. If your goods will have to be stored for a while at your destination, containers are convenient.

Some full-service moving companies are experimenting with containerized moves in which the containers are placed on rail cars for transportation. Ask your company representative if your goods will be shipped by container.

To find a do-it-yourself moving company, look in the telephone book under *moving equipment rental; moving, self-service;* or *storage.*

Sample moving schedule

Finding a week-by-week schedule of suggested moving-related tasks is easy. Truck rental firms, van lines, real estate and relocation companies all offer their own free lists. Some include more detail than you'll ever need. Here are simplified suggestions. Use this as a framework and add your own concerns and requirements.

Eight weeks before:
• Call van lines to obtain estimates. Collect literature on self packing and truck or container rentals. (If you're planning a mid- to late-summer move, give the movers as much advance notice as possible.)

• Start collecting records from schools, physicians, dentists, etc.

• Contact your insurance agent to find out your coverage options for moving, truck rental, fire and liability insurance in your new home, etc.

Four to six weeks before:
• Get seasonal clothes you won't need, dry cleaned and sealed for packing. Also have rugs and drapes you're taking dry cleaned and wrapped for moving.

• If you're going to pack yourself, start collecting boxes, tape, packing materials, labels, and other necessary items.

• Start sorting your belongings. Decide what will be moved, stored, discarded, sold, or given away.

• Decide if you will have a garage sale. (Movers and real estate agents have booklets on how to hold a garage sale.)

• Find out how to dispose of paints, solvents, and other toxics hiding in your garage.

• Arrange for outside help, if necessary, to prepare for moving items such as satellite dishes, built-in home entertainment centers, exercise equipment, hot tubs, and spas. If in doubt, discuss these items with your moving company representative.

• Start establishing financial contacts in your new city with a savings and loan, credit union, or bank. Obtain a checking account, safety deposit box, line of credit, and other services.

• Make reservations if you're going to board your pets before or after the move.

• Obtain change-of-address forms from the U.S. Postal Service. Address changes for magazines, organization memberships, and catalogs, among others, may take many weeks before they take effect.

Three weeks before :
• If you're packing yourself, get busy. First, pack the things you won't be needing before you go. Schedule plenty of time for packing, especially if you think you'll get sidetracked on memory lane as you look through old treasures.

• Make hotel/motel reservations if necessary.

• Make reservations to get your pets' shots as necessary. Obtain new rabies certificates as needed. Ask your vet about the use of tranquilizers for your dog or cat if you have a long trip ahead.

• Arrange to cancel your utilities at your old house and have them turned on, ready for you, at your new home.

One to two weeks before:

• Cancel newspapers and other local services such as pest control.
• Get your car serviced.
• Decide what you are going to do with your house plants.
• Start eating all your frozen and other perishable food.

One to three days before:

• Have movers pack all your goods. Arrange/adjust your time so that someone is always home during the packing.

• If the packers don't have an open-me-first box for your TV remotes, extension cords, etc., make one yourself.

• Point out any especially fragile items to the packers.
• Isolate and label any items you do not want packed or loaded.
• Defrost refrigerators and freezers and allow them to dry.
• Turn off televisions and computers. Allow internal parts to cool to room temperature before packing.

• Put together your get-at-it-quick collections: tool kit, first aid kit, checkbook and important papers, first nights' kitchen supplies.

• Drain your waterbed.

• Obtain cash and traveler's checks for the trip and be prepared to pay the movers as you have agreed.

• Plan some tasks your children can do to help the move without getting in the way of the movers as they load the truck.

Moving day:

• Have specific, written instructions for your driver on how to get to your new home. Your moving company sales rep should have obtained this from you already. But if you have simple instructions handy for the driver, you'll be sure he knows where to go.

• If at all possible, give the driver a phone number where he can contact you at your destination.

• Get the driver's name in case you have to contact him.
• Stay until the van is packed with all your belongings.
• Make a last check of the house, looking in closets, cabinets, lofts, storage sheds, etc.

Resources

American Movers Conference
1611 Duke St.
Alexandria, VA 22314
(703) 683-7410

Information brochures are available from this trade group. Send a stamped, self-addressed No. 10 envelope for each brochure: *Moving and Children; Guide to a Satisfying Move; Household Goods Dispute Settlement Program.*

Federal Highway Administration, HMT-25,
Office of Motor Carriers
1201 Constitution Ave. N.W.
Washington, DC 20423.

This is the moving industry regulatory agency. A booklet, *Your Rights and Responsibilities When You Move,* is available from the agency. Van lines estimators also offer the booklet when they visit you. Obtain a copy and read it thoroughly.

Address Express
P.O. Box 9133
Boston, MA 02155-9133
(800) 248-6683

A free service which will handle all your changes of address with magazines, catalogs, associations, and clubs.

Design Your Home
3-D Walkaround

Software that lets you create (and easily change) room arrangements for every room of your house. Then you can switch to three-dimensions and see how your furniture will look in your new home. You can even add carpeting and wall coverings.

Web sites

World Wide Web of Moving and Storage *http://www.snapse.net/~tall/*
Includes information on insurance, packing, estimates, moving-related legislation, newsgroups, how to move plants and fish, and more.

The Virtual Mover *http://www.mfginfo.com/mover.htm*
Contains resources for both consumers and people in the moving industry.

12

Where to go: Southwest

In Ely, Nevada, the average daily low temperature can dip below freezing for half the year. This tiny ranching and mining town is near Great Basin National Park, where 13,000-foot Wheeler Peak is host to bristlecone pines and pristine alpine lakes, icy cold year round. Does this sound like your picture of Nevada? Or do you think of slot machines, neon lights, and blazing sun?

Like California, all Western states contain diversities and contrasts. Calling an area a "land of extremes" is the biggest cliché in travel writing, yet it's hard to avoid when discussing the West. Virtually every climate, size of community, and geographic variation is available in the West: thriving mountain towns, gussied up coastal villages, huge desert communities. Alabaster cities gleam, and vast open spaces lie beneath spacious skies. Tying it together is a pioneering spirit that's almost palpable. From the San Jose computer scientist now working in Albuquerque, to the grizzled, third-generation Montana rancher, pride and enthusiasm about the West is unbridled.

So, where should you go? This and the next chapter provide a few possibilities. Included is information on each Western state, plus some selected cities. The brief profiles that follow offer a starting point. If a town sounds appealing, use the research techniques discussed earlier to get more details. Or search a map for nearby communities.

Addresses and phone numbers for chambers of commerce for each city mentioned are at the back of this chapter. The cities listed were selected in part to demonstrate the broad range of possibilities. Towns with populations from 17,000 to 2.4 million are profiled. Edge cities near larger metro areas are described, as are small towns located hours from the nearest metropolis. This is a small sample; thousands more communities are there for your inspection.

This listing is not intended as a rating or ranking, only as a prelude to your search for a new hometown. Arbitrary ratings, such as those in magazines and books, are only as helpful as the criteria used to select them. Your preferences in climate, priorities in job fields, and many other variables will influence your search.

This chapter and the next cover towns in only the Western states—the states that attract the most Californians. You can apply the research techniques already discussed to create your own city profiles and to explore the South, Midwest, or other region.

Figures can lie and . . .

As you gather material on potential hometowns, be wary of statistics. They're one way to analyze a destination, but not the only way. Although this book contains statistics in narrative and table form, it contains fewer statistics than it could. Statistics on states and cities are only useful if they (1) are accurate, (2) are easy to understand, (3) measure the conditions they purport to measure, and (4) come with useful comparisons or benchmarks. Without reams of background explanations, statistics can be deceiving. For example, *Facts About the Cities* (cited in Chapter 3) lists, among other things, the average commute times in various cities. For Las Vegas and other, smaller, cities, the times are about 20 minutes. Compared to L.A. or the Bay Area that would be a dream of a commute, right? But what does the book say about the average commute time in Los Angeles? Only 25 minutes. Twenty-five minutes?! To get a figure that low, you'd have to average in retirees, elementary school children, and people who work at home. Soccer moms drive longer than that.

Then there's the weather. The weather table in this book uses the average highs and lows for January and July. That gives some idea at least how hot (and cold) it gets on an average winter and summer day. Some relocation guides and chamber of commerce publications show *one* average monthly temperature. How is that calculated? Is it the average of the mid-point temperatures for each day of the month? Perhaps it's an average of all highs and lows. In other words, it's a pretty useless figure. Do you know the average temperature where you live now?

There are other problems with statistics and surveys. How, when, and where are the data are collected? And by whom? For example, the murder rate in Oklahoma City skyrocketed in 1995. That statistic doesn't indicate a crime wave or a trend. It was simply a mathematical result of the bombing of the federal building. Statistics or facts alone can be deceiving. It's easy to celebrate a community's low home prices, without considering that if some condition makes it undesirable, prices will naturally be low. In addition, statewide—or even citywide—averages for various quality-of-living-factors may not be indicative of the town or suburb you're investigating.

What this shows is that you can consider statistics as advisory information, but you should gather your own specifics. Talk with people in your potential destinations. Collect information first hand. Weigh your experiences and impressions with the statistics. In other words, see for yourself.

ARIZONA

On a map, Arizona is to the right of California. That describes its politics as well as its geography. But the state has more than just a history of electing Republicans, from Senators Barry Goldwater and John McCain to majorities in the state legislature. Arizona shares with nearby states a Western self reliance and a skepticism about Eastern establishments—including the federal government. Arizona also has the lowest unionization rate of any Western state except Texas.

About half the state's population of more than four million people live in the Phoenix area. Tucson is the second-largest metro area, with the balance of the population in much smaller communities sprinkled around the state.

Dramatic and diverse scenery makes tourism a leading industry. It gives Arizonans vast recreational choices, from the Grand Canyon in the north to the saguaro-filled Sonora Desert to the south. The canyon from which Arizona draws its nickname draws visitors from all over the world; the Grand Canyon is the monarch of natural wonders. But Arizona has a splendid royal court, including Sedona, Oak Creek Canyon, Monument Valley, Meteor Crater, the Petrified Forest, Sunset Crater, and Canyon de Chelly. And many of these marvels are within easy driving distance of Phoenix.

Geographically, the northern and eastern portions of the state—with mountains, canyons, and forests—are a contrast to the state's central and southern desert areas. The highest point in Arizona is Humphreys Peak, one of the San Francisco Peaks north of Flagstaff.

Services and wholesale and retail trade account for the most employment in the state's expanding economy, with high tech, aerospace, and financial services representing small-but-growing areas. Arizona's $7.3 billion tourism industry represents a larger segment of the economy in rural areas than it does in the more diversified metro areas of Phoenix and Tucson. Fueled by a growing population, home construction has also been a key industry in the state. Mining, ranching, and agriculture are important to the economy although they provide a small percentage of jobs. Although Arizona is home to many retirement communities, the state's average age is slightly below the national average. An influx of young families offsets the seniors.

Although neighboring New Mexico has a higher percentage of Native Americans and people of Hispanic descent, Arizona has more people in each category. Only Oklahoma and California are home to more Native Americans than Arizona. More than 200,000 Californians have moved to Arizona since the late 1980s, as have smaller numbers of people from every other state.

Two of the state's popular, smaller communities worthy of investigation are Flagstaff and Lake Havasu City. Flagstaff, population 53,000, is appealing because sunshine predominates—even though its altitude of nearly 7,000 feet means it receives nearly 100 inches of snow annually.

Northern Arizona University brings sports, culture, and other diversions to the town, but for many, the greatest attractions are the natural ones. The Grand Canyon is about 75 miles away; the San Francisco Peaks ski areas are even closer. Within easy driving distance are lush pine forests, eerie volcanic craters, and the remarkable red-rock landmarks of Sedona. For a smaller town, Flagstaff offers a variety of shopping—including an indoor mall with several department stores and a downtown shopping area of boutiques, specialty shops, and bookstores. The cost of living is lower than Tucson, and the average price of a home is $130,000.

Another smaller town, Lake Havasu City, was practically unknown before 1971. Then Robert McCulloch, Sr. bought the London Bridge and had it reconstructed over an inlet of Lake Havasu. At the time, the sleepy desert community had less than 6,000 residents. Today chain-saw maker McCulloch Corp. and other companies employ many of the city's 41,000 residents. Some people have tourist-related jobs (such as employees of the shops and restaurants of the English village alongside one end of the bridge). But don't let photographs of the town—nestled along the east coast of the 45-mile long lake—convince you it has a consistently cool climate. Although winters are mild, and rain is scarce, the summer heat bakes the town with 100+ temperatures.

Phoenix

Pop. 2.4 million (metro area)
Elev. 1,110 ft.
Maricopa County
Newspaper: *Arizona Republic*

Phoenix and surrounding communities share the summer heat with Lake Havasu. They also have clear skies nearly 300 days per year and they get less annual rainfall than one or two good storms drop on Seattle in a week. The winters are among the mildest and most pleasant on earth. But come summer, when it's still over 100 degrees at 9 in the evening, you know why it's called the Valley of the Sun.

And Phoenix is big. It's the seventh largest city in the country. When you approach the outskirts of town along Interstate 10 from California, signs say you've still got 20 miles to go to reach Phoenix. The city also is one of the top communities in the country for particulate air pollution, according to the National Resources Defense Council. The brown cloud that settles over the city from time to time didn't exist just a few decades ago when Phoenix was more like a frontier town.

One thing that hasn't changed since the frontier days is the importance of water to the city's growth. Aqueducts from the Salt River and Central Arizona projects bring irrigation and drinking water to Phoenix through a series of channels. Man-made lakes east of Phoenix, including Theodore Roosevelt lake, provide water and recreational opportunities.

Like the metro areas of California, Phoenix is not one city, but many. Six of the top 10 largest cities in the state are Phoenix suburbs: Mesa, Tempe, Scottsdale, Glendale, Chandler, and Peoria. Upscale Scottsdale, with more than 135,000 people, has the highest average income and highest home prices. Leading employers include tourism, advertising, insurance, banking, and software. The town has more than 100 art galleries (nearly half of them within a five-block area of Main Street). Tempe is the home of Arizona State University, with more than 40,000 students and a PAC-10 athletic program. To the east of Tempe is Mesa, one of the fastest growing cities in the U.S., an area of expanding housing developments and several Fortune 500 manufacturing firms.

Some of the outlying residential areas of metro Phoenix are connected by freeways, but many are not, and thus commuters take surface streets. Congestion clogs some streets and freeways at times, but it thins out much more quickly than in California.

In exchange for all this bigness you have services, resources, and amenities that few Western cities offer: When the Rattlers baseball team starts play, Phoenix will have four major-league sports franchises. Massive Sky Harbor International Airport, home to America West Airlines, is one of the busiest in the nation. Local public libraries, sprinkled throughout the valley, are supplemented by ASU's central library and six other specialized libraries. The Phoenix Art Museum recently completed a major renovation; the Heard Museum preserves the art of American Indians; and Taliesin West in Scottsdale showcases the architecture and art of Frank Lloyd Wright. Large, indoor shopping malls dot the residential landscape, and more than 100 golf courses mean that you're never far away from the game.

While Phoenix's size may remind you of urban California, Arizona is still a small, growing, and relatively unbureaucratic state.

Tucson

Pop. 765,000 (metro area)
Elev. 2,584 ft.
Pima County
Newspapers: *Tucson Citizen, Arizona Daily Star*

Tucson is smaller and slightly cooler than its neighbor, Phoenix, two hours to the northwest via Interstate 10. It has a Southwest pueblo atmosphere, more like Albuquerque than Phoenix. The cost of living is a little lower than Phoenix, but median housing prices are about the same. (See Table 10.1.) Some Tucson residents refer to sprawling Phoenix as "L.A. East." Tucson lies in a high-desert valley, with mountain ranges on four sides. The highest range is the Santa Catalinas, topped by 9,157-foot Mt. Lemmon, a ski area.

The four major economic influences in Tucson are the military, University of Arizona, increasing numbers of industries, and tourism. Davis-Monthan Air Force Base, with its huge aircraft-storage facility, is a leading employer. So is the university, located in the central part of town. The university provides jobs for about 10,000 people, entertainment in the form of cultural activities, and Arizona Wildcat PAC-10 sports. The campus serves about 35,000 students.

The business and industry segment of the economy has grown within the last few years, due in part to the activities of the Greater Tucson Economic Council. The council has helped attract employers from California and other states. (See Appendix B.) Hughes Missiles, American Airlines, and Microsoft are some of the well-known corporate names to establish facilities in the Tucson area in the 1990s. Tourism, the fourth major economic influence, produces employment at hotels, motels, dude ranches, and attractions such as Old Tucson Studios, an old-west movie set.

Thousands of people from all over the U.S. and Canada spend their winters in Tucson. These *snowbirds* contribute to the economy and occasionally irritate full-time residents who complain that stores and roads are more crowded in the winter. The out-of-state license plates of snowbirds are also a common sight throughout Arizona, Nevada, and New Mexico.

During summer, when the snowbirds move out, thunderstorms move in. If you've never visited southern Arizona, Tucson (or other desert communities) might bring to mind miles of undulating, naked sands. Actually, areas of bare sand dunes (e.g. Death Valley, Calif., Great Sand Dunes National Monument, Colo.) are rare in the United States. Most of the desert is home to a fascinating variety of plants and animals. But since the desert flora and fauna are different from even the semi-arid portions of urban California, they need to be understood to be appreciated. The desert around Tucson, for example, is rich with growth. Nature has adapted trees and other plants to cope with the dry, warm weather.

COLORADO

With 54 peaks more than 14,000 feet high, it's no wonder Colorado is called the Rocky Mountain State. Denver and nearby cities, which contain a majority of the state's 3.8 million residents, are actually on the eastern foothills of the Rockies. The Rockies—a combination of several mountain ranges—extend from north to south, occupying the central portion of the state. To the east, a high grassy plain stretches across one-third of the state to Nebraska and Kansas. The far western portion of Colorado is a high plateau carved with valleys and canyons. Eleven national forests take up more than one quarter of the state's area.

The stunning mountains provide recreational opportunities and jobs in world-famous ski and resort areas, such as Vail, Breckenridge, and Steamboat Springs. If you're a skier, this is as close to heaven as you can get. But it comes with a price tag. Vail, for example, has higher home prices than many areas of urban California. In other parts of the state, however, housing prices are generally lower than California cities.

Employment in Colorado is concentrated primarily in these areas: services, 29 percent; retail trade, 20 percent; government, 16 percent; manufacturing, 10 percent; construction, 6 percent; utilities and communications, 7 percent. Mining and wholesale account for the balance. The largest private employers include US West, King Soopers/City Market, Wal-Mart, Lockheed-Martin Astronautics, AT&T, Safeway Stores, Hewlett Packard, and Coors Brewing Co. Colorado has more than 25,000 farms producing cattle, wheat, hay, corn, and other crops.

The state's percentage of employment in the various industrial categories and its list of leading employers closely match that of Denver, the capital and largest city. The Denver metro area contains more than 2 million people. It includes a number of suburbs and separate cities, and it extends into portions of five counties. The largest suburbs are Aurora, Arvada, Lakewood, Littleton, and Westminster. A short drive up Highway 36 is Boulder.

In the shadow of the Rockies, Denver is the state's center for a variety of cultural, business, sporting, and educational resources. Denver residents are nuts over pro sports. The overwhelming support the local teams have received over the years is in contrast to the sometimes fickle relationship California fans have with local teams. John Elway, of Bronco's football fame, is one of the state's most well-known citizens.

Denver has an extensive park system, many museums and theatres, and two daily newspapers (the *Rocky Mountain News* and the *Denver Post*). The city has relatively mild weather, given its altitude of 5,282 feet, and like many parts of the state, there's an abundance of sunshine with low humidity.

The state's per-capita income is one of the West's highest. The cost of living for many cities is mid-range—lower than many California cities, but higher than towns in neighboring states. The unemployment rate has been among the lowest in the United States. Colorado has a ratio of physicians to the population close to California. According to the American Medical Association, California has 246 physicians per 100,000 people, Colorado 240.

Fort Collins

Pop. 104,000
Elev. 4,984 ft.
Larimer County
Newspaper: *Fort Collins Coloradoan*

Fort Collins is a mid-sized, recreation-oriented, college town. It's smaller than Colorado Springs, but big enough to support large shopping centers, libraries, major employers, theatres, more than 100 restaurants, several microbreweries, and transportation facilities. Colorado State University has been in Fort Collins for nearly 120 years. CSU has more than 21,000 students, 1,400 faculty, and NCAA Div. I athletics.

Hunting, fishing, hiking, boating, and skiing in the Rockies are a few of the reasons Fort Collins residents place a premium on the outdoors. Rocky Mountain National Park and the town of Estes Park are a short drive away. Extending the appeal of the town for outdoors people is the system of more than 50 miles of hiking and biking trails that run through town along the Poudre River and Spring Creek. The trails are accessible from many streets in town. With climate similar to Denver, Fort Collins has nearly 300 days of sunshine annually, 50 inches of snow in winter, and summers in the 80s and 90s.

The municipally owned Lincoln Center of Fort Collins is home to a symphony orchestra, ballet, and theatre company. The city's Discovery Science Museum and Fort Collins Museum of history are other cultural attractions. The largest local employers are Colorado State, the local school district, Hewlett Packard, and Poudre Valley Hospital. Other employers include Anheuser-Busch, Teledyne Water Pik, US West Communications, and the city.

Weekend drives in any direction will take you to a variety of cities, forests, lakes, and rivers. Denver is 65 miles south on Interstate 25; Cheyenne, Wyo., is 45 miles north. Colorado towns of Greeley, Loveland, and Windsor are even closer. Horsetooth Reservoir is a 15-minute drive.

This mid-size town with an exceptionally low crime rate was named the third best place in U.S. to raise a family in a recent survey by the *Reader's Digest*. Editors cited its many activities for young people and its sense of community. The town is growing steadily, as are home prices. The cost of living is higher than that of Denver (and the other two Colorado cities profiled below) but still lower than Los Angeles, San Diego, or San Francisco.

Colorado Springs

Pop. 326,000
Elev. 6,145 ft.
El Paso County
Newspaper: *The Gazette*

The second-biggest metro area in the state lies about 70 miles south of Denver. Depending on how far out you measure the metro area, greater Colorado Springs can include more than 450,000 people. That's almost a half million more people than were here in 1806, when Zebulon Pike spotted the 14,110-ft. peak that now bears his name. Pike's Peak offers recreational and sporting activities and provides a dramatic backdrop for the city. You can ascend to the top via car, on foot, or along a famous cog railway. Other nearby attractions include Garden of the Gods, a park containing huge sandstone formations; the historic gold rush town of Cripple Creek; museums; and extensive scenic mountain drives. Tourism is an economic force in Colorado Springs.

The unemployment rate has hovered around 4 percent recently. The diverse economy provides jobs in manufacturing, services and retail trade, finance and real estate, and the military. The United States Air Force Academy is in Colorado Springs, as is Peterson AFB, Fort Carson Army base, and the North American Air Defense Command (NORAD).

Housing prices are rising, as is the population. (Check out the huge number of Web sites sponsored by Colorado Springs real estate agents.) The town receives an average of 43 inches of snow; summer temperatures are in the 80s.

Pueblo

Pop. 102,000
Elev. 4,684 ft.
Pueblo County
Newspaper: *Pueblo Chieftan*

For years, Pueblo was the state's grimy industrial center, complete with coal mine and steel mill. With the mill now closed, the city is cleaning up its image. Replacing the mill are a variety of smaller firms recruited to town. Pueblo's negligible growth in the 1990s, however—when many towns were booming—says that city fathers have more to do if they want to attract new residents.

One project that may help is the Historic Arkansas Riverwalk, an ambitious multi-year downtown redevelopment. The aim is to create commercial and retail development along the Arkansas River including trails, cafés, public art, an amphitheater, and conference center. Rows of restored red brick buildings along Union Avenue also show the city's interest in revitalization. West of town, construction of the Pueblo Dam created a reservoir with 60 miles of shoreline.

Recently, the majority of new homes in the area have been started in Pueblo West, a self-contained community developed by the McCulloch Corp. Pueblo West has its own schools, industrial park, and recreational facilities. Victorian homes can be purchased in the Mesa Junction and Northside areas of Pueblo.

With only one airline, United Express, air transportation is limited, but the Colorado Springs airport is about 40 miles north. Pueblo is the home of the University of Southern Colorado and site of the annual Colorado State Fair.

As the city works to improve itself, one positive aspect of its past is low prices. In 1994, *Money* magazine said Pueblo was the 18th best place to live and that it had the lowest cost of living of all cities surveyed. The cost of living in Pueblo is still low and home prices still a bargain. The Pueblo Board of Realtors reports the average price of an existing home is $90,000.

Grand Junction

Pop. 37,000
Elev. 4,843 ft.
Mesa County
Newspaper: *Daily Sentinel*

Grand Junction is not a smaller version of Fort Collins, but it does have some of the latter city's appealing elements: local culture including a symphony; riverside trails; an abundance of outdoor activities; dry, warm summers; and lots of sunny days.

The name Grand Junction refers not to the point where Highway 50 joins with Interstate 70, but the junction of the Gunnison and Colorado rivers. Both connections make the town—and the smaller communities surrounding it—a center of transportation, recreation and commerce for Colorado's vast, sparsely populated western slope, also known as the Colorado Plateau. The city and its surrounding area, called Grand Valley, contain about 100,000 people.

As the trading center for a large area, Grand Junction offers more shopping, banking, and business services than a town under 40,000 might normally have. Major stores include J.C. Penney, Mervyn's, Herberger's, Sears, Sam's Club, Wal-Mart, and Target. Employers include government, education, health care, retail trade, services, and manufacturing. It's a good thing that Grand Junction is self-contained, because it's a long drive to a major city: Denver, 245 miles; Salt Lake City, 285; Albuquerque, 382.

The 42-acre campus of Mesa State College, with about 5,000 students, borders a residential area of town. Athletics, fine arts programs, and a campus radio station connect the college to the community.

Being a day's drive away from major cities has plenty of advantages for locals. They can enjoy the forests, rivers, and mountains without the press of humanity. Excellent ski areas lie east and south; national parks, monuments, and forests lie in all directions. The thousand-foot-deep canyons of colorful Colorado National Monument are just outside of town.

NEVADA

The Silver State led the nation in population growth and job creation for the 1990s. And it leads all states in attracting Californians. Most of the growth, jobs, and population are concentrated in the Las Vegas area, but Reno, the second-largest city, has shown substantial progress and prosperity as well. Unless you've lived on the moon for the past few decades, you don't need to be told what the state's largest industry is. But development groups have been successful in luring a variety of other enterprises to Nevada. Light manufacturing, warehousing, financial services, even a sprinkling of high technology, are among the new, growing industries. Mining and ranching, the reasons why people came to Nevada originally, are still dominant outside of the state's two metro areas. The vast majority of land in Nevada is owned by the federal government, giving the Bureau of Land Management, among other agencies, a strong, and sometimes resented, presence.

Almost all of Nevada lies within the Great Basin, an area of ancient inland seas where all rivers, except the Colorado, flow inward, ending in lakes or dry lake beds. Rising from the basin floor are row after row of north-south mountain ranges. They create a series of valleys, particularly prominent in the northern half of the state. While deserts take up vast portions of southern Nevada, the northern mountains and valleys are cooler and have more vegetation.

Nevada is the seventh largest state in area, but its population is one of the smallest. The state's few cities and towns are spread out. It's farther from Las

Vegas to Reno than it is from Los Angeles to San Francisco. And Reno, near Lake Tahoe and the California border, lies 385 highway miles from Great Basin National Park on Nevada's eastern border. The state's highway system is adequate to handle the small volume of cars that traverse the state. Interstate 80 stretches across the northern portion of Nevada, from Utah to Reno. I-15 connects Southern California with Las Vegas and continues on through Utah.

In some ways, modern Nevada is not far removed from its origins in the gold and silver mines of Virginia City. A pioneering, self-sufficiency and can-do attitude still characterizes Nevada natives. And they pass that frontier spirit on to newcomers. Politically, the state is almost evenly divided between the two parties, but Nevadans' independence was demonstrated in Ross Perot's strong vote-getting in the state during the 1992 presidential elections. The state's high unionization rate is due largely to unions representing casino and hotel employees. Nevada has no state income tax.

Las Vegas

Pop. 1.07 million (metro area)
Elev. 2,162 ft.
Clark County
Newspapers: *Las Vegas Review Journal, Las Vegas Sun*

Las Vegas is hyperbole. Where else can you find a 350-foot tall, gleaming-black pyramid, the skyscrapers of New York, an ongoing pirate battle (complete with roaring cannons and a sinking sailing ship), and frequent volcano eruptions—all within a few blocks of each other?

Visitors rarely venture from the exaggerated world of the Las Vegas Boulevard "Strip" or Fremont Street downtown. And locals not employed there rarely venture down the strip, unless it's to attend a civic event or escort visiting friends and family. Las Vegas residents sometimes have to explain to out-of-towners that yes, Las Vegas does have schools, churches, stores, and offices, just like a real city.

Las Vegas is, in fact, full of surprises for newcomers. There are so many newcomers (3,000 to 6,000 per month during the 1990s) that being from somewhere else is almost the norm. Ex-Californians are usually astonished by the lack of bureaucracy at any level of government, from the state DMV to the local planning department. Most newcomers usually expect hot, dry summers, but they're not prepared for winters that call for overcoats and gloves and are cold enough to damage exposed water pipes at night. New Las Vegans are often surprised by—but soon become accustomed to—the 24-hour nature of local commerce. Many retail and service businesses have extended hours to cater to hotel/casino employees on night shifts. An unpleasant surprise for new residents with children is the crowded Clark County School District, with double sessions at some schools.

The city itself includes only about one-third of the area's population and doesn't encompass the famous hotel strip. New housing developments are available at all compass points, with major growth areas in the North, Northwest, and Southeast. Home prices have been rising but are still well below California levels. The constant supply of new homes keeps existing home prices reasonable, while providing thousands of jobs in the city's robust construction industry.

The exploding growth, coupled with the round-the-clock gaming business, gives Las Vegas an energy and optimism that drives not only the entertainment/hotel industry, but seems to affect everyone who works in the city. The gaming business fuels the economy by creating thousands of jobs in support businesses from advertising to industrial-laundry services. The Nevada Development Authority—located in Las Vegas and supported by hotels and other businesses—has attracted such diverse employers as Ocean Spray and Silicon Graphics to the area to broaden the employment base. Other non-tourist employers include Citibank, University of Nevada, Nellis Air Force Base, Kerr-McGee Chemical Corp., Nevada Ready Mix, Levi Strauss, the Community College of Southern Nevada, and Nevada Power.

Residents have extraordinary recreation/entertainment options. And those options extend beyond the lounge and dinner shows to include the university's cultural and athletic events, boating on Lake Mead, skiing at 11,918-ft. Mt. Charleston (Las Vegas's best-kept secret), and hiking in Red Rock Canyon National Conservation Area and in Valley of Fire State Park. For the time being, the fastest growing city in the country is still growing, still adding to its list of hotels extraordinaire. The city's future depends largely on two factors: the continued vitality of the U.S. economy, which feeds tourists to the Strip, and the continued flow of water from all available sources into Las Vegas faucets.

Reno

Pop. 210,500 (metro area)
Elev. 4,404
Washoe County
Newspapers: *Reno Gazette-Journal, Sparks Tribune*

Nevada's principal northern city is not a Las Vegas with snow, a thought that would make Reno natives shudder. Reno, along with its smaller neighbor, Sparks, is older, more formal, and more traditional than its brasher, faster-growing sister to the south. Reno is to Las Vegas what San Francisco is to Los Angeles. Reno was the state's largest city for most of Nevada's history. The city's Ivy-League-looking University of Nevada campus was founded in 1874—90 years before students received degrees at what later became the University of Nevada - Las Vegas.

The venerable Reno arch—proclaiming Reno the Biggest Little City in the World—and the huge dome of the new Silver Legacy Hotel, are as close to a volcano or pyramid as you're going to find in Reno. But don't be misled; tourism is still the biggest game in town. Reno, like Las Vegas, is diversifying, but nearly half the private sector employees work in service industries—reflecting the casino/hotel/tourist influence on business. Reno-Sparks is also a warehousing and transportation center due to its strategic location near major California cities, yet close to other states' metro areas as well. Manufacturing and construction are other components of the local economy. Unemployment is below 5 percent and housing costs are slightly higher than Las Vegas, due in part to a smaller supply of new homes.

The lofty peaks of the Sierra Nevadas form a dramatic backdrop for Reno, beckoning residents and tourists to Lake Tahoe and the ski areas and national forests that circle the huge, clear lake. Housing is costly in the Nevada communities along the lake, and waterfront home sites in Incline Village are among the state's priciest real estate.

The climate of the Reno area is cooler than the southern portion of the state. In summer, temperatures are routinely in the 90s during the day, but when the sun drops behind the Sierras the temperature drops too, cooling Reno to the 60s and sometimes lower. The winters bring light snow and freezing temperatures. Although rainstorms in the winter of 1996-97 brought disastrous floods to portions of Reno along the Truckee River, the city averages only about 8 inches of rain per a year.

In 1996, *Money* magazine ranked Reno as 98th out of the top 300 best places to live in the U.S., citing, among other things, a physician/population ratio higher than California.

Carson City area

Pop. 49,000 (metro area)
Elev. 4,660
Carson City and Douglas Counties
Newspaper: *Nevada Appeal*

Just south of Reno, in the agricultural valley along the base of the massive Sierras, lie the state capital and three other communities, all worth exploring. At about 40,000 people, Carson City is one of the smallest state capitals, yet it's the third largest metro area in the state, after Reno and Las Vegas.It has a reasonable cost of living, affordable housing, and a relaxed, almost country atmosphere. Every other January the town starts to hum when the legislature is in session. Much of town, including residential areas, shopping, and the state capitol, is just a few blocks off Carson Street (U.S. 395), which runs down the middle of the north-south oriented town. Various state divisions are leading employers in town as are tourist-related businesses.

To the northeast is Virginia City, from whose silver mines the state got its nickname. Today, Virginia City—which once contained half the population of the state—is a tourist destination and has few full-time residents. Carson City shares the outdoor recreational opportunities available in the Reno/Tahoe area, and like any self-respecting state capital, has museums and capitol tours.

Close to Carson City, and also in the shadow of the mountains, are the small communities of Gardnerville, Minden, and Genoa. This quiet trio is a long commute to Reno, unless you're a veteran of the Irvine-to-West L.A. or San Rafael-to-San Jose runs. But the towns offer inexpensive homes, clear air, and inviting rural ambiance. Homes in Gardnerville and Minden usually come with more land than homes in Carson City, but the median price is about $10,000 higher.

HAWAII

White sand beaches, gentle trade winds, a relaxed pace, and tropical weather make the 50th state a dream vacation destination for millions of Americans. For a special few, it also is a new place to live. But Hawaii, and its largest city, Honolulu, represent relocation trade-offs taken to the extreme.

First the pluses. Okay, you know what they are.

Now the minuses. It's expensive. The Chamber of Commerce of Hawaii estimates the cost of living to be 35 to 40 percent higher than in most mainland cities. And per capita income in Hawaii is only slightly higher than other Western states, not nearly enough to compensate. According to a Coldwell Banker Co. survey, a home that would cost $124,000 in College Station, Tex., or $187,000 in Eugene, Ore., costs $430,000 in Honolulu. Studio apartments rent for $700 per month and up, and a large percentage of the population lives in condos rather than single-family homes. If you think it's costly to have the van lines haul your belongings down the interstate, imagine how much it will cost to float your furnishings across the Pacific.

And the Hawaii chamber doesn't even seem to want you. Its relocation brochure says: "Oahu is classified as a tight labor market area. This situation exists because of the lack of diversified industries and the relative immobility of the work force. . . .

"Employment service officials advise that chances of getting a job in Honolulu in many occupations are slim, and by mail they are next to impossible." The chamber also warns job seekers to bring along enough money to buy a return ticket in case they are unable to find employment. Cautionary terms also are used for people thinking about starting a business.

New residents have not been flocking to Hawaii. From 1990 to mid-1996 the population increased by less than 7 percent. People do relocate to Hawaii; it just takes more work. If you have a skill or experience that is uncommon in the islands, then you have a much better chance of obtaining an interview. If your potential employer is sufficiently interested in you, the company will pay your travel expenses to talk with you. If expenses for an interview are on you, you can minimize the costs by booking a discount "vacation" package on a group tour to Honolulu that includes airfare and hotel. The hotel will not be the most exclusive, but the entire package could cost less than $500—excluding meals and rental car. Connecting with a Hawaii headhunter, business colleague, or other local resident who is willing to help you, will give you an advantage. Also, remember that the pace and style of business in Hawaii are different from California. The pager-fax-cell-phone-voice-mail-power-lunch attitude will not impress locals.

If you're thinking about retiring to Hawaii, and can afford the move and the higher cost of living, consider a less encumbered life with a smaller home. The Hawaii style of living promotes a more casual existence. With temperatures in the 80s every month of the year, you don't need seasonal clothes. People tend to spend more time outdoors, so you don't need as many square feet of space for indoor furniture. And, in addition to a seemingly healthy lifestyle, Hawaii has the highest physician/population ratio of any Western state.

NEW MEXICO

During the 1996 Olympics in Atlanta, someone from Santa Fe called the Olympic ticket office to inquire about seats for upcoming events. The caller was told that tickets could not be sold over the phone to people in foreign countries. Misunderstood by many Americans, New Mexico, "The Land of Enchantment," could as easily be called the land of confusion. But it's the outsiders who are confused, not New Mexicans. A few years ago Intel announced a major corporate expansion in Albuquerque. Until that time, many Californians may not have thought much about the business side of New Mexico—or even knew it had a business side. Today people speak of Silicon Mesa, referring to Intel, Motorola, and other high-tech companies that employ thousands in New Mexico's largest city.

By the time the first Spanish explorers traveled across the New Mexico mesas in the early 1500s, Native Americans had been living there for thousands of years. The Indian and Spanish cultures shared the territory—alternately warring or living in peace—for another 300 years until the Santa Fe trail brought American settlers from Missouri. Today, this blend of cultures is evident in New Mexico's architecture, food, festivals, customs, and people. Nineteen different Indian pueblo communities can be found, ranging from small settlements, to the 2,000-square-mile Navajo Reservation in the northwest corner of the state. New Mexico's current population is about 10 per cent Native American, 40 percent Hispanic, 45 per cent white, and the balance African- and Asian-American.

Geographically and climatically, New Mexico is as diverse as its people. In the lower Sonoran flatlands, across the southern portion of the state, herds of javelinas (wild boar) wander among the yucca and creosote bushes, while the sun pushes the summer temperature into the high 90s. In the mountainous areas that characterize northern portions of the state, huge winter snowfalls support the skiing business in Taos, Sandia Peak, and other locales. Albuquerque lies at 5,311 feet (29 feet higher than Denver), between the Sandia Mountains on the east and a range of mesas on the West.

Albuquerque's summer temperatures are in the 80s and 90s, and the city receives about the same amount of sunshine as San Bruno, Calif., which is to say plenty.

Albuquerque is not just the largest city in the state, it's more than six times as large as the next largest city, Las Cruces. A healthy business climate, competitive housing market, and strong tourist industry lure residents from California and other states. The largest employers in Albuquerque, excluding local government and education, are concentrated in high tech and military/defense. In addition to Intel, which employs more than 4,000 people, major employers are Motorola Ceramic Products, Kirtland Air Force Base, Sandia National Laboratories, Phillips Semiconductors, Honeywell Defense Avionics, and GE Aircraft Engines. The University of New Mexico and Albuquerque Public Schools are other leading employers.

As home to more than 400,000 people, in a state with just over 1.7 million, Albuquerque is also a center for banking, marketing, and other services. Low property taxes and home prices still below California add to the appeal of this Southwest city. But like Las Vegas, water is a question mark in the city's future. Politically, Democrats have dominated both houses of the state legislature, but congressional seats and statewide offices are more evenly divided between the parties.

Las Cruces

Pop. 66,000
Elev. 3,896
Dona Ana County
Newspaper: *Las Cruces Sun-News*

Agriculture, education, regional business, retirement, and rocketry are the chief concerns in New Mexico's second largest city. It lies in the Mesilla Valley, near the Mexican (that's old Mexico) border. Cotton, chilies, pecans, alfalfa, and other crops grow in the valley, irrigated by water from the Rio Grande. Academically, agriculture is one of many majors available at New Mexico State University, located in the southern section of town. As the largest town in the lower half of the state, Las Cruces provides banking, shopping, and other services. The city also is attracting new industry. Northeast of town is the White Sands Missile Range. A growing number of retirees are moving to Las Cruces for its dry, warm climate and low cost of living. Home prices in town have been shooting upward—more than a 25 per cent increase from 1990 to 1996—but the average price is still less than $100,000.

Less than an hour's drive south is El Paso, Texas, with its shopping, business services, large airport, and recreational opportunities.

Santa Fe

Pop. 59,840
Elev. 7,000
Santa Fe County
Newspaper: *The New Mexican*

The Spanish colonial architecture, winding narrow streets, rich cultural mix, and wealth of Indian art, make Santa Fe the quintessential New Mexico (and Southwest) city. If Santa Fe is not the center of New Mexico enchantment, then it's probably just a short drive away in Taos, a charming mountain town known for art galleries and winter skiing. As mentioned in an earlier chapter, all this intriguing appeal does not necessarily mean the welcome mat is always out. Sante Fe will accept you, but on its terms. The heritage of this centuries-old city is guarded by natives, some of whom decry the business and commercial growth of Albuquerque, not to mention Santa Fe.

Rising home prices and a relatively high cost of living keep Santa Fe out of the bargain-basement-community category. The city's relocation guide also cautions newcomers that salaries may be lower than expected. But economic factors seem not to be the reason people are moving to Santa Fe; retirees who don't need to rely on local jobs, for example, find it a rewarding place to live.

Tourism is a leading industry in New Mexico's capital city. Visitors wander shaded streets; spend hours in galleries displaying local pottery, sculpture, and paintings; and take meandering country drives among stands of aspen and Douglas fir.

Due to its elevation, temperatures in summer are mild by Southwest standards. But winters bring freezing temperatures and up to 40 inches of snow. Santa Fe has a local symphony; a nationally known opera with a modern opera house; a community college; two private, four-year liberal arts colleges; an international airport served by several airlines; and the capitol and other state offices. In Santa Fe, "The Plaza" refers to the open area in the center of town bordered on the north by the Palace of the Governors. The palace, dating from 1610, has been the seat of government under Spanish, Indian, Mexican, and U.S. rule.

TEXAS

Texas has become a target for what could be called the second wave of California emigrants. In the first half of the 1990s, Texas was not high on the list of destinations. But according to California DMV figures, the Lone Star State is now drawing more Golden State expats. Many have gone to Austin, the booming capital city. Others are scattered throughout the vast number of Texas cities and towns. Texas is, after all, huge. As the second most populous state—and home to three of the country's ten largest cities (Houston, Dallas, San Antonio)—Texas offers some of the same urban and bureaucratic maladies as California. But it has no personal or corporate income tax, and many of its small- to medium-sized towns offer lower home prices and a lower cost of living than anywhere in urban California.

The vastness of the state expresses itself in the wide open plains that make up the panhandle and much of central Texas, as well as in the distances between major cities. From west to east, El Paso is 750 miles from Houston. Roughly north to south, Amarillo is more than 800 miles from Brownsville via Abilene.

Geography influences Texas weather. Most of the state is farther south than the California-Mexican border. This gives that portion of the state a subtropical climate—warm and humid. West Texas, however, is drier, with climate similar to southern New Mexico.

To explain the business opportunities in a sentence or two would be simplistic; the Texas economy is large and diverse. Oil and gas production, refining and related enterprises remain leading money makers. Other industries include manufacturing, food products, and chemicals. Only California has a higher agricultural output than Texas, and fishing (along the Gulf Coast) also creates jobs. Tourism and computer hardware and software are growing industries.

Texas ranks about the middle of Western states in per-capita income, and is on par with California in SAT scores. The state lags behind about half the Western states in the percentage of physicians in the population. Texas is a Western state, but it belonged to the Confederacy during the Civil War. It shares many Western traditions with California and other states, but it has many of its own, unique customs as well. Of the 13 Western states, only Hawaii represents broader social and cultural differences compared to California (excluding differences due solely to the size of communities).

Austin

Pop. 514,000
Elev. 587 ft.
Travis County
Newspaper: *Austin American-Statesman*

Not every city can be the new Silicon Valley, but the concept seems to have appeal to many chambers of commerce. The reality is that high-tech companies are growing, multiplying, and driving the economy in many states. Austin's part of the high-tech pie is substantial and includes thousands of jobs in manufacturing as well as software development. Supporting the large high-tech industry is local research, conducted at several facilities in town— including the semiconductor research center at the University of Texas. The capital city of Texas is also the capital of Dell Computer and Advanced Micro Devices. Those high-tech corporations—along with branches of Motorola, Samsung, and others—have been expanding manufacturing space and creating jobs. Just two local computer employers, Dell and IBM, employ more than 10,000 persons. Local software companies add another 8,500 jobs. Austin led Texas in job growth from 1994 to1996, and posted one of the lowest unemployment rates in the country during that period. It remains one of the healthiest, fastest-growing economies in the nation. A large segment of service jobs in Austin are in back-office operations of such companies as Harte Hanks and MCI. About one-quarter of the workers in Austin are employed in government, half in state government, half in local and federal government.

The setting for this business expansion is a genial city on the edge of the Texas Hill Country, with a metro area that's approaching 1 million. The Colorado River (a different one) flows through parks and feeds Lake Travis west of Austin, then meanders through downtown. *Money* magazine, in 1996, rated Austin one of the top 10 best places to live and called it "an enclave of liberalism in otherwise conservative Texas." The city's liberal attitudes are influenced by the university and its 48,000-member student body. (Southwest Texas State and Austin Community College add another 47,000 students.)

More than liberal or conservative issues, what really gets citizens steamed up is the heat and humidity in the summer. Austin is south of all other Southwest cities mentioned in this book, except Honolulu. The subtropical weather means the humidity can reach 80 percent and higher in summer, while the temperatures are comparable to inland Southern California. Annual rainfall is nearly 32 inches per year.

The cost of living is still low, although home prices have been increasing almost as fast as prices in Salt Lake City (the nation's leader). In addition to supporting the city's high-tech environment, the University of Texas provides Big-12 Conference football and other sports, arts programs, and one of the largest libraries of any college in the country. Austin calls itself the live music capital of the world because of the dozens of small clubs and bars that nightly offer everything from country to jazz and blues. A new airport is scheduled to open in a few years on the site of a former air base. And Del Webb Corp. is planning a retirement development 30 miles north of town.

Bryan/College Station

Pop: 120,192 (metro area)
Elev. 376
Brazos County
Newspaper: *Bryan-College Station Eagle*

With little fanfare, this pair of college towns has been attracting new residents by the carload. People are drawn to the mixture of relaxed, small-town charm combined with the culture of a major university, albeit an agricultural one. Bryan/College Station is deep in the heart of Texas—tucked away in the gently rolling hills of the Brazos Valley, more than 30 miles from the nearest interstate. Houston is about 100 miles southeast, Austin an equal distance to the southwest. The town is served at Easterwood Airport by three airlines that connect to Houston and Dallas-Ft. Worth.

Texas A & M University, with its 42,000 students and nearly 20,000 associated employees, sparks the local economy. The university, the oldest in Texas, was founded in 1876 in open farmland south of Bryan. A community—called College Station for the name of the local train depot—grew up around the college and was incorporated in 1938. Texas A & M is known for its agriculture, engineering, veterinary, and ROTC programs. The TAMU Aggies play in NCAA Div. I.

Both communities are encouraging growth and have new industrial parks. Both also have downtown redevelopment projects underway. Local hospitals, county government, the school districts, Redman Industries, GTE Southwest, and Westinghouse are among the leading employers. The Bryan/ College Station unemployment rate has, at times, been an almost nonexistent. Yet home prices are what they were in urban California 20 years ago.

UTAH

The Beehive State combines vast outdoor wonders, a strong economy, a range of climatic choices, and a social climate that emphasizes the family.

The southern portion of Utah seems to be one big national park full of red-rock canyons and mesas. The northern half features the Great Salt Lake and a multitude of ski slopes. Utah has five national parks, six national monuments, seven national forests. In addition, southern Utah provides the main access to the North Rim of the Grand Canyon. In northern Utah there are 12 major ski resorts, the majority within an hour's drive of Salt Lake City and boasting some of the best ski slopes in the country.

Climate and topography in Utah ranges from the hot, arid, high desert, surrounding Lake Powell in the south to Park City at 6,900 feet in the Rockies near Salt Lake City, where winter brings many feet of snow. Most of the state lies on a high plateau above 4,000 feet.

All of the state's major cities are located in the north at the foot of the 150-mile-long Wasatch Range of the Rockies. Much of the eastern portion of the state contains the high plains and mountains of the Great Basin. The Great Salt Lake and Bonneville Salt Flats take up most of the northwest corner of the state. To the southeast are portions of the Colorado Plateau and the parks of Utah's famous red-rock country.

Although people of all faiths live in Utah, about 70 percent of the population is Mormon. Teachings of the Church of Jesus Christ of Latter-day Saints exert a strong influence on the state's cultural life and to a lesser extent on local business. As a result of this influence, communities throughout the state emphasize family values and hard work. The Mormon culture promotes close family ties, personal development, and abstinence from alcohol and tobacco. The population of the state recently topped 2 million; about half of them live in the Salt Lake City metro area.

Education is a high priority in the state, and Utah posts the highest SAT scores of any Western state, despite a high pupil-teacher ratio. (Utah residents tend to have large families. The state's average of 3.15 people per household is the nation's highest.) The state has five major universities and many state and community colleges.

Salt Lake City is the state capital, the headquarters for the LDS Church, and the state's largest and most well-known city. Founded in 1847 by Brigham Young, the city is booming. Home prices have been rising faster than any city in the U.S. According to *U.S. News and World Report,* prices increased an average of 12.8 percent per year from 1992 to 1996. As is the case with many Western cities, even dramatic increases have not pushed home prices beyond those of California, although in the super-heated Salt Lake City housing market, it won't take long. Tens of thousands of jobs are being created every year in the Salt Lake area, and unemployment over the past few years has dipped below 3 percent. Just about anyone who's willing and able to work has a job.

Development officials have been successful in attracting back-office banking centers, high-tech companies, and corporate call centers to the Salt Lake area. The city can expect a continuing boost—economically and symbolically—from the 2002 Winter Olympics to be held there. The city has the Utah Jazz basketball team; the Crossroads Plaza, one of the largest covered shopping malls in the country; and the University of Utah.

In spite of the notable success of some women politicians in Utah, the state ranks near the bottom in a survey of women's salaries. The Center for Policy Alternatives and the Institute for Women's Policy Research said women in Utah earn only 61 percent of what men do, compared to the national average of 72 percent. Only three other states had a wider gap (including Wyoming, which, according to the survey, pays women 60 percent of what men earn). Utah exceeds the national average, however, in the percentage of its businesses that are owned by women.

Provo/Orem

Pop: 92,630 / 73,600 (291,000 metro)
Elev. 4,550 / 4,700
Utah County
Newspaper: *Daily Herald*

The two towns that sit just east of Utah Lake and south of Salt Lake City, were named best places to live in the West by *Money* magazine in 1994. Citing a low crime rate, low unemployment, an expanding job base, low housing costs, and more than 200 sunny days per year, the magazine's editors also lauded the towns' scenic location. Since then, housing prices have continued to climb, but not enough to stop people from moving into the county at the rate of more than 1,000 per month. *Reader's Digest,* in 1997, named Provo the 12th best place in the United States to raise a family.

The Provo/Orem area has the economic vitality and recreational opportunities of Salt Lake, in a smaller, college-oriented community. Dozens of high-tech companies have flocked to Provo/Orem, making it, too, a version of Silicon Valley. Companies are attracted by the climate, surroundings, and the presence of Brigham Young University. With a strong engineering school and computer sciences department, the university provides skilled employees for the growing high-tech business community.

Like most big universities, BYU serves its community in many ways, including providing cultural opportunities, continuing education, and big-time athletics. The campus takes up a large part of Provo, and is about a mile southeast of Orem. BYU, one of the largest independent universities in the United States, is affiliated with the LDS Church.

The area is far from being an exclusive Mormon town; the chamber of commerce lists 38 other local religious denominations.

Cedar City

Pop. 17,000
Elev. 5,800
Iron County
Newspaper: *Daily Spectrum*

Cedar City is the smallest community profiled in this book. Its combination of scenic beauty, expanding job base, low costs, and enrichment from a state university make it difficult to understand why it has escaped the notice of "best places" writers. The town lies on a high plateau with 10,000-foot mountains immediately to the east. Within an hour's drive of town are the deep canyons of Zion National Park, the broad vistas and curious rock formations of Cedar Breaks National Monument, and the winter skiing resort center of Brian Head. About an hour's drive in another direction is Bryce Canyon National Park. Cedar City is considered a semi-arid area, which means it receives only about 10 inches of rain per year. Yet it's surrounded by higher, heavily forested country containing lakes and streams.

On the business side, Cedar City has been as successful (for its size) as any community in the state in attracting new jobs, says the state's national business development director. A furniture manufacturing plant, for example, is one of the city's recent acquisitions. The presence of a four-year college, plus rail and interstate highway transportation, make Cedar City attractive to new business. The town even has commuter airline service.

One attraction for businesses and would-be ex-Californians alike is the low home prices. Flipping through a real estate booklet on the area will make an urban Californian drool. In one booklet, only one home is priced above $200,000; many homes are listed below $100,000.

The mile-high elevation brings about 40 inches of snow in winter. But like other Southwest mountain communities, the sun shines most of the time. And in Cedar City, you never have to worry about bad air days.

What's left? Just the event for which Cedar City is best known: the Utah Shakespearean Festival. Held on the university campus, the festival brings thousands of visitors to Cedar City from June to September each year. Six plays, at least three by the Bard, are offered during the season—along with Elizabethan dancing, craft shows, dinners, and other events. Plays are performed in a replica of the Old Globe and in two other theatres.

St. George

Pop. 38,000
Elev. 2,840
Washington County
Newspaper: *Daily Spectrum*

About 50 miles south of Cedar City is St. George, a community that more Californians seem to have discovered, perhaps because of its proximity to Las Vegas. St. George is larger and warmer than Cedar City, its neighbor to the north. Three thousand feet in elevation makes the difference in climate. Although snow in the winter is a rarity, in summer, St. George cooks. Low humidity and cool evenings, however, make summers more tolerable. Washington County is one of the fastest growing areas of the country.

Its size and location make St. George a commerce center for a large area of southern Utah. Shopping includes the 70-store Red Cliffs Mall and a manufacturers-outlet shopping center. New housing is springing up in several directions, including the suburban areas of Bloomington Hills to the south and Santa Clara to the north. According to the chamber of commerce, an average 1,500 sq. ft. home sells for $110,000. St. George is home to a regional medical center and to Dixie Community College. Local boosters identify the town as a year-round golfing center; it has eight courses within a few minutes drive of each other. St. George is on Utah's southern border about a two-hour drive from Las Vegas—a trip that takes you though a deserted corner of Arizona.

For isolated living in a spectacular setting, check out the tiny communities of Hurricane and Springdale, between St. George and the main entrance to Zion National Park.

Resources

Arizona

Arizona Office of Tourism
2702 N. 3rd St. Suite 4015
Phoenix, AZ 85004
(602) 230-7733

**Flagstaff Visitor and
Convention Bureau**
211 W. Aspen Ave.
Flagstaff, AZ 86001
(520) 779-7611

**Lake Havasu City Visitor
and Convention Bureau**
1930 Mesquite Ave. Suite 3
Lake Havasu City, AZ 86403
(520) 855-4115

Scottsdale Chamber of Commerce
7343 Scottsdale Mall
Scottsdale, AZ 85251
(602) 945-8481

**Tucson Convention and
Visitors Bureau**
130 S. Scott Ave.
Tucson, AZ 85701
(520) 624-1817

**Valley of the Sun
Convention and Visitors Bureau**
400 E. Van Buren Suite 600
Phoenix, AZ 85004
(602) 252-5588

Colorado

**Colorado Travel and
Tourism Authority**
P.O. Box 3524
Englewood, CO 80155
(303) 799-5965

**Colorado Springs Convention
and Visitors Bureau**
1 N. Cascade Ave. Suite 110
Colorado Springs, CO 80903
(719) 635-1551

**Greater Denver
Chamber of Commerce**
1445 Market St.
Denver, CO 80202
(303) 534-8500

**Fort Collins Convention
and Visitors Bureau**
P.O. Box 1998
Fort Collins, CO 80522
(970) 482-5821

**Grand Junction Area
Chamber of Commerce**
360 Grand Ave.
Grand Junction, CO 81501
(970) 242-3214

**Pueblo Chamber,
Convention and Visitors Bureau**
P.O. Box 697
Pueblo, CO 81002
(800) 233-3446

New Mexico

Department of Tourism
P.O. Box 20002
Santa Fe, NM 87503
(505) 827-7400

**Albuquerque Convention
and Visitors Bureau**
P.O. Box 26866
Albuquerque, NM 87125
(505) 243-3696

**Las Cruces Chamber
of Commerce**
P.O. Drawer 519
Las Cruces, NM 88004
(505) 524-1968

**Santa Fe Chamber
of Commerce**
P.O. Box 1928
Santa Fe, NM 87504
(505) 983-7317

Nevada

Nevada Commission on Tourism
Capitol Complex
Carson City, NV 89710
(800) NEVADA 8

**Boulder City
Chamber of Commerce**
1497 Nevada Hwy.
Boulder City, NV 89005
(702) 293-2034

**Carson City
Chamber of Commerce**
1900 S. Carson St. Suite 100
Carson City, NV 89701
(702) 882-1565

**Carson Valley
Chamber of Commerce**
1524 Highway 395 Suite 1
Gardnerville, NV 89401
(702) 782-8144

**Reno-Sparks
Chamber of Commerce**
P.O. Box 3499
Reno, NV 89505
(702) 686-3030

**Las Vegas
Chamber of Commerce**
711 E. Desert Inn Rd.
Las Vegas, NV 89109
(702) 735-1616

Texas

Texas Commerce Department
P.O. Box 12728
Austin, TX 78711
(512) 936-0172

**Bryan-College Station
Chamber of Commerce**
P.O. Box 3579
Bryan, TX 77805
(409) 260-9898

**Greater Austin
Chamber of Commerce**
P.O. Box 1967
Austin, TX 78767
(512) 478-9383

Utah

Utah Travel Council
Council Hall/Capitol Hill
Salt Lake City, UT 84114
(800) 200-1160

Cedar City
Chamber of Commerce
286 N. Main St.
Cedar City, UT 84720
(801) 586-4484

Orem Chamber of Commerce
51 S. University Suite 215
Orem, UT 84057
(801) 377-2555

St. George Area
Chamber of Commerce
97 E. St. George Blvd.
St. George, UT 84770
(801) 628-1658

Salt Lake Convention
and Visitors Bureau
180 S. West Temple
Salt Lake City, UT 84101
(801) 521-2822

References

Data on each city come from a variety of sources. Unemployment figures come from the Department of Labor, Bureau of Labor Statistics, first quarter, 1997. Per-capita income information comes from the U.S. Bureau of Economic Analysis (cited in the 1996 *U.S. Statistical Abstract*). Details of state populations by race come from "Resident Population by Race, Hispanic Origin, and State: 1992," *U.S. Statistical Abstract,* 1996. Annotations in the statistical abstract indicate the 1992 U.S. Census Bureau figures are consistent with 1995 estimates. Data on family size is also from the U.S. Census Bureau, cited in the statistical abstract.

Home prices (unless otherwise specified) come from either an individual city's board of realtors or from the National Association of Realtors. All prices are based on 1996 average or median prices. Identification of many local employers comes from brochures and Web sites from chambers of commerce. (Many chambers provide extensive employer lists that could be helpful in a job search. Only the top few employers are listed here for the sake of brevity.) Unionization rates come from the Bureau of National Affairs' *Union Membership and Earnings Data Book.*

Climate data for the cities come from the *Climatic Averages and Extremes for U.S. Cities,* published by the National Climatic Data Center of the National Oceanic and Atmospheric Administration, June 1995. More detail on most cities' climates is found in Table 5.1. (The elevation for each city also comes from the NCDC.)

Information on air pollution comes from the National Resources Defense Council's *Technical Report: Breath Taking,* revised May 7, 1996. The report lists U.S. cities by amount of particulate air pollution and by the number of annual deaths per 100,000 population due to air pollution. Phoenix is listed seventh on the list of amount of pollution. (The top six cities are all in California.)

According to the Council's *Technical Report,* the number of annual premature deaths, per 100,000 population, in a few Western cities are: Riverside-San Bernardino, 122; Bakersfield, 115; Los Angeles, 79; Las Vegas, 76; Phoenix, 74; San Diego 64; Reno, 61.

Population figures for each city in this chapter are estimates. U.S. Census Bureau estimates were used in some cases, chamber of commerce or municipal figures were used in others. State populations were taken from U.S. Census Bureau estimates as of Dec. 31, 1996. Data on the number of physicians per state come from a Jan. 1, 1996 report of the American Medical Association. (Hawaii's rate of 263 physicians per 100,000 population was the highest of the Western states.) Figures on the number of people who have moved to Arizona come from the California Department of Motor Vehicles' annual migration report, 1996. Quotations regarding employment in Hawaii come from *Living and Working in Hawaii*, published by the Chamber of Commerce of Hawaii. Crime figures come from the FBI Uniform Crime Report for 1995, released Oct. 13, 1996. Tax information comes from the Federation of Tax Administrators.

The statistics on women's salaries in Utah and Wyoming come from an article, "Gender Gap is gaping in Utah, study finds" in the July 29, 1996 (Salt Lake City) *Deseret News*. Figures on home price increases come from the April 1, 1996 *U.S. News and World Report*, in an article: "The Hottest Markets." *Reader's Digest* for April, 1997, ranked 50 cities as the best places to raise a family.

13

Where to go: Northwest

Shimmering blue-green waters, dense forests, and snow-capped peaks characterize much of the Pacific Northwest. Crisscrossed by the Columbia, Snake, Missouri, Yukon, and other rivers, the land ranges from rain forests to deserts, from tundra to tide pools. Evergreen countryside attracts Californians accustomed to seeing the hillsides turn golden brown with the coming of summer. But the green abundance of the Northwestern states is caused by rain—something else many urban Californians are not accustomed to.

The states north of California have enough variety of cities, terrains, and climates, however, to let you compromise. Southern Idaho and the eastern portions of Washington and Oregon, for example, have more sunshine and less precipitation than other parts of the Northwest. While these areas are removed from the ocean, they are endowed with lakes and rivers. As with all other states in the U.S., the Northwest provides plenty of opportunities for you to locate the town of your dreams, one that has just the right blend of population, recreation, employment, climate, and schools to fit you and your family.

As you read through the summaries that follow, remember that this information is just a sample of the details available in exchange for a little research. These short profiles are just examples. If you're going to develop a relationship with a new town, you need to take the next steps. Addresses and phone numbers for the chambers of commerce for all cities mentioned are listed at the end of the chapter.

ALASKA

Alaska dwarfs almost everything in the lower 48 states. It has higher mountains than California, a longer coastline than Florida, more lakes than Minnesota. And a larger population than Vermont or Wyoming. This vast, sparsely populated land is the United States' last frontier, and living here can be a challenge. If you're up to the rigors, it can be rewarding. But more than a move to any other state, leaving for Alaska requires preparation. Living and working in Alaska is guaranteed to be unlike anything you've experienced in California.

Job availability varies. In the mid-1990s unemployment in Alaska was on par with California, which is to say, not great. Production had declined in the oil industry, the state's largest revenue producer. But in late 1996 and early 1997, announcement of new oil discoveries promised to rejuvenate the industry—and fuel environmental protests. Fishing and lumber, the other traditional Alaska industries, have had problems too. In fact, employment in the lumber industry, due in part to closure of a major pulp and sawmill, has declined in recent years. Predictions vary on the possibility of job growth in the future.

But demand for various specialities creates opportunities in Alaska, as elsewhere. For example, in remote areas, teachers have been in demand. In urban areas, however, the state employment service advises that teaching positions are difficult for out-of-staters to obtain. Anchorage is the site of most job opportunities, and the city's unemployment rate has been a point or two below the statewide average. As with many states, retail trade, services, and government are the three largest sources of employment. Civilian positions working for the military have always been a significant area of Alaska employment, too. These jobs make up a larger percentage of the work force in Alaska than in other states—a situation that is likely to remain.

For a more detailed look at jobs in Alaska, write the Alaska Employment Service for a brochure on employment. See the end of this chapter for the address. (The only way to know for sure about employment opportunities in *any* city or state is to study the market carefully before you make a job or moving decision.) Alaska state officials warn people from the lower 48—using language similar to that found in Hawaii literature—that travel to Alaska can be expensive, and moving to the state without a job is risky.

Generally, the cost of living, except for housing, is higher in Alaska than in the lower 48 states—comparable to San Francisco or New York. Salaries are higher in Alaska too, but not always enough to compensate. Housing is less expensive than urban California, and Alaskans pay no state sales or income taxes.

Climate and terrain also pose challenges depending upon where you live. Anchorage, for example, is relatively temperate; weather conditions are moderated by ocean currents. In winter it is sometimes colder in some upper Midwest towns than in Anchorage. The city does, however, receive an average of 70 inches of snow annually. In summer, the highs are in the 60s, the lows in the 50s.

Some 350 miles north of Anchorage is Fairbanks, where the temperatures can be in the 70s in summer and 50 degrees below zero—or colder—in winter. Juneau, in the southeast panhandle of Alaska, is colder than Anchorage—and far wetter. Anchorage averages 15 inches of rain per year, Juneau, 54.

No highways connect Juneau, the capital city, with Anchorage. The most direct route to get your car to Juneau is via ferry. Alaska's ferry system is the key transportation link among Ketchikan, Sitka, and other towns in the panhandle. Modern roads do connect Anchorage to Fairbanks, but winter weather conditions can making driving difficult at best. Transportation to and from Alaska's smaller towns and outposts is via floatplane. Scheduled airlines and charter pilots use a variety of pontoon aircraft to connect remote portions of the state. Alaska has many times more pilots and private aircraft per capita than any other state.

Anchorage

Pop. 257,000
Elev. 114
Anchorage Municipality
Newspaper: *Anchorage Daily News*

With forty percent of the population of Alaska, Anchorage has a strong influence on the politics and economics of the state. The city is situated in south central Alaska, on the Cook Inlet, sheltered from the Gulf of Alaska by the Kenai Peninsula. It's a cosmopolitan city—no igloos in sight—offering a range of recreational and cultural opportunities. Anchorage has the Center for Performing Arts, the Anchorage Museum of History and Art, the Alaska Heritage Library and Museum, many galleries, and the University of Alaska - Anchorage, serving 19,000 students at several area campuses. (Anchorage even has Mexican restaurants.)

The transportation/communication segment of the economy is fourth in the number of jobs, according to the state labor department (after services, government, and retail employment). Anchorage is an air transportation hub and stopover for travel within Alaska and also for flights connecting points throughout North America and Asia. Between 1991 and 1996, air freight tonnage at Anchorage International Airport doubled. Anchorage's other leading airport, Lake Hood Air Harbor, is the busiest floatplane base in the world, with more than 800 takeoffs and landings during busy summer days.

The air harbor is one of many interesting sights in the largest U.S. city north of Seattle. Other sights, along the Seward Highway south of Anchorage, include bald eagles, Dall sheep, and killer whales in the Turnagain Arm of Cook Inlet. Within town you can cycle along a paved coastal trail that runs along Cook Inlet or fish for salmon in Ship Creek. The bike trail is part of the city's 259 miles of hiking, biking, skiing, and dog-mushing trails. That may sound like a lot of trails for one medium-sized city, but the Anchorage Municipality covers nearly 2,000 square miles. (Alaska has no counties; areas are generally governed by mayors and councils.)

Like the state as a whole, per capita income in Anchorage is higher than the U.S. national average, while home prices are on par with the more expensive Western cities outside California. The crime rate is lower than Los Angeles, but higher than San Francisco and San Diego.

Perhaps the biggest adjustment for people moving from California—in addition to the weather—is the daylight. Alaska is truly the land of the midnight sun. Anchorage days range from more than 19 hours of sunlight in summer to less than six at the winter solstice. On the bright side, in summer, golfers can book 8:45 p.m. tee-off times at Anchorage courses

IDAHO

Another state often associated with snow and pine forests is Idaho. The upper two-thirds of the state is generally mountainous and moist, but that's not two-thirds of the story. The lower portion of the state is a high, arid plain drained by the Snake River. Sage and chaparral dominate much of the landscape, and it is here that most of Idaho's cities are located. Many communities in southern Idaho have warm summers and limited rainfall, typical of Southern and Central California.

Along with Nevada, Idaho has been a national leader in the percentage of population and job growth throughout the 1990s. A growing tourist industry, steady energy-related employment, native high-tech companies, and successful recruitment of out-of-state firms have kept the economy rolling ahead. A number of large corporations also have headquarters in the state, adding to the prosperity. It's almost enough to make you forget that agriculture—with emphasis on one particular vegetable—is key to the state's economy.

The cost of living in Idaho is relatively low, with home prices and utility rates especially reasonable. The unemployment rate for the state in the mid-1990s has been about 5 percent (Boise is even lower). But the per capita income ranks Idaho slightly below many other Western states. Idaho also has a lower percentage of doctors than any other Western state, with only 136 per 100,000 population.

Idaho education figures show fewer students per teacher than in California which translates into higher SAT scores. And crime statistics indicate that

Idaho is one of the safest states, with a violent crime rate one-third that of California. As with other Western states, however, conflicts among environmental groups, business interests, and government entities sometimes arise concerning the best use of natural resources.

One of the best known natural resources in the state is the Snake River, which figures prominently in Idaho in several ways. The river begins its journey in Yellowstone Park (in neighboring Wyoming) and then makes a broad arch, running first southwest, then northwest, across the state. In western Idaho the river flows north, forming a portion of the border with Oregon and Washington, eventually leaving Idaho for the Columbia River.

The lower arc of the Snake is paralleled, approximately, by the major interstate route in southern Idaho: I-15 to I-84 to I-86. Most of the state's major cities and towns are near the river. Unlike many Western states, Idaho has no giant metropolis that dwarfs all other communities. The capital, Boise, is the largest city, but there are many other medium-sized towns. From east to west along the curve of the Snake are: Idaho Falls, 50,000 people; Pocatello, 60,000; Twin Falls, 32,000; Boise, 163,000; Nampa, 36,000, and Lewiston, 30,000. A variety of other, smaller towns—such as Rexburg, Mountain Home, and Caldwell—fill in the crescent of the Snake.

Along the Snake's route, from Wyoming to Washington, the water turns turbines to create power for Idahoans and is diverted into channels to irrigate the state's crops. To the north, the river flows through Hells Canyon, a national recreation area, where the water rushes between black basalt walls deeper than the Grand Canyon.

In the northern portion of the state, where mining- and lumber-related jobs have been the main forms of employment, a growing tourism industry and base of small manufacturing firms are contributing to the economy. The area contains two large, beautiful lakes, Lake Coeur d'Alene and Lake Pend Oreille. The latter is so large it contains a Navy submarine research center. The entire state is actually stuffed with outdoor recreational opportunities and contains six designated wilderness areas covering more than four million acres.

Boise

Pop. 163,000
Elev. 2,838
Ada County
Newspaper: *Idaho Statesman*

Although it contains less than 20 percent of the state's population, Idaho's largest city is still a strong economic influence with an active, prosperous business community. Boise is the headquarters for many of the state's largest companies including: Albertson's, Inc.; Idaho Power; Boise-Cascade Corp.; T.J. International; Micron Technology; and Morris-Knudsen Corp. Including neighboring cities of Nampa and Caldwell, the metro area contains more than 200,000 people.

The capital city—named by French trappers for "the woods"— Boise is an oasis of trees and flowing water in an otherwise dry, hilly plain. About 25 miles north of the Snake River, the city sits astride the Boise River with the capitol and state buildings on one side, the tree-shaded Boise State University campus along the other side of the river. The university, known for its business, nursing, and high-tech education, has 12,000 students. The campus borders the city's 10-mile greenbelt and bicycle path, which follows the river through town. The city has a number of parks—including 153-acre Ann Morrison Memorial Park along the river in the southwest portion of town. Among the many recreational areas outside of Boise are the Bogus Basin ski area to the north, (hence the phone book snowmobile listings) and the Snake River Birds of Prey Natural Area to the south.

Boise has several museums including the Basque Museum and Cultural Center and a science and industry Discovery Center. The heritage of the area is preserved in the Old Boise historic district with 120-year-old brick and stone structures, in Pioneer Village featuring historic homes, and even in the restored 1870s Idaho Penitentiary.

Statistically, the crime rate is low—on par with Fort Collins—but the median home prices are lower than the Colorado city. The city is busiest during the first few months of each year when the legislature is in session. Temperatures in Boise are high in summer, low in winter. The city receives only 20 inches of snow and about 12 inches of rain per year.

Twin Falls

Pop. 32,500
Elev. 3,745
Twin Falls County
Newspaper: *Twin Falls Times-News*

Driving through the Magic Valley toward Twin Falls tells you this is an agricultural community. Idaho's famous potatoes—as well as sugar beets, corn, and alfalfa—come from the rich, irrigated fields that surround the town. Beef cattle and commercial trout also are raised here. Companies with the well-known names of Green Giant, Pet, and Ore-Ida operate processing facilities in the area. Food processing and some small- to medium-sized manufacturing firms are the chief industrial enterprises. The city is also a commercial and service center for a large portion of southern Idaho and a section of northern Nevada. It has a 60-store enclosed mall, two hospitals—one a 165-bed medical center—and a regional cancer center.

Twin Falls lies on the southern edge of the Snake River Canyon, roughly half-way between Pocatello and Boise. Varied recreational areas are nearby, giving the town significant tourism business. Close-by attractions include: Shoshone Falls, lakes, ski areas (in the mountains to the north) and gaming in Jackpot, Nev., to the south. If you move to Twin Falls and need to bust out of the bucolic lifestyle once in a while, Boise is your best bet. Salt Lake City is 222 miles away, Reno, 453.

The town is home to many ex-Californians, including Seastrom Manufacturing, which relocated from Glendale in 1995. The reasonable home prices—the average cost is well under $100,000—are an attraction. And the high desert climate is not a big adjustment for many Californians.

Twin Falls gets but 10 inches of rain per year. Winters are cold and bring about 17 inches of snow. The rate of violent crime is low, but FBI reports show a significant number of burglaries. Getting around in Twin Falls can be disorienting for first-timers. Numbered streets in the town's center all run diagonally either southwest to northeast, or southeast to northwest. In newer areas, surrounding the city's core, all streets are oriented north and south.

At the north end of town, toward the Snake River, is the College of Southern Idaho, a two-year community college that also offers four-year degrees through extension programs with the University of Idaho and Idaho State. The college has a library and planetarium, an active theatre arts program, and a range of intercollegiate athletics—including a national championship women's volleyball team.

OREGON

Between Idaho and the Pacific is Oregon, where the Cascade Mountains march north through the western portion of the state, from California to Washington. The mountains separate Eugene, Portland and the state's other major cities from the eastern two-thirds of the state. West of the mountains and south of Portland lies the fertile Willamette Valley, agricultural center of the state. Farther south are lakes, rivers and hills, the geography of Ashland, Grants Pass, Medford, and other communities. Along the coast is a 400-mile string of state parks and beaches, interspersed with colorful fishing villages and occasional resorts. The eastern side of the Cascades is a high plateau broken by several east-west mountain ranges. Weather in the small towns sprinkled about is warmer and dryer than the coast side of the Cascades.

Oregon is also home to the Rogue River, Crater Lake, the Columbia River Gorge, and some of the most beautiful boulder-strewn beaches in the world. It offers a variety of recreational activities, from fishing, hunting, and hiking, to boating, skiing, and camping.

Politically, Oregon has a reputation as a progressive state. It was one of the first states to enact a direct primary, and provide for initiatives and referendums. Oregonians also are known for their interest in preserving the environment. Legislators are in session every two years in the capital, Salem. The state has no sales tax and low car registration fees.

Employment in the state ranges from high tech, biotech, and manufacturing in Portland, to agriculture and ranching in the Willamette Valley and eastern Oregon. Banking, retail trade, and services also are key employment areas in the major cities. Traditional areas of employment—wood products and fishing—are still solid portions of the state's economy. In the Willamette Valley and southern portions of the state, wine making is a growing industry. (And to accompany the wine, Oregon produces Tillamook cheese, from the town of the same name.) The unemployment rate for the state for 1995-96 was about 5 percent. Oregon has 3.2 million people, making it the 29th largest state.

Portland

Pop. 1.6 million (metro area)
Elev. 21 ft.
Multnomah, Clackamas, Washington, and Yamhill Counties
Newspaper: *The Oregonian*

On a sunny spring day, there's no major city in the U.S. prettier than Portland. Commercial boats and pleasure craft float along the Willamette River, in front of a downtown that hasn't been deserted by business. High-rise office buildings—including examples of postmodern architecture—stand between Waterfront Park along the river and the green hills of Washington Park, home to a zoo, arboretum, and famous rose garden. Just north is the mighty Columbia River, and rising in the east is the majestic profile of snow-capped Mt. Hood. The pine-scented air is crisp and clear.

If this image makes you want to head north, you're not alone. Along with Seattle, Portland was a prime destination for escapees in the late 80s and early 90s, and home prices have not been the same since. On average, homes are still less costly than in California and Seattle, but you have to be selective.

The economy is solid and, if not setting national growth records like Austin, Texas, or Provo, Utah, it's attracting its share of corporate relocations and expansions. People come to Portland because it's a sprawling city with jobs and housing, but the greenery, the rivers, and even the rain combine to make it seem less urban, more inviting.

About the rain. According to the National Climatic Data Center, Portland receives 36.30 inches of rain in a normal year. It receives *some* rain 150 days out of the year, and it has an average of 222 cloudy days each year. A number of major cities in the U.S. receive more rain than Portland—including Houston, Atlanta, Orlando, and St. Louis—but Portland seems stuck with the wet reputation.

The diverse economy of the area is demonstrated by a list of large local employers: Fred Meyer Inc. (grocery, discount store chain); Intel Corp.; Kaiser Permanente; Tektronix, Inc.; U.S. Bancorp; James River (paper) Corp.; Willamette Industries (wood products); Freightliner Corp.; United Parcel Service; and Nike, Inc. These and other industries benefit from transportation that includes the Port of Portland, where ships carrying automobiles from Japan pass ships carrying wheat and a variety of other products headed out to sea. Portland's per capita income, at more than $23,000, exceeds Oregon's statewide average.

Portland is surrounded by a variety of suburbs. East toward Mt. Hood is Gresham, connected to downtown by the Metropolitan Area Express (MAX) light rail system. The 15-mile run is expected to be supplemented with a line extending west from downtown to the communities of Beaverton and Hillsboro and later, a line to Vancouver, Wash. Gresham is home to Mt. Hood Community College, one of three community colleges in the Portland metro area. Directly south of Portland is the upscale community of Lake Oswego. Home prices may remind you of California, but the lush river, lake, and mountain views remind you why you're looking in Oregon. Beaverton, to the west, is headquarters for Nike, Inc., the shoe and sportswear manufacturer. Hillsboro is a growing center for area high-tech companies.

Across the Columbia River to the north is a community that's part Portland suburb, part separate city. Vancouver, Wash., is a port and commerce center for southern Washington. Residents don't have state income taxes, and when they shop in Portland, they avoid sales tax too. The Clark County community has a population of 65,000.

Although the University of Oregon and Oregon State are in other cities, Portland is home to a variety of two- and four-year colleges and universities—including Portland State University, University of Portland, and Reed College. The colleges add cultural and entertainment opportunities to a community that also has 75 galleries, many museums, a symphony, an opera, and an annual jazz festival.

Eugene

Pop. 122,000
Elev. 359 ft.
Lane County
Newspaper: *Eugene Register-Guard*

Eugene and nearby Springfield sit in the middle of lush Lane County. To the east are the Three Sisters—Cascade Mountain peaks each over 10,000 feet tall. Sixty-one miles due east is Florence, on the Pacific coast. The MacKenzie River meets the Willamette at Eugene, and several other rivers and lakes punctuate the forests and farmlands that surround the city. Recreational activities span the seasons; they include skiing, ocean and river fishing, hiking, exploring lava beds, camping, cycling, boating, and many others. The area chamber of commerce says Eugene has 49 parks covering 1,996 acres, 98 miles of bikeways, five jogging trails, 23 tennis courts, 11 golf courses, five bowling alleys, and an ice rink.

Eugene is the state's second largest city and metro area. It lies less than two hours south of Portland, via Interstate 5. County population is about 300,000. Among the institutions in town are the University of Oregon, home of the PAC-10 Ducks and 18,000 students; Sacred Heart General Hospital, a 432-bed facility with intensive care, emergency, pediatric and other departments; and the Fifth Street Saturday Market. The latter is a March-through-December tradition featuring crafts, food sales, and street entertainment. The city also has a 145-store enclosed mall and downtown retail and speciality shops.

Employment in Eugene is a mixture of government, education, and private industry. Sacred Heart Health System and the university are among the largest employers. Leading manufacturers include Weyerhaeuser Company, Willamette Industries, Agripac, SMC Corp., Symantec, Springfield Forest Products, and Spectra-Physics. Seventeen financial institutions operate 59 local branches. Farms in the area raise a variety of livestock, fruits, and vegetables. Lane Community College (with 35,000 students), provides job training and retraining, as well as university transfer programs. The Eugene Airport is served by regional and national carriers.

About a two-and-a-half-hour drive west from Eugene, over the Cascades, is Bend. It's one of the most popular small-town destinations in the Pacific Northwest. The community is surrounded by forests, parks, lakes, and rivers. Many newcomers are attracted by the weather, which is warmer and dryer than towns on the ocean side of Oregon.

Coos Bay, North Bend, Charleston

Pop. 32,000
Elev. 15 ft.
Coos County
Newspaper: *Coos Bay World*

The three towns that make up "Oregon's Bay Area" represent the largest metro area on the coast, although metro area is an overstatement. Nonetheless, this area has a daily newspaper, commercial airline service to Portland, the largest hospital on the coast, a community college, and the University of Oregon's Institute of Marine Biology. The most prominent feature of the area is the port. The sight of ocean-going freighters tied up in this small town seems almost incongruous at first, but Coos Bay has been an important shipping point for more than 100 years. Wood and wood products are shipped to U.S. and foreign ports. Along with the lumber industry, fishing is a mainstay of Coos Bay. The unincorporated town of Charleston, at the mouth of Coos Bay, is home to a commercial fishing fleet and fish processing facilities. Just north of town is the Oregon Dunes National Recreation Area, a 40-mile ribbon of sand dunes, grasslands, and marshes along the coast.

The entire Oregon coast is practically one, long, state park. Tourism and fishing are the main industries; the towns small and the views breathtaking. Lighthouses, tiny harbors, beaches guarded by rock monoliths, green headlands, and miles of unspoiled hiking trails await visitors. Summer is by far the busiest time. Fall and winter bring uninterrupted weeks of overcast and rain. (Coos Bay receives about 60 inches annually.) With few industries present on the coast, outside of some manufacturing in the Coos Bay area, high-paying jobs are scarce.

Home prices along the coast vary with the topography. Homes closest to the beach, or with sweeping views, fetch the highest prices. Brookings and Newport are among the more pricey coastal communities. An Oregon ocean-front home (of which there are few) costs far less than its urban California equivalent—but it's still not cheap. Small homes, without views, in coastal towns can be found in the $100,000 range and up. The median home price in the Coos Bay area, for example, is between $90,000 and $100,000.

MONTANA

Montana doesn't have isolated ocean bays and coastal fog like Oregon, but it's nonetheless a mystical place. Robert M. Pirsig wrote about his transcendental journey of discovery to Montana in *Zen and the Art of Motorcycle Maintenance*. Montana was home to American artist Charles M. Russell, who helped create our quintessential images of cowboys, horses, and the Western landscape. Montana is a collection of interests—from ranchers and miners to environmentalists, social philosophers, and representatives of the state's nascent business community. Montanans seem to be in a constant debate over the best use of the *last best place* and over the introduction of outsiders into this vast, largely unpopulated state.

"Montana has become an escapist vision," says Professor William E. Farr, of the University of Montana in Missoula. "Books and movies advertise the image. . . . Starlets glitter against rural skies. Ted Turner raises buffalo on the Flying D, and too many others fish, hunt, ski, and gawk in a wild environment that is not only close by but close to a pervasive nostalgic dream," he says. "Space and spaciousness have given us an enviable scale."

In the late 1980s and early 1990s, when other Western states were luring corporations and setting business and population growth records, Montanans continued their debate. Many expressed trepidation about a possible influx. "It's a bumper-to-bumper raceway—Jeeps and Winnebagos and Harleys, Californians and Canadians, illicit drug vendors on holiday, fly fishing nuts who saw *A River Runs Through It*," writes Missoula author William Kettredge in *Time* magazine in late 1993. "Who knows? Some of them are tourists, but some of them are coming to stay."

Californians have relocated to Montana, but not in the same numbers as they have in nearby states. From 1990 to mid-1996—when Nevada grew by more than 30 percent, Arizona by more than 20 percent, and Idaho by more than 18 percent—Montana grew by about 10 percent, to 879,000 people. Recent population projections by the state show growth slowing to less than one percent annually through the year 2000.

Is the slower growth due to the well-publicized reticence of Montanans? The freezing-cold winters that can last five months? Certainly it's not for lack of natural beauty or inviting small cities. The fourth-largest state in area, Montana encompasses broad plains, jutting mountains, and vast forests. The eastern three-fifths of the state belong to the prairie, the balance to the Rockies. The state has 10 national forests, 13 wilderness areas, and two national parks.

In addition, Montana is the most peaceful state in the West. According to FBI estimates, Montana averages 177 incidents of violent crime annually per 100,000 population. The average for the Western U.S. is 805.

The state Department of Labor and Industry predicts a job growth of about 2 percent per year through the year 2000, with most of that in service industries. Job opportunities in retail sales, food service, bookkeeping/accounting, and general management positions are expected to increase the most.

Other openings will be for general office clerks and registered nurses. According to a labor and industry department report, jobs for farm and ranch workers will decline the most. Jobs in coal and metals mining will be increasing slightly.

Montana has no statewide sales tax and no city with more than 100,000 people. Billings, established as a railroad stop in the 1880s, is the largest with 82,000 people. Next are Great Falls, 56,000; Missoula, 43,000; and Butte, 34,000. Missoula is the state's unofficial cultural center—home to a number of Western writers and site of the University of Montana, with its 11,000 students. One of the West's many inviting cities on a river, Missoula is nearly surrounded by wilderness areas and national forests. Helena, a former mining town, is the capital. It is minutes from forests, wilderness areas, and Canyon Ferry Lake, one of the state's largest. Butte, a mining town in southwestern Montana, is home to Montana Tech University. It is also the site of the Berkeley Pit, a one mile wide, mile-and-a-half-long abyss on the edge of town. Water has filled the abandoned open-pit mine, and acidic chemicals, leached from the walls, have contaminated it.

Great Falls

Pop. 56,000
Elev. 3,663
Cascade County
Newspaper: *Great Falls Tribune*

Not all communities that have riverside biking/hiking trails through the center of town are ideal destinations, but a trail certainly beats a packed freeway. The River's Edge Trail in Great Falls starts at a park near where the Sun River flows into the Missouri River and continues for 11 miles.

Great Falls is the commercial center for central Montana. It lies 120 miles south of the Canadian border, on Interstate 15. Like most of the larger towns in Montana, Great Falls is minutes from lakes and national forests. Located 50 miles east of the Continental Divide, the town is something of a dividing point for the state as well. For hundreds of miles to the east are wheat fields, ranches, and undulating prairie; to the west, the Rocky Mountains.

The Missouri River flows through Great Falls and over the cascades the town is named for. The falls were discovered in 1805 by Meriwether Lewis of Lewis and Clark fame. Just outside town is Malmstrom Air Force Base.

Tourism is a key industry, and for Western-art aficionados, Great Falls is Russell Central. Artist C.M. Russell lived and worked in Great Falls. His memory and works are celebrated at the C.M. Russell Museum Complex, which includes a large collection of his work, along with his original log-cabin studio. Great Falls is also the home of the University of Great Falls, a private Catholic university, and Montana State University-College of Technology, a two-year school offering associate degrees in health, business and trades, and technology.

WASHINGTON

Why would anyone want to move from California to cloudy Washington, particularly the Puget Sound area? The attraction could be low crime rates, sparkling blue waters, good schools, lush rain forests, a growing economy, world-class shopping and dining, universities, symphonies, miles of unspoiled coastline, and the inviting Canadian cities of Vancouver and Victoria just a short distance away. These qualities and more put various Puget Sound communities on "best places" lists year after year. Bremerton was picked by *Reader's Digest* as one of the top 10 best places to raise a family; Bellingham was ranked No. 36. Whidbey Island was picked by *Money* as one of America's 50 hottest little boomtowns. Seattle also finds its way to high spots on city lists.

Western Washington has, for years, been a popular destination for Golden State expatriates (not to mention people fleeing other metro areas). As a result, home prices are not the cheapest in the West. Tables 8.1 and 10.1 show that Seattle prices are only slightly lower than major California cities. Bellevue, an upscale suburb, is priced on par with parts of Orange County—but cheaper than San Jose or San Rafael. The Seattle area is appealing because of its blend of new and old. The town began in the mid-1800s as a logging port. When the Klondike gold rush began in 1897, Seattle became the leading jumping-off point. Outfitters became more prosperous than most of the miners. By 1962, Seattle had been a city for nearly 100 years, but the successful World's Fair in that year started a new period of growth.

For many years Seattle's economic fortunes tended to rise and fall with aircraft sales at the city's Boeing Company plant. Today, however, the city, and its dozens of neighborhoods and suburbs, are more diversified. The Seattle area may be better known now as the home of Microsoft, rather than Boeing. But both large, local employers have been successful of late, and the town's unemployment rate for the 1990s has been lower than California's.

The housing boom of the 1990s, fueled in part by demand from ex-Californians, pushed the suburbs out from Seattle in all directions. Across the sound are suburban areas where commuters reach Seattle via a short ferry ride.

The city has nearly a century and a half of traditions and all the signs of a modern metropolis: major-league sports teams, high-tech employment, growing world trade, and a profile of skyscrapers that dwarf older buildings along the waterfront. Yet unlike Los Angeles, San Diego, or even some San Francisco Bay Area cities, downtown Seattle is within minutes of the trees, lakes, and quiet harbors that surround the city. But don't mistake Seattle for a large Coos Bay, or even Portland; its metro area has as many people as Phoenix and its commuter congestion snarls roads from time to time. Nevertheless, Seattle is a city with charisma, and the rain keeps it looking green and clean.

Spreading out from Seattle, around Puget Sound, are the majority of the state's cities and population. The cities include Tacoma, Olympia, Bellingham, Bremerton, Everett, and Federal Way. You also find many tiny, picturesque getaways such as Friday Harbor on San Juan Island and Coupeville on Whidbey Island. The San Juan Islands are beautiful weekend destinations, but they offer few year-round jobs and they depend on ferries for auto transportation to the mainland.

Whidbey, on the other hand, is a narrow, 45-mile-long island connected to the mainland by a bridge at its north end and a brief ferry ride at its south end. Oak Harbor, at about 20,000 people, is the largest of several towns on the island. Employment is concentrated in tourist/service fields and the local Naval air station. Parts of the island are easy commuting distance from other cities.

Outside of Puget Sound, Washington is geographically similar to Oregon. Washington's portion of the Cascades runs north from Oregon to Canada and contains the towering peaks of Mt. Rainier, Mt. Baker, and the now slightly-less-towering Mt. St. Helens. East of the mountains are miles of grain and other crops, several large lakes, including 150-mile-long Roosevelt Lake behind Grand Coulee Dam, and towns scattered here and there.

Agriculture is a major economic force in the state. Washington is known for its apples, but milk and other dairy products, cattle, wheat, hops, cherries, and potatoes are also important crops. In addition, Washington is the second-leading wine producing state in the nation. The state's population of more than 5.5 million makes it the third most populous Western state, after California and Texas. The state levies no income tax; per capita income is about the same as California; and the cost of living in cities other than Seattle is comparable to like-size cities in other Western states.

Bellingham

Pop. 58,000
Elev. 68 ft.
Whatcom County
Newspaper: *The Bellingham Herald*

The city's aging downtown doesn't have quite the quaint charm of Port Townsend, yet Bellingham—which started as a coal mining town and turned to lumber and salmon in the late 1800s—has much to offer. Bellingham has a low crime rate, reasonably priced housing (read *cheap* by California standards), a state university, a commercial port, a huge pleasure/fishing boat marina, and just outside of town, some of the greenest country imaginable. The historic Fairhaven District is in the process of being restored, and several marina and park trails offer peaceful strolling.

Bellingham is 60 miles south of Vancouver, British Columbia, and 90 miles north of Seattle. Mount Baker dominates the horizon on the east, and the Mt. Baker Wilderness area is about a 40-mile drive away. A finger of Lake Whatcom extends into town. Locate Bellingham on a map and you'll see it's actually north of Victoria, British Columbia, and just northeast of the San Juan Islands. This location makes Bellingham an ideal spot from which to explore by boat. The marina at Squalicum Harbor has thousands of slips. (If you're attracted to Puget Sound, you may already have a boat in mind.)

Shipping is a part of the local economy. The port facilities provide for passenger and cargo traffic. Passengers can board ships for the Alaska Marine Highway or take smaller vessels to Canada or local destinations. At the Whatcom cargo terminal, aluminum, pulp, lumber, and wood chips are exported. In addition to the port, other Bellingham employers (excluding government and education) are St. Joseph's Hospital, Georgia Pacific (wood products), Haggen's, Inc. (retail grocery), Intalco Aluminum Corp., and ARCO.

Sitting just above town is Sehome Hill Arboretum, a 165-acre preserve that offers spectacular views of the city, the harbor, the San Juan Islands, and Mt. Baker. The Sehome Hill area is also an old residential neighborhood of Victorian homes. Adjoining is Western Washington University, looking out over Bellingham Bay. The university serves about 10,000 students, offers innovative music, theatre, and NCAA Div. II sports, including football and women's basketball.

For shopping, Bellingham has a 900,000-sq. ft. mall. The mall appeals not only to locals, but to British Columbia shoppers looking for bargains in the United States. Another mall is located in Mt. Vernon, about 30 miles south. Mt. Vernon and nearby Anacortes are two other nearby towns that deserve exploration.

Spokane

Pop. 196,000
Elev. 2,573
Spokane County
Newspaper: *Spokesman-Review*

While Puget Sound seems to get most of the attention, Spokane, at the other end of the state, also has been attracting newcomers. With outdoor activities that rival Eugene and Portland—yet lower home prices and half the rainfall of the two Oregon cities—Spokane is a star of the Pacific Northwest. New home developments are rising in several parts of town, and the local business development program is bringing in new companies.

Given the huge areas of farmland in the western portion of Washington, the Spokane economy has a large agriculture base. According to the chamber of commerce, the city also employs a large number of people in health care industries, making it a medical center for western Washington. In fact, Spokane's size and location makes it a commerce and support center for not only western Washington, but portions of three other states and British Columbia. Employment is oriented toward trade and service. The lumber industry contributes jobs in the creation of pulp, paper, and plywood.

Spokane does not have a state university campus, but it fills this void in several ways. It is home to several small private institutions, including Whitworth College and Gonzaga University. The latter, a Jesuit institution, has about 4,700 students, a law school, and offers NCAA Div. I sports, including baseball and basketball. Spokane also has two community colleges, and a state university (Eastern Washington in Cheney) is less than 20 miles south. On the banks of the Spokane River is Higher Education Park, where Eastern Washington and Washington State will both offer courses and degree programs in the near future. The education park is also the site of the Spokane Intercollegiate Research and Technology Institute, a joint project of the area's universities and colleges. The institute will provide research and educational opportunities to help local businesses.

Spokane's downtown is a mixture of historic buildings and modern office towers. At the center of town is Riverfront Park, providing playgrounds, views of Spokane Falls, walking trails, and areas for festivals and concerts. The park was site of the 1974 World's Fair. In addition, Spokane offers minor-league hockey and baseball, galleries, museums, theatre, a jazz orchestra, and wineries. Near downtown is the city's new 12,500-seat arena for sporting events and concerts.

Spokane is another city with a biking/hiking trail along a river. Its river trail runs completely through Spokane and continues to Lake Coeur d'Alene, Idaho, 33 miles to the east. The eastern end of the trail is the beginning of Spokane's connection to the lakes, ski resorts, and forests of north Idaho. And 19 golf courses are within 45 minutes of Spokane.

Although the National Resources Defense Council placed Spokane number eight on its list of particulate-polluted cities in 1995, *Readers's Digest* pegged the city as the eighth-best place in the country to raise a family. The article cited the city's many cultural events and its small-town feeling.

WYOMING

Relocating to anywhere in Wyoming is like moving to a small town. Life is less complicated in this state that has a smaller population than many California *cities*. You can't move to a big city in Wyoming, because there aren't any. Cheyenne, the capital, is the largest town at 53,700 people. The next largest communities are: Casper, 49,100; Laramie, 27,200; Gillette, 18,800; and Sheridan, 14,800. The state's small population and large area (481,000 people and 97,000 square miles—making it ninth largest) tend to provide a unique common bond for its citizens. As a small state, Wyoming needs less bureaucracy. It has no DMV, for example. You get your license plates from your county. The slogan on the Wyoming visitors book, "like no place on earth," is true in several ways.

The landscape visible from interstate 80—which spans the lower portion of the state, connecting Cheyenne and Laramie with western Wyoming—provides a good look at the state's vastness. But it only hints at its diversity. Much of the state is high grasslands, at an average of about 6,000 feet. Several mountain ranges punctuate the plain, most notably the Grand Tetons, part of the Rocky Mountains, and site of Grand Teton National Park.

North of the Tetons, in the northwest corner of the state, is Yellowstone National Park. Yellowstone and Grand Teton parks are filled with the awe-inspiring views that help Wyoming draw more than seven million visitors each year. Other natural wonders include Devil's Tower National Monument, Fossil Butte National Monument, and Flaming Gorge National Recreation Area.

The state's economy is anchored by three industries: mining/oil, tourism, and agriculture. According to the state's Economic Analysis Division, Wyoming leads the nation in coal production and is fourth in crude oil. Natural gas is also a major Wyoming resource. Agriculturally, the state has more than 9,000 farms. They produce sheep (Wyoming is second in the country in wool production), cattle, sugar beets, dry beans, hay, and vegetables. These three industries bring in roughly $6.5 billion annually. Many other jobs in the state are in the familiar service and retail areas.

Laramie, less than 50 miles west of Cheyenne, is a cultural center. It's home to the University of Wyoming, the only four-year college in the state. The university, in turn, is home to NCAA Div. I sports, including Western Athletic Conference football and a geological museum featuring a brontosaurus skeleton. About 12,000 students attend the university, which has a law school and agricultural extension service.

Weather in Wyoming is on the cool side, owing to the altitude. Cheyenne and Casper have sunshine about half the time, but June through September are the only months the average high temperature exceeds 70 degrees. In many areas of the state the air is dry and the winds are strong.

The state has no corporate or personal income taxes and no sales tax on fuel. In the mid-1990s Wyoming's two senators, its congressman and governor were all Republicans. (The first woman governor in the U.S. was Wyoming's Nellie Tayloe Ross in 1925.)

Cheyenne

Pop. 53,000
Elev. 6,130
Laramie County
Newspaper: *Wyoming Tribune Eagle*

Wyoming's capital city began when railroad builder Grenville Dodge built a settlement on the site in 1867. The town is situated on a high, grassy plain at the edge of Medicine Bow National Forest and separated from the town of Laramie by the Laramie Mountains. Cheyenne is near several Colorado cities. Ft. Collins is the closest at 45 miles, and Denver is just over 100 miles away.

Aside from state and local government, one of the leading area employers is F.E. Warren Air Force Base. The base actually dates back to the early days of the state when it was a cavalry fort housing troops to protect settlers and railroad workers. Fort D.A. Russell, as it was originally named, became a U.S Air Force facility in 1958. Other leading employment areas are retail and service industries.

Home prices in Cheyenne are slightly less expensive than neighboring Fort Collins. FBI figures show Cheyenne to be one of the safest cites in the West. Its overall crime rate is lower than the Western and national averages, and its low violent crime rate would put three-quarters of the cops in California cities out of work. Imagine, no murders in an entire year in the state's largest town! For local recreation, the city offers 17 parks, a botanical garden, and three golf courses. Shopping opportunities include a 75-store mall.

The biggest local event is Cheyenne Frontier Days in early July, featuring a huge professional rodeo, parades, musical entertainment, and other activities.

Conclusion

The cities reviewed in this and the previous chapter are just a sample of the communities waiting outside California. And of course there are many potential hometowns outside the West. Many towns in North and South Carolina, for example, offer sunbelt weather, growing economies, and many recreational opportunities. Several Wisconsin towns have made "best places" lists due to a combination of healthy economies and strong community spirit. The Orlando area of Florida offers a lower cost of living than urban California with a lifestyle similar in some ways to Southern California.

Using these city chapters, the tables, and other resources in this book, you can identify communities that have the combination of characteristics you want. In a way, it's like custom building your own hometown.

Resources

Alaska

Alaska Employment Service
P.O. Box 25509
Juneau, AK 99802-5509

Alaska Division of Tourism
P.O. Box 110801
Juneau, AK 99801-0801

Anchorage Convention and Visitors Bureau
524 W. Fourth Ave.
Anchorage, AK 99501
(907) 276-4118

Idaho

Idaho Dept. of Commerce
P.O. Box 83720
Boise, ID 83720
(800) 847-4843

Coeur D'Alene/Hayden Lake Convention and Visitors Bureau
P.O. Box 1088
Coeur D'Alene, ID 83816
(208) 664-0587

Boise Chamber of Commerce
168 N. 9th St.
Boise, ID 83702
(208) 344-7777

Twin Falls Chamber of Commerce
858 Blue Lakes Blvd. No.
Twin Falls, ID 83301
(208) 733-3974

Montana

Travel Montana
P.O. Box 200533
Helena, Mont. 59620
(406) 444-2654

Great Falls Chamber of Commerce
815 2nd. St. South
Great Falls, MT 59405
(406) 761-4434

Oregon

Oregon Tourism Commission
P.O. Box 14070
Portland, OR 97214
(800) 547-7842

Bay Area Chamber of Commerce
P.O.Box 210
Coos Bay, OR 97420
(800) 824-8486

Bend Chamber of Commerce
63085 N. Highway 97
Bend, OR 97701
(541) 382-3221

Convention & Visitors Assn. of Lane County
P.O. Box 10286
Eugene, OR 97440
(800) 547-5445

Portland Visitors Association
26 W. Salmon St.
Portland, OR 97204
(800) 962-3700

Washington

Washington State Community, Trade and Economic Development
P.O. Box 48300
Olympia, WA 985043
(360) 753-7426

Bellingham/Whatcom County Convention and Visitors Bureau
904 Potter St.
Bellingham, WA 98226
(360) 671-3990

Seattle/King County Convention and Visitors Bureau
520 Pike St. Suite 1300
Seattle, WA 98101
(206) 461-5840

Spokane Convention and Visitors Bureau
926 West Sprague Ave. Suite 180
Spokane, WA 99204
(800) 248-3230

Vancouver/Clark County Visitors and Convention Bureau
404 E. 15th St. Suite 11
Vancouver, Wash. 98663
(800) 377-7084

Wyoming

Wyoming Division of Tourism
I-25 at College Dr.
Cheyenne, WY 82002
(307) 777-7777

Cheyenne Chamber of Commerce
301 W. 16th
Cheyenne, WY 82003
(307) 638-3388

Laramie Chamber of Commerce
800 So. Third St.
Laramie, WY 82070
(307) 745-7339

References

Data on each city come from a variety of sources. Alaska data come from the Alaska Department of Labor, Alaska Employment Service, Alaska Division of Tourism, the Municipality of Anchorage, and the Anchorage Visitors and Convention Bureau.

Unemployment figures come from the U.S. Department of Labor, Bureau of Labor Statistics, first quarter, 1997. Per-capita income information comes from the U.S. Bureau of Economic Analysis, cited in the 1996 *U.S. Statistical Abstract.* Home prices (unless otherwise specified) come from either an individual city's board of realtors or from the National Association of Realtors. All prices are based on 1996 average or median prices. Figures on home price increases come from the April 1, 1996 issue of *U.S. News and World Report,* in an article: "The Hottest Markets."

Identification of many local employers comes from brochures and Web sites from chambers of commerce. (Many chambers provide extensive employer lists that could be helpful in a job search. Only the top few employers are listed here for the sake of brevity.)

Climate data for the cities comes from the *Climatic Averages and Extremes for U.S. Cities,* published by the National Climatic Data Center of the National Oceanic and Atmospheric Administration, June 1995. More detail on most cities' climates is found in Table 5.1. (The elevation for each city also comes from the NCDC.)

The information on air pollution comes from the National Resources Defense Council's *Technical Report: Breath Taking* revised May 7, 1996. The report lists U.S. cities by amount of particulate air pollution (The top six cities are all in California) and by the number of annual deaths per 100,000 population due to air pollution.

Population figures for each city mentioned in the chapter are estimates—U.S. Census Bureau estimates in some cases, chamber of commerce or city figures in others. State populations were taken from U.S. Census Bureau estimates as of Dec. 31, 1996.

Data on the number of physicians per state come from a Jan. 1, 1996 report of the American Medical Association. Crime figures come from the FBI Uniform Crime Report for 1995, released Oct. 13, 1996. The Federation of Tax Administrators is the source of information on state taxes. (See Table 2.1)

Reader's Digest for April, 1997, ranked 50 cities as the best places to raise a family. Quotations from Professor William E. Farr come from *Montana Business Quarterly,* October, 1995. William Kettredge's essay on Montana appeared in the Sept. 6, 1993 issue of *Time* magazine.

14

How to fit in, settle in, and avoid Caliphobia

There's no anti-California sentiment in Oregon, says a state business development official in Portland. She's even an ex-Californian herself, she says. But then she adds, "We lived in Colorado for a year before we moved here, so we covered our tracks."

So, what kind of reception *can* you expect when you show up with your suntan and your California plates?

The possibility of anti-California feelings is a basic concern of would-be expatriates. It's high on the list, right after rainfall, taxes, and crime. The issue dates back at least to the 1980s, when the first wave of Californians arrived in Seattle with pockets full of home-equity cash. When Washington locals started to blame Californians for everything from higher prices to lower moral standards, the backlash attracted media attention. *Caliphobia* was conceived. Since then, magazine and newspaper articles have perpetuated the antagonistic attitudes through a continued—and sometimes exaggerated—focus on adverse local reactions.

As a result of this on-going, negative press, some ex-Californians expected worse conditions than they found. Many people interviewed say they encountered little out-of-state animosity. "One of the biggest surprises was that there isn't the anti-California sentiment that we had heard about," says Sheila White, a Seattle-area resident transplanted from Orange County. Susan Gonzales—also from Orange County—whose family moved to a small town in southwest Washington, says they were expecting trouble. "The year we moved up here, we heard that we would have to change our license plates right away because people would egg our car." The Gonzales's car was not vandalized, and the family members quickly became comfortable in their new community. In Fort Collins, Colo., ex-Californian Scott Gordon says he found no anti-California attitudes. "Fort Collins is like California was when we were growing up. Everyone is from somewhere else, so people are very open."

In another state, local bumper stickers say, "Welcome to Wyoming. We don't care how you did it back home." A common sentiment toward would-be newcomers, says ex-Bay Area resident Michael McKown, is: "Keep moving until you get to Colorado. You'll like it much better there." Beyond these outward messages, however, says McKown, Wyoming is hospitable enough. The state is "not as nasty as the locals will tell you. This place is a hidden gem, and nobody wants me to talk about it."

Whether Wyoming or some other state is in your plans, it's difficult to know for sure if you'll receive a warm welcome, a cold shoulder, or something in between. Anti-newcomer sentiment can be found almost anywhere, says Sam Hill, a Helena, Mont., real estate agent. Hill lived in New York, Texas, Florida, Alabama, and Colorado before moving to Montana. In each state, he says, he found resistance to newcomers. The resistance comes from "generally friendly people who want to preserve their way of life. It's only the fear of change," he says, "or the unknown that results in an ugly mood swing."

Fear of the unknown is universal. When you move to a new town, most everything is unknown. And to the locals, you are too. It's no wonder there are misunderstandings. But you can influence what happens, first by your destination research, and second by your behavior. Since news articles are not necessarily a precise guide for avoiding hostile natives, you can do some first-hand research. When you visit, tell people that you're from California and you're thinking of moving in. See what happens. Bear in mind, of course, that real estate agents and other local boosters are not necessarily going to volunteer how many Californians have been tarred and feathered recently. School officials and local business contacts probably will be more candid. Another way to avoid Caliphobia is to look for growing cities and towns that already have a sizable immigrant population. When other residents are newcomers too, they're less likely to prejudge you simply because you're from out of town, says Gordon.

Another way to connect with other newcomers is to buy a home in a new neighborhood. This idea is suggested by several expats. New residents to an area—even if they just moved from another part of the same town—may have more in common with you than neighbors who have lived on the same street for years. New neighborhoods don't have longstanding relationships or cliques. Also, if you move to an expanding area of new homes, you won't be the newcomer for long. In a week or a month, when some family moves in down the block, you'll be an established resident by comparison. New neighborhoods are also fertile ground for trying new techniques to meet your fellow residents. (See the list of ways to meet your neighbors, later in this chapter.)

Finally, you might consider the size of the city itself. A derogatory, but sometimes valid stereotype, is that people in smaller towns are more skeptical of outsiders than are city folk. "The smaller the town, the higher the level of mistrust in newcomers," says Montana real estate agent Hill. "Everyone in town knows everything about everyone, and thus it takes a little longer to fit into the community."

The flip side of this—to revisit trade-offs for a moment—is that once you are settled in a smaller community you may find it's more friendly than the city. When he moved to Flagstaff, Ariz., from Los Angeles in 1996, Clint Rosser's whole life improved. "I came alive again. I don't feel the need to hide inside at night [because of crime]. . . . There's no graffiti because everyone loves their little town. It's easy to meet people here, because they're friendlier."

Finding out in advance precisely *how* friendly locals are going to be, however, is impossible. Your research will tell you only so much. Once you've picked a town that otherwise fits your criteria, fitting in and enjoying yourself is up to you. For the most part, you'll have to take the first steps to meet people, make friends, and avoid antagonizing locals. If you're like many of the people who have left California, it shouldn't be an intimidating task. You're probably interested in moving because you want to try something new, expand your perspectives, and make changes in your life. Going out of your way to meet people is one of those changes. "The Californians I have worked with have not been afraid of being outsiders," says Carson City, Nev., Realtor Victoria Williams, "As a matter of fact, they embrace the community."

Fitting in

This chapter contains a variety of suggestions for meeting people, fitting in, and embracing your new community. The first step in becoming a citizen of another city is to recognize that the way you treat others will greatly influence how they treat you. You're not in urban California any more, and you don't want to be anonymous. So smile, and make the first move to say hello. Greet coworkers, neighbors, church members, and others. Introduce yourself. Be natural and friendly, but don't force yourself on others. Just as you may have stereotypes of people in smaller towns, small-town people may have preconceived notions about big city folk. For example: Californians have lots of money, know all the answers, and are not too approachable. That may not describe you at all, but it may be how you're perceived simply because you're from California.

A way to sidestep this categorization, of course, is to avoid broadcasting your origins—at least at first. "Some people you meet are shy about it," says

Lloyd Thompson with the Idaho Commerce Dept. "They sort of whisper it under their breath: 'I'm from California.'" Fact is, you don't need to say it at all unless someone asks you. Ideally, if you get to know someone, even slightly, *before* he or she finds out you're an ex-Californian, you have a chance to elude that stereotypical first impression. That's the reason out-of-state DMV offices are early stops for ex-Californians. Savvy transplants know the value of first impressions, and they don't want neighbors to single them out as interlopers because of their license plates.

Unless you live in Colorado for a year before you move to your ultimate destination, there are times when you'll just have to fess up. Lying is not a good idea. Eventually your tell-tale Golden State roots will show. Then you will have convinced the people you lied to that you're a typical, scheming Californian. In casual conversation—at work or on your block—you may have the opportunity to explain that you didn't always live in California. If you are originally from somewhere else, that could have a mitigating effect. But don't pretend you're really a Minnesotan who was just passing through California (for 25 years).

If you get desperate, and you have relatives in your new state, you can always talk about your family. Says Scott Sullivan, the teacher who moved to a small Oregon town in 1995: "I have an aunt in Portland and other relatives in central Oregon. If I sense any hostility from people, I always throw my relatives at them."

Regardless of the strategy you adopt regarding the secret of your origins, a good sense of humor can help to diffuse any repugnance you may encounter. For example, in the early days of anti-California sentiments in Seattle, some immigrants from down south decided to proudly advertise their origins. They wore t-shirts featuring a California license plate that read: BLAME ME. Under the plate was the word "for" followed by a facetious list of offenses ranging from the introduction of tanning salons to the black plague. Self-directed humor that doesn't make fun of locals can ease the strain or pain when you have to admit where you're from.

Learn the local landscape

Once you've found a comfortable way to handle your California background, start becoming a local by learning about your new home. If you didn't grow up in your new state, you won't have the benefit of high school civics and state history classes. You probably won't know when the state was admitted to the union, who the local historical heroes and villains were, or even the name of the governor. It's also likely that you won't know the local social and political issues.

Most important—at least to covering your identity as an outsider—you won't know the local lingo. Every state and town has its own vernacular, its own slang terms and expressions. Learning the local jargon can help you understand and fit in with the locals. It also can help you avoid labeling yourself as an outsider by the way you pronounce place names. In an earlier chapter, I mentioned some of the puzzling terms I heard when we first moved to Las Vegas. If *you* move to Las Vegas, in addition to knowing that *Trop* is the name of a street and *RJ* one of the newspapers, you'll need to learn the proper way to pronounce Nevada. It's not Nev-ODD-dah, but *Nev-ADD-dah*. If you're going to Oregon, mispronouncing the name of one of the state's prominent rivers will immediately classify you as an outsider. *Will-AM-met*, not WILL-a-met, also is the name of a large valley, a local corporation, and a river that flows through Portland. Or perhaps you settle in Medford or another inland Oregon town and one day you decide to visit the ocean. If you say you're going to the *beach*, locals know you're from California; Oregonians go to *the coast*.

Where can you pick up local lingo? Just about anywhere. You only have to be alert to it. Should you hear something you don't understand, ask (discreetly, of course).

Television news also helps. Listen to Salt Lake City or Phoenix evening newscasts for a week or two, for instance, and you'll get a crash course in Utah-speak or Arizona-speak. (If you're planning to move to Texas, you'll have distinctive regional accents to cope with as well.) Newspapers also are a good source of local terminology, except that you don't get pronunciations in print.

The local news media is also an excellent source for information on local issues. Who are the movers and shakers in your community and state? Who holds the balance of political power? Who are the local wags? How are the local sports teams doing? What controversial issues are being debated in town? What's the latest gossip or scandal? These and other questions about your community are answered in the news media, particularly in your daily newspaper. If you read a local paper regularly before you move, you'll be able to hold up your end of a conversation on local issues the day you arrive in your new town.

Being knowledgeable about community issues and personalities not only permits you to engage in small talk, it also can give you insight into local feelings on controversial subjects. For example, in a number of Pacific Northwest towns you might want to consider who you're talking to before you expound your views (pro or con) on logging. By reading and listening, you can learn how the tide of local opinion flows.

If you want to go all the way with your local education, learn the geography and history of your new home state. The museums, state parks, libraries, galleries, and monuments of your new state can be the classrooms where you learn all about your new citizenship. For me, that was the most fun part of my Nevada education. On weekends my wife and I traveled around the Las Vegas area. On our first extended vacation in Nevada, we hit the back roads to find out what the Silver State was all about. We visited a newspaper museum in Eureka, poked into an active gold mine in Ruth, and hiked in the magnificent Ruby Mountains near Lamoille. In the state capital we toured the Carson City Mint and checked out the railroad museum. In Virginia City we sipped a beer in a bar Mark Twain frequented more than 100 years before.

Getting involved

The more you know about your new hometown, the more likely you are to get involved in it. Becoming an active part of their new community is the goal of many expatriates. Many who have settled into new hometowns strongly advise it. "Getting involved" may sound platitudinous, but the advice points to three goals that can make life worth living when you relocate: meeting people, making friends, and contributing to the well-being of your new community. The three goals are interrelated. By working—both through your job and volunteer opportunities—to improve your new town you will inevitably meet people and have an opportunity to make friends. And making friends can help you advance your career, and your ability to make more contributions.

When asked what they miss about California, most expatriates—particularly recent ones—say they same thing. It's not their jobs, their towns, or their favorite restaurants they miss the most; it's their friends. Transplants who spent many lonely months adjusting—and those who moved back to California— found it difficult to connect with locals. Idyllic weather and magnificent scenery are fine, but if your neighbor has a grudge against you, and you can't seem to find things in common with co-workers or others in the community, clear air and wonderful scenery can lose their attraction.

In a previous chapter I said that most people want to be friendly, but sometimes need an excuse. (For the people I talked with before and just after I moved, belonging to the same association was their reason for helping me.) The reverse of the theory can also work for you. You can use a variety of common bonds as your way to connect with others when you move. Working for the same company, belonging to the same community organization, or even playing golf at the same course can be your excuse to meet people you might not otherwise talk to. Special interest groups, charities, just living in the same neighborhood are all links to other people. When you relocate, you need to find or create those links. You need to take risks and be friendly. Meeting your neighbors is a good first step.

Painless ways to meet your neighbors

Meeting your neighbors can be an art. When you move into a new community, guard against perpetuating old urban habits—city ways that isolate you from those around you. For instance, it's not uncommon for city folks to come and go without so much as making eye contact with neighbors. One ex-Californian says he hardly knew his Golden State neighbors because they all came home and "went into the bat cave." What an apt analogy: Modern commuters drive home and, keeping their personas protected, punch the garage door remote control and drive—unidentified, if not unnoticed—into their bat caves. Holy isolationism! Isn't this the mind-set you want leave behind? To do that, take off your mask and enjoy your new Gotham.

To get you started, here are 10 ways that ex-California city dwellers can break the ice in their new neighborhoods. Not all of these ideas will be applicable in your situation. Use your common sense and try the following:

1. *Hang out in your front yard.* If you stay in your bat cave you're never going to meet anyone. Washing your car, tending to the flowers, installing a new mailbox—or just sitting on a porch—gives you opportunities to say hello to your neighbors. It also gives them an opportunity to stroll by and meet you.

2. *Watch for opportunities.* When your neighbor is washing his car, or taking out his trash, or even picking up his paper, it gives you a chance for a greeting. (Timing is important. When your neighbor is running his power lawn mower is not a good time.)

3. *Take walks.* Neighborhood strolling is the easiest and least stressful or contrived way to meet your neighbors. If you have a dog, so much the better; your pooch can be the first topic of conversation. Jogging, cycling, or skating in your neighborhood are other options, but the speed and intensity of these activities might keep you from lingering long enough to talk.

4. *Ask about local services.* When you move into a new house, condo, or apartment, you'll need to know about such things as trash collection, cable TV, and mail. Ask a neighbor. You also can talk to neighbors about school bus routes, local baby sitters, grocery stores, a dentist, and other necessities of family life.

5. *Volunteer to help.* Do you see a neighbor loading up a pickup or station wagon? Why not volunteer to help for a few minutes? Neighbors help neighbors; one way to meet and get to know yours is to volunteer to help. Rosser of Flagstaff says he met people after snowstorms, when he used his four-wheel drive vehicle to pull cars out of drifts.

6. *Welcome other newcomers.* If you're in a new development, you won't be the new family on the block for long. Welcome others with a plate of cookies; you'll have your newness in common. Use a variation of this if you relocate during a holiday. Call on established neighbors and share Christmas, Valentine, or Halloween cookies.

7. *Join a homeowners association committee.* Housing tracts, planned unit developments, and condominiums may have associations that need volunteers. At regular meetings you will meet and work with neighbors.

8. *Meet neighbors of neighbors.* Once you meet one or two neighbors, see if you can find ways to meet neighbors they know. Neighbors may invite you and other neighbors over for coffee, a drink, dinner, etc.

9. *Organize a Neighborhood Watch.* The first rule in suggesting anything in your new neighborhood is restraint. As the outsider, you don't want to insist, dictate, or push. Depending upon your area, however, a Neighborhood Watch could be welcomed by others. Fighting residential crime is a cause most people can agree upon. A start-up project such as this is best accomplished with others, rather than on your own. Make a suggestion and let a consensus form.

10. *Hold a block party or progressive dinner.* One of these projects can be an enormously enjoyable way to meet neighbors, but like the Neighborhood Watch idea, it's best done as part of a group. Incidentally, a progressive dinner—something I'd never heard of until one was organized by our Las Vegas neighbors—is a multi-site dinner party. One family hosts the neighbors for drinks; the whole group then walks to the next house for appetizers, then to the next house for salad, and so on until someone hosts the coffee and tea at the end of the meal.

Obviously this advice isn't necessary (or suitable) for everyone. If you're a natural joiner, or gregarious enough that you automatically generate opportunities to meet people, this advice may seem extraneous or superficial. In contrast to the stereotype of small-town people being standoffish, it is people with small-town backgrounds that seem to adjust the best when they leave California. One ex-Californian from a small town laughed when he was asked what techniques he used to meet his new neighbors. "I just talked to them," he said, as if finding some excuse to introduce yourself was silly.

Lee Taylor—who moved to Telluride, Colo., from the Bay Area— was originally from a small town in North Carolina. So adjusting to a tiny mountain community was easy for him. Taylor said that during the first winter that he and his wife were in their home in Mountain View (Calif.), they held a Christmas party for the neighborhood. "We wound up introducing people to each other who had lived there for years and not met," he says.

With that background, the Taylors moved easily from Mountain View to a Rocky Mountain view. "One of the reasons we moved up here was to get involved in the local community," he says. One way he met people was while writing grant proposals for the local school district. "The biggest plus for me here is the community. I've done such a range of interesting things in the past three years that I simply never would have thought of in California."

Involvement and meeting people go together. Who do you meet when you work on community service projects? People like you who are interested in helping others. They're often genuinely unselfish people who are content with themselves and looking for ways to help others.

Joining groups

So, how do you go about "getting involved?" The easiest place to start is at work. Your office or place of employment provides day-to-day opportunities to meet people. At lunches you can explore common interests and look for people with whom you and your spouse might like to socialize. Beyond the obvious social connections through work are business- or profession-sponsored organizations and events. After-work volleyball games, bowling teams, corporate golf tournaments, training classes, and even such standards as company parties and employee committees offer you chances to extend your circle of acquaintances. Any one of these activities—as well as others—could become a regular part of your life. You could become an officer of a company tennis league or help set up continuing-education classes at your office. If you and your spouse work for different organizations, you have twice the possibilities for work-related social activities. If you or your spouse is self-employed, or if for some other reason your work-related contacts are limited, then church and community organizations become more important.

Many ex-Californians joined a church (or synagogue) soon after they relocated. "The church is the main support," said Susan Gonzales. (She and her husband Gene, joined a church soon after they relocated to Chehalis, Wash.) Depending upon the size and denomination of your church, you may have a variety of involvement opportunities—from Bible study classes to bazaars to charity projects.

Beyond business- and church-related activities, most communities have hundreds of ways you can meet others who have things in common with you. Many expats choose charity or community work, but you could also join a computer club, political party group, or other special interest organization— or any combination.

Figure 14.1, an outline of settling-in strategy, includes a list of ways to get involved in your new community. For example, the Hessons, who moved to Sandpoint, Idaho, joined a country western dancing group. Pattie also enrolled in craft classes and Vern joined Kiwanis, having been an active Kiwanian in California.

When Anne and I moved to Las Vegas, I was self-employed so I knew I'd have to create opportunities to meet people and get involved. In addition to joining the local chapter of IABC (the business communicators group) I became a member of a Miata-owners club as well as a volunteer seminar leader for the American Cancer Society. In addition, I was elected to the board of directors of my homeowners association.

Joining the homeowners board is not something I set out to do. In fact, as a newcomer, I would not have presumed to run for the homeowners board, except for one thing: there were more vacancies than candidates. The development in which we lived was small, and only partially completed. Few families lived there, but a homeowners board was necessary, so I decided to try it.

After a few years in town, I also joined a Toastmasters club and became a member of a writers roundtable. All these organizations may seem to add up to a massive commitment. Occasionally I was excessively busy, but I wasn't active in all the groups at the same time. At times, my involvement in an organization amounted to attending a luncheon once a month. Other times I was setting up special events, conducting publicity drives, or—in the homeowners association—studying legal issues.

My involvement in these groups, coupled with a variety of local business organizations that my wife belonged to, helped me find some of the best friends I've ever had. Naturally, I didn't hit it off with everyone I met. But exploring different possibilities turned up rewarding volunteer work and gave me a chance to meet a variety of people in my new community.

If you need help in finding organizations, try your local newspaper or chamber of commerce. The *Las Vegas Review Journal,* for instance, runs a weekly column listing charity and community service organizations seeking help. In Vancouver, Wash., the newcomer package sent out by the chamber of commerce lists the phone number of the United Way, which serves as a clearing house for organizations that need volunteers. "Making new friends is an enriching way to become comfortable in your new home and new neighborhood," says the Vancouver chamber's booklet. "One of the most satisfying ways to meet new people is by serving as a volunteer. . . ."

If you have school-age children, it's important to help them find opportunities to make friends, too. As discussed in Chapter 2, if your children can learn in advance about the school they will be attending—and even about some of the local social norms—they will be more comfortable.

Helping your children settle in will yield benefits for the whole family. When Andy and Teresa Schneider moved from Southern California to Coeur d'Alene, Idaho, they quickly got their twin 11-year-old daughters involved in school track events. Within months the girls were winning awards and eventually represented their school in an Idaho regional meet.

School athletics, the PTA, and extra-curricular endeavors are all good ways for you to make friends. Whether you're coaching a Bobby Sox, Little League, or AYSO team, serving on a parents' committee, becoming a scout leader, or simply taking turns driving kids to team practice, you will meet parents and other local adults. As your children make friends in school, you'll likely have an opportunity to meet their friends' parents. Just *attending* a school sporting event is an opportunity to meet people. If your community supports local high school teams, for example, you will find people from all walks of life in the stands.

"We're heavily involved in PTA and sporting events in the community," says Susan Gonzales. "We've met wonderful people just by going to high school basketball games. It gives you a form of common bond."

Avoiding an attitude

Joining youth groups or other local organizations not only gives you an opportunity to meet people and feel a part of your community, it can head off hostility. Through charity or other volunteer work, you demonstrate your interest in the community and your willingness to help others. The attitude you display toward your new community will make a huge difference to long-time residents. "Do not try to tell people how it was in California and how things should be changed here," says ex-Bay Area resident Julien Wagenet, now of Santa Fe. "Fit in, or you'll be left out."

That advice is echoed by many California transplants in different states. "If you come here with the intention to assimilate and contribute [to the community], then where you come from is not an issue," says Taylor in Colorado. In Brookings, Ore., former Southern Californian Jim Frisch says, "I think if people up here know you're going to move here and blend in

Making friends and settling in
Here's a checklist of suggestions to help make the transition
to a new community easier.

Before you leave:
- ☐ Read newspapers from your destination town.
- ☐ Watch TV news when you visit your new hometown prior to moving.
- ☐ Read articles about your destination town.

Once you arrive:
- ☐ Replace California license plates.
- ☐ Learn the vernacular.
- ☐ Meet your neighbors.
- ☐ Smile and be friendly, but don't push.
- ☐ Follow local trends, such as how to dress when you go out for dinner.
- ☐ Find other escapees with whom you have things in common.
- ☐ Don't lose touch with friends back home.
- ☐ Avoid saying, "Back in California, we used to do it this way."
- ☐ Don't criticize local customs.
- ☐ Use your big-city business advantages with care.
- ☐ Don't focus attention on your origins by asking others where they're from.

Volunteer, join, get involved:
- ☐ Use your business opportunities to meet people at:
  Conferences, seminars, meetings with clients/customers;
  Company sponsored athletic events, employee committees, parties
- ☐ Service clubs: Kiwanis, Civitan, Rotary, Lions, etc.
- ☐ Fraternal organizations: Elks, Eagles, Knights of Columbus, etc.
- ☐ Charities
  Many local newspapers publish listings of volunteer opportunities.
  Check with your local chamber of commerce, United Way.
- ☐ Junior chambers of commerce
- ☐ Church, church committees
- ☐ Political party organizations

☐ Special interest clubs:

Photography, computers, sewing, crafts, gardening, cooking, dog obedience, woodwork, travel, sports, ballroom and square dancing, etc.

☐ Twelve-step support groups

☐ School, youth activities with/for your children:

Bobby Sox, Little League, Pop Warner, AYSO, PTA, dance, drama, band, special events, fund raising, remedial classes, after-school activities

☐ Adult education/community college classes

To fit in:

☐ Enjoy your surroundings. Take advantage of local recreational opportunities.

☐ Initially, avoid refusing social invitations. Don't give the impression you're not interested.

☐ Smile at people and be ready to volunteer.

☐ Cultivate a positive attitude.

☐ Slow down and go with the flow. Enjoy the slower pace.

Figure 14.1 This list focuses on the social side of your move. Lists and suggestions in other chapters cover job- and house-hunting and preparing for the movers.

with their community, they have no problem with that. But if you're com-ing up here to change things, that's what they don't want."

For years Frisch and his family lived in the small San Bernardino County community of Yucaipa. They moved to the Oregon coast when the conges-tion and smog of the greater Los Angeles area reached their once-isolated California community. Before he left Yucaipa, Frisch experienced a newcomer attitude that doesn't win the esteem of longtime residents anywhere. He was mowing his front yard one day in Yucaipa and a new neighbor came by. She asked him to sign a petition to get rid of a local chicken ranch. Frisch reported the subsequent exchange this way:

"She wanted me to sign a petition to get rid of Hoover's Chicken Ranch. I chatted with her and asked her where she was from. She said Orange County. I said: 'Why do you want to get rid of the chicken ranch?' She said: 'The flies up here are terrible.' I said: 'Didn't you notice that when you first came up?" She said, 'Well not really, but we notice it now.'

"I said: 'Do you know Rick Hoover? No? Well I went to high school with him. Did you know his father and his grandfather operated that ranch?'"

"Because of an inconvenience," says Frisch, "the woman wanted to get rid of a three-generation family livelihood."

Ugly Californians

When you move, remember, not all the California expatriates before you were sensitive to local traditions. As a result, you may have to overcome a negative reputation established for you by other ex-Golden Staters. A recent manifestation of the "ugly Californian" appeared in southern Nevada. According to KVBC-TV channel 3 in Las Vegas, California attorneys who spe-cialize in construction litigation have started moving into Nevada. They file lawsuits against Las Vegas builders on behalf of new homeowners. The home-owner suits stem from various alleged construction flaws in new homes. The station's news report gives an example of one California attorney who started prospecting for clients among new home buyers while he studied for the Nevada Bar exam. Four times as many California attorneys passed Nevada's Bar exam in 1996 as in 1991.

In addition to being alert to the possible effects of ugly Californians, guard against becoming one yourself—even accidentally. For example, in business or social situations you may find local practices that seem inefficient, too com-plicated, or just plain unnecessary. But unless you want to risk alienation, forego telling people that the way you used to do it back in San Diego is better. Or that in San Francisco you would never have done it that way. This advice sounds so self-evident as to be superfluous. Unfortunately, it's easy to slip and let a, "here's how we did it in California," pass your lips. Bite your tongue; minor physical pain is a fair exchange for maintaining goodwill. If this point is not crystal clear, imagine for a moment that you're meeting with a new co-worker in your present office. How would you react if he told you he didn't understand what you were doing and offered to show you how they do it in New York.

Ultimately, your California way of doing things may not even *be* better. Other ways of doing things may be appropriate for other cities in other states. Different is not synonymous with wrong. If the pace is a little slower than you're used to, relax and enjoy it. If you want a high-pressure job, stay in California.

One difference that delights ex-Californians—in smaller cities and towns from the Oregon coast to the New Mexico plains—is that work is not the beginning and end of life. Instead, emphasis on family activities, recreation, and outdoors seems to be a common denominator. Business people are no less professional; they just don't take a cell phone and fax machine to bed with them. Even Las Vegas, a city of about one million people—which has one of the highest number of cell phones per capita in the U.S.—has a slower pace than urban California. Says Glenn of Fort Collins, "In California, people are interested in money. It's number one. Here hunting and fishing are number one and two; money is about number 10."

A slower pace may take getting use to, but it's worth the effort. Take the time to talk with people you meet for the first time and to say hello to people you already know. When you first move in, make a special effort to accept social invitations. You don't want to give the impression that you don't want to socialize. Even if you don't want to be Mr. or Ms. Civic Responsibility, and you are comfortable with limited social outlets, take time for people. The consideration you offer will be returned.

First aid for homesickness

No matter how hard you try to socialize and fit in, you may be homesick at times. You'll go through a period of adjustment. Some people are lonely for friends, others miss the daily routines of California life. Regaining your balance or making your life more harmonious may take a little time. Here are a dozen tips to help you adjust:

1. Expand your social circle. At first, living in your new hometown will seem strange because you know so few people. Your social circle will revolve around work. Find opportunities early to meet people outside your place of employment. Even shopping at the same supermarket and getting to recognize the store employees will help make you feel at home.

2. Subscribe to a California paper. If you're in a small town, with an equally small newspaper, and you miss the scope of the *L.A. Times, San Jose Mercury*

News, etc.—subscribe. After a while, however, you probably will adjust to the local paper. You'll take pleasure in seeing stories about people you actually know. How many times have you seen the names of people you know in an urban California paper? In St. George, Utah, or Las Cruces, N.M., if your neighbor gets a big promotion, opens a new business, wins a civic award, or even catches a record trout, you'll see his or her name in the paper. If you still hunger for detailed national news, you can read news magazines, the *Wall Street Journal,* or *USA Today.*

3. Get satellite TV. If you miss your favorite California sports team, you can follow them via satellite TV. With the explosion of sports stations, you may even be able to follow your California team on standard cable TV. Satellite or cable TV may also give you access to local California programming and news.

4. Shop by mail or the Web. The Hessons, of Sandpoint, Idaho, didn't do much catalog shopping when they lived in California. But now they buy things through the mail when they cannot find them in their new hometown. "Shopping is limited in a small town," says Pattie. "Everything from curtains to car parts has to be ordered."

If you haven't browsed through a mail-order catalog in a while, you'll be surprised at the variety and quality of merchandise you'll find. From the giant mail-order clothing merchants—such as Lands' End, L.L. Bean, and Spiegel, Inc.—to speciality catalogs such as Wireless, which sells old-time radio programs on tape, you can find just about anything you need. If you're connected to the World Wide Web, your options are multiplied. Most large mail-order firms have Web sites and new, specialty Web merchants offer unique services. For example, Web-based music merchant "CD Now" offers more than 160,000 different selections. And it lets you read reviews and listen to the music before you buy.

5. Go back for a fix of what you miss. Although he loves Nevada, Mark Dorio says he and his family visit Los Angeles occasionally. They browse in Westwood bookstores and eat in their favorite Los Angeles restaurants. Depending on where you relocate, you could go to Denver, Phoenix, or elsewhere for your big-city fix.

6. Avoid remorse. If you return to California for a visit, look at your old hometown realistically. Remember that you probably won't be driving during rush hour. You will probably be on vacation so you will not have any business concerns. Although you may not have had much time to visit friends when you lived in California, when you return, friends will make time for you. The harder your adjustment in a new state is, the rosier your old California haunts may seem.

7. Stay busy. Loneliness is a problem for some people who move. Staying busy is often the best antidote. After Jim and Kathy Frisch had moved to Brookings, Ore., in 1993, Jim went through a period of depression. At first he was involved in running his Shaklee distribution business long-distance and building a home. After a year, when their home was completed, and he was less busy, Jim says he took a number of trips back to California. Ostensibly the trips were about his Shaklee business, but really they were about his uncertainty.

"Eventually," he says, "I realized that what I was missing was not reality, but the old days that I couldn't go back to. A lot of my friends had moved out too." As his level of activity picked up again, so did his spirits. The family has since bought a Brookings restaurant that keeps him exceedingly busy and happy.

8. Let your kids stay in touch with California friends. While you're providing many opportunities for your children to connect with local kids, letting them stay in contact with friends left behind will help in the transition. Phone calls, letters, e-mail, and, if feasible, even a visit, are ways your children can keep in touch with old friends while they make new ones. You can do the same thing.

9. Have California friends and relatives come for a visit. Expatriates say their visits with family and friends—either in their new hometown or back in California—are often more enjoyable than before they left. Visits out of state usually last several days, so they allow you more time with friends and relatives than you normally would spend when you live in the same city.

Depending upon where you go, you may find that many people want to come for a visit. When we moved to Las Vegas, we heard from people we hadn't seen in years.

10. Expect to be noticed. During the time that Andy Schenider was moving his small company from Southern California to north Idaho, his progress was regularly reported in the local newspaper. He says he received more publicity in Idaho in a few months than he did during the years he'd operated the business in Southern California. In a small town, such as Post Falls, Idaho, where Schneider moved his business, any company relocating from another state is news. This doesn't mean that you're going to get press coverage just for moving into a small town. It does mean that a small town affords you little opportunity to be anonymous.

11. Learn to appreciate your new surroundings. This too, is a matter of slowing down and taking time. The United States is filled with so much natural beauty you won't have to look far to find the treasures all around you. Even if you move to an area that seems austere, you may just have to look a little deeper.

When we moved from Orange County to the Nevada desert, we traded an area where the vegetation is brown much of the year to an area that didn't seem to have *any* vegetation. It's there; it just took us a while to appreciate it and to realize that desert plants are different—they have to be to survive. Yucca, ocotillo, mesquite, cholla, and hundreds of other desert plants have a complex ecological system for survival. Life in the desert is just as marvelous as it is anywhere else—maybe more so, because conditions can be harsh.

12. Acclimate yourself physically. If you live at high altitude, what you think is homesickness could be something else. Many cities and towns in the West are thousands of feet high. Denver and Albuquerque are a mile high. Santa Fe, N.M., and Flagstaff, Ariz., are 7,000 feet high. These altitudes adversely affect some people. According to Lovelace Health Systems of New Mexico, altitude sickness is puzzling because of its unpredictability. Living at high altitude means thinner air and the increased need to use sunscreen. The air is usually drier, so there's more chance of dehydration. People also experience a decreased tolerance for alcohol. If you have a physical condition that may be affected by high altitude, or if you think you may be suffering from altitude sickness, consult your doctor.

Staying for good?

If, in spite of your best efforts, you just can't make a go of it in your new town—economically, socially, or emotionally—you have two choices: move back to California, or move on to somewhere else. Maybe the idea of moving is still strong—you just need a different destination. Even if you move back to California, as some people have done, it's likely that you will have gained much for your investment of time. You'll have some understanding of another state and another town. You may even have a better understanding of yourself.

But don't let a temporary period of loneliness discourage you. Thousands of transplanted Californians have felt homesick, but they stayed put and found satisfaction in a new life. Cynics may tell you that you'll be forced to move back, just like thousands of others. "I hear people saying that all the time—that the ex-Californians are moving back," says Frisch of Oregon. "And I always ask: 'Who's moving back?' I don't get too many names."

"We are very pleased with our decision," says Glenn Sweitzer, formerly of Burbank, now of Nashville. "Everybody thought we would not last a year here, that we'd come crawling back to California. I think not. We're here to stay."

Appendix

Internet research basics

The World Wide Web is a marvelous research tool. If you already know the fundamentals of using the Web, you can skip this appendix. If you're new to Web research, what follows may be helpful—it's a beginner's look at finding information.

Before you can use the Web, you must, of course, have access to it. If you don't, consider getting it. Many excellent books, CDs, and videos are available to get you started. Or you can shorten your learning time by enlisting the aid of a knowledgable friend or co-worker.

Finding information on the Web is mostly a matter of moving from one Web page or site to another, reading the material you find, then moving on for more. Here are ways you can first locate a Web site, then maneuver around.

1. *Type in the address (URL).* When you start a search, you'll begin by activating your World Wide Web browser, (such as NetScape Navigator or Microsoft Internet Explorer.) If you know the precise Web address you wish to visit, type in that address in the proper line on your browser screen. (Addresses usually begin with http://.) Be sure to write the exact address; missing one slash or period will keep you from finding your location.

2. *As appropriate, click on "forward" or "next" page buttons.* You find these buttons at the sites you visit. (Some sites lead you from one page to the next with prompts.)

3. *Click on a link.* Highlighted or underlined words on Web-site screens indicate that by clicking the word, you can be transported to another site to find related information. Some sites, for example, consist mainly of lists of other sites plus links to them. (Many city, chamber of commerce, and real estate sites feature lists of links.)

4. *Use a bookmark.* To save yourself the trouble of retyping an address site every time you want to go to it, use your browser to bookmark the site.

Bookmarked sites appear in a special list in your browser software. You can return to any bookmarked site by clicking on the bookmark name. (Your browser contains instructions on how to establish and use your list of bookmarked sites.)

5. *Click forward or back.* When you move from one Web page to another, the pages you visit usually are logged within your computer's memory. You can return to any logged page by clicking the back button on your browser. Once you sign off the Web and end a session, however, you lose the ability to return to these pages via the back button; hence the value of bookmarks.

6. *Use a search engine.* For most Web research, your first stop will be a search engine. These sites are online indexes. They find the addresses of sites for you, based upon criteria (key words or phrases) you supply.

Using a search engine

To find information on the Web when you don't know the exact address, use a search engine. (Type in the search-engine address on the appropriate line on your browser, and hit the return key.) Many search engines contain helpful hints on the way to effectively structure a search. For example, if you want information on Colorado, you could simply type in the name of the state. But using most search engines, that would lead to thousands of Web sites. With *Alta Vista* (which indexes titles, topics, and text in Web sites) a "Colorado" search yields more than one million responses. You might as well go to a library and start with the first book on the first shelf and keep going, book by book, until you find what you're looking for. Narrowing your search—by using more specific terms in your query— produces more manageable results. It is essential to use words specific enough to find what you want but broad enough that you get at least a few responses. For example, using the search engine *HotBot*, a "Colorado" search yields more than 600,000 responses. A "Colorado employment" search yields 33,000, but searching for "Colorado employment, sales" yields a manageable 60 replies.

Web addresses for popular search engines:

Alta Vista *http://www.altavista.digital.com*

Yahoo *http://www.yahoo.com*

Lycos *http://www.lycos.com*

Excite *http://www.excite.com*

HotBot *http://www.hotbot.com*

New-generation search engines:

LookSmart *http://looksmart.com*

Meta-crawler *http://metacrawler.cs.washington.edu*

Capturing information

When you want to save the information you see on your screen, you have two options: printing or downloading. Your browser has a button for each function. Printing out material allows you to read it at any time and also to share it with others.

If you're gathering large quantities of information, downloading will be faster than printing—almost instantaneous. You can print it out later. To download, click on the proper button. You can download to your hard drive, floppy, or removable disk cartridge.

Web terminology

Browser A software program that allows you to move from one Web site to another. Netscape Navigator and Microsoft Internet Explorer are two examples.

Home page The main or entry page for accessing a Web site. Usually it's the first page you see when you log on to a Web address. From there you can move to all the other pages that make up that personal, company, or organization site.

Link A connection that allows you, with a click of a mouse, to move instantly from one URL or Web site to another. Links also let you move to separate pages within a single Web site. Usually highlighted text on a Web page indicates that there is an underlying link to the information referenced. When you move your cursor to a highlighted word and the arrow changes to a pointing finger, you know there is a link.

Mailing List Not to be confused with unsolicited e-mail lists, a mailing list is like a newsgroup. The difference is that all the messages are sent to group members via e-mail, rather than being posted at a site.

Newsgroup Also called usenet newsgroup. A group of people who share an interest in a particular subject and who read (and sometimes post) messages about that topic. Newsgroups are organized around any of thousands of subjects from architecture to zoology.

Search engine A Web site that offers index-like information about Web sites and Web-site content. You usually use a search engine by typing in a topic, name, or other words, and then having the engine scan its index of Web sites for those words.

URL Uniform Resource Locator, another term for Web address.

Visitor In Web lingo, someone who logs onto a Web site.

Appendix

Company relocation

Want to move your company or get your company to move?

While you're pondering how you, personally, can move out of state, economic development specialists in other states are thinking how they can entice entire companies out of California. More than two dozen organizations in the West are engaged in the business of luring companies from California.

Competition among out-of-state corporation raiders can be intense. At stake are thousands of jobs and millions of dollars in state and local taxes. Incoming companies help diversify local economics, create employment, and support other area businesses—from construction companies to stationery stores to restaurants. Representatives of Western states' economic development groups agree that California state and local governments have revised many policies and regulations previously unfriendly to business. ("Basically," says one executive of a relocated company, "we were encouraged to move.") San Diego, for example, has cut its business fees substantially and the governor and state legislature are trying to improve the state's image among business. But that hasn't halted inquiries from California companies—still a large portion of the business for out-of-state raiders.

Nevada has been a leader in attracting California firms; about half of the companies that relocated to Nevada in the 1990s came from California. The percentage of California relocations is smaller in Arizona, but the Golden State still provides more new operations to Arizona than does any other state. And, in 1996, the number of jobs created in Arizona through California relocations increased.

The business of stealing companies, transplanting them from one tax base to another, is little-publicized in California. But it can hold some positive implications for you and your plans to move. First, the relocation of hundreds of California companies during the past 10 years means that no matter what size town you're considering—from Phoenix, Ariz., to Drain, Ore., (population 1,011)—you're likely to find former California companies. Second, the continuing economic migration means that moving out with your company is at least a possibility, albeit a remote one. Third, if you're a company executive, or occasionally have the big boss's ear, economic development experts from other cities and states have news for you.

Why leave California?

Reasons for leaving vary depending upon the company and the destination. Bill Torres, president of Serrot Corporation, which moved from Huntington Beach to Henderson, Nev., near Las Vegas, in 1993, can quickly rattle off a list of reasons why his plastics manufacturing firm bailed out:

• No corporate or personal income tax in Nevada.

• Low industrial real estate costs. Depending on the area, says Torres, "I could buy ten acres in Nevada for the price of one acre in Southern California."

• Cheaper electrical power. Torres says the process his firm uses to make plastic is energy intensive. "Our energy costs here are a half million dollars. In California, it would have cost us a $1 million a year in energy."

• Rail access. Very few sites in Southern California, says Torres, would provide a rail siding. In Henderson the company has a siding that can accommodate 14 rail cars at once.

• Low residential real estate prices. "Our employees could buy a house for considerably less than in California." Torres said several clerical employees who moved with the company became first-time home owners in Nevada. "They were paying $800 to $900 a month in rent in Southern California. Here they bought $90,000 to $100,000 homes and their payments were $600."

• Friendly business climate. "We closed escrow on January 3 and had the factory operating on July 12," says Torres. "In California we would still have been looking for the permits . . . doing environmental impact studies, and going through the bureaucracy."

• Sales-tax payment plan. When the company relocated, it bought $6 million in new equipment. Nevada allowed the company to pay the sales taxes over a five-year period.

With financial incentives, clear skies, and uncrowded roads as bait, corporation raiders from Nevada and other states have been trolling for California companies. Many of the development groups—such as the Greater Tucson Economic Council, the Economic Development Corporation of Utah, and the Seattle-King County Economic Development Council—are hybrid organizations funded by private and public sources.

Theoretically, every local chamber of commerce is also in the running to attract corporations. And in at least two Western states, Utah and Washington, each county has an economic development director (or someone with that function as a part of his or her job). Usually though, it's the larger development groups—sometimes working in conjunction with local chambers—that land the big fish.

Economic-development organizations use trade-show exhibits and various other techniques to attract the attention of California executives. Direct mail and trade journal advertising are two tools used by the Arizona Department of Commerce, according to Steve Vierck, the department's national marketing director. Vierck says when companies respond to the advertising, his department follows up with calls and visits to California. Inquiries generated from trade-journal advertising declined in 1995-96, Vierck says, but Arizona still heard from nearly 200 California companies. He says his department also reaches companies by staying in contact with relocation consultants who are hired by companies interested in moving.

The simple technique of cold calling yields results for Bob Potter, president of Jobs Plus, a small economic-development organization headquartered in Coeur d'Alene, Idaho. Potter got started by calling company presidents. He says he began with no leads and just zeroed in on small- to medium-sized companies. Potter looked for companies that were financially strong and that manufactured products that were not dependent on a specific location. He wanted companies that could ship their products out of state and bring revenue and jobs into the state. He also looked for companies that were in "high-cost areas." Southern California was a match for this last criteria.

"To get our foot in the door," Potter says, "we would do a business case study of Idaho vs. California. And obviously that comparison came out heavily in our favor," he says.

Varying his strategy little in seven years, Potter attracted about 50 companies to the Coeur d'Alene area, nearly all from Southern California. Potter's biggest prize is Harpers, an office furniture manufacturer that moved from Torrance. The company's 470,000 sq. ft. plant, just off Interstate 90 in Post Falls, Idaho, employs nearly 500 people. Potter, himself an ex-San Franciscan, says that today he has widened his scope to recruit from other states as well, but California remains a major target.

Companies seek benefits

If you've already begun to plan your family relocation, you have an idea how complex the task can be. Now imagine the difficulties in moving an entire company from one state to another. Even with business-friendly governments inviting companies in, the decision to move is complicated and challenging. And once a decision is made, it often cannot be implemented for months or even years, until myriad issues are resolved. According to company executives and state economic development directors, corporate officials should consider these factors when contemplating a move:

• Fewer or less onerous regulations on business in general— with emphasis on environmental requirements.

• Workers compensation insurance rates lower than California.

• Help in working with the various levels of government that regulate and/or tax business.

• A skilled work force.

• Reasonable labor costs.

• Housing for officers and employees at lower costs than in California.

• Availability of low-cost land, or existing office/industrial space.

• Convenient transportation for people, raw materials, and finished goods.

• Vendors who can supply raw materials, products, and services.

• Abundant supplies of energy and water at reasonable prices.

• Local colleges and training programs.

• A local armed services base that can be a source of employees in the form of military spouses.

• Conditions that contribute to a satisfying quality of life.

John Teets, vice president of the Wilkinson Co., a small dental-products company in north Idaho, says his firm conducted detailed research before relocating from Southern California in mid-1994. Many economic factors such as wages, taxes, regulations, property values, and workers compensation costs were charted on a grid. Teets says his team researched locations in Arizona, Utah, Washington, Colorado, Oregon, and Idaho. They narrowed their list to four cities, then visited those locations and met with local officials before making a decision.

Incentives

The National Business Development program of Utah posts a list of the state's business advantages on its Web site. Custom training, a computerized job-matching system, and enterprise zones are among the benefits listed. Enterprise zones, available in a number of states, are typically districts of lower income and higher unemployment than surrounding areas. States offer tax incentives to companies to locate in the zones.

In the Pacific Northwest, cities promote the availability of water and low energy costs, two attributes attractive to semiconductor manufacturers, among others. Austin, Texas, emphasizes its high-tech community which, according to the Austin chamber's Economic Development Division, spends $1.4 billion annually on research and development. Arizona and Nevada cities stress their proximity to California markets via interstate trucking. Arizona also has a low unionization rate. Las Vegas offers access to high-tech companies from all over the world at the huge electronics conventions held twice annually in town. Portland offers access to the Pacific rim via its port. But among all the reasons that companies relocate, the most persuasive probably are tax credits and rebates.

Corporate relocation is not without opposition in some target states, however. According to opponents, tax credits or tax abatement that entice companies, reduce the money a city has to create infrastructure. Yet more companies mean greater demand on local municipal services. Community leaders may oppose a relocation when an incoming company is not planning to hire a large percentage of its employees locally or make substantial infrastructure improvements. Economic development officials also say that some companies use periodic relocation as part of their strategic business plans. Once tax incentives are used up, the company may ask for more tax credits, threatening to move again if credits are denied.

For more information on corporate relocation, contact the economic development authority in your target area. Development specialists can provide you with reams of information, including the names of officials at companies that have already relocated. The resources section that follows includes some of the many agencies available. To gather business relocation information for a city or area not listed, contact the nearest chamber of commerce and ask for the number of the local economic-development agency.

Resources

Arizona Department of Commerce
3800 N. Central Suite 1400
Phoenix, AZ 85012
(602) 280-1300

Economic Development Division, Greater Austin Chamber of Commerce
P.O. Box 1967
Austin, TX 78767-1967
(512) 322-5608

Greater Tucson Economic Council
33 N. Stone Suite 800
Tucson, AZ 85701
(520) 882-6079
http://www.futurewest.com/gtec/history.htm

Idaho Department of Commerce
700 W. State St.
Boise, ID 83720-0093
(208) 334-2470
http://www.idoc.state.id.us

Jobs Plus
202 Sherman Ave.
Coeur d'Alene, ID 83814
(208) 667-4753

Nevada Development Authority
3773 Howard Hughes Parkway Suite 140-S
Las Vegas, NV 89109
(702) 791-0000

Portland Development Commission
1120 S. W. Fifth Ave. Suite 1100
Portland, OR 97204
(503) 823-3200

Seattle-King County Economic Development Council
701 5th Ave. Suite 2510
Seattle, WA 98104
(206) 386-5040

Spokane Area Economic Development Council
221 N. Wall St. Suite 310
Spokane, WA 99210-0203
(509) 624-9285

Utah Department of Community and Economic Development
National Business Development
324 S. State Street Suite 500
Salt Lake City, UT 84114
(801) 538-8800
http://www.ce.ex.state.ut.us/national/welcome.htm

**Washington Department of Community,
Trade and Economic Development**
101 General Administration Bldg. AX-13
Olympia, WA 98504
(206) 753-5630

Index

A

Adjustable Rate Mortgages (ARM), 153-154
Advertising
    newspapers, 44-45
    strategy for selling your home, 120, 130-131
    your home on the Internet, 132
Aggravated assault
    number of offenses known to police by city, 50
    rates by city, 48-49
Alaska
    Anchorage, 213-214
    profile, 211-213
    visitor information addresses, 230
Animals, and moving, 175
Anti-California sentiment. see Caliphobia
Appraisals, 123
Arizona
    Phoenix, 185-186
    profile, 184-185
    Tucson, 187-188
    visitor information addresses, 207
ARM. see Adjustable Rate Mortgage
Associations
    finding employment in your field, 88-89
    real estate, on the Internet, 142
    see also Organizations

B

Beale, Calvin, rural migration trends, 6
Bolles, R. N., finding employment through college connections, 90
Brainstorming
    relocation priorities, 14-16
    résumé writing, 78-79
Brubaker, Suzzanne, financial planning advice, 20-22
Budgets, 20-21
Burglary

    number of offenses known to police by city, 50
    rates by city, 48-49
Business
    advantages in smaller towns, 71
    plan summary, 105-106
    publications, 116-117, 118
    start-up kits, 107
Business opportunities
    company relocation, 256
    newsgroups, 95
Buy-out packages, 137
Buyer's market, defined, 145
Buying a home
    applying for a mortgage, 150-152
    avoiding Caliphobia, 234
    bargain homes, 162
    closing, 164-165
    considerations, 139, 156-158
    disclosure statements, 160
    finding an out-of-state real estate agent, 145-147
    inspections, 159-161
    Internet resources, 143, 144
    new homes, 161-162
    pre-approval, 152
    publications, 140-141, 148, 166
    real estate attorneys, 160
    termites, 161
    types of loans and lenders, 154-155
    video tours, 144
    vs. renting, 140
    World Wide Web sites, 142

C

Caliphobia
    attitude, 243, 246
    destination research, 234
    emigrants' expectations, 2, 74-75, 233
    finding employment, 91
    fitting in, 235-236

reasons for, 9-10
"ugly Californians," 246-247
Car theft
    number of offenses known to police by
        city, 50
    rates by city, 48-49
Chambers of Commerce
    addresses in the Northwest, 230-232
    addresses in the Southwest, 207-209
    destination research, 32, 43, 52
    finding employment, 92
    Internet resources, 34-35, 36
    job market information, 101
    Service Corps of Retired Executives, 107
Checklists
    checking out your potential hometown,
        54
    making friends and settling in, 244-245
    pre-move financial checklist, 19
Children
    circle the city game, 30-31
    destination research, 55-56
    fitting in, 243
    homesickness, 249
    involving in relocation plans, 23, 25-27
    movers, 175
    selling your home, 128
City networks on the Internet, 35-36
Classified ads
    destination research, 44-45
    finding employment, 94
    on the Internet, 95
    selling your home, 131
Climate
    considerations, 62-63
    destination research, 42-43, 56
    publications, 43, 57
    quality of life factor, 17, 60
    resources, 57
    for selected cities, 64-65
    vs. pollution, 66
    weather terms defined, 65
CMA. see Comparative Market Analysis
Cold calling, 90
Colorado
    Colorado Springs, 190
    Denver, 188-189
    Fort Collins, 189-190
    Grand Junction, 191-192
    profile, 188-189
    Pueblo, 190-191
    visitor information addresses, 207

Commissions
    real estate agents, 147
    when selling your own home, 120-121
Community involvement
    fitting in, 238-239
    joining groups, 1, 241-242
    vs. privacy, 69-71
Company relocation
    considerations, 257-258
    corporation raiders, 255-256
    economic-development organizations, 254
    reasons for, 7-8, 256-257
Comparative Market Analysis (CMA), 121,
        122-123
Contracts
    buying a home, 158
    movers, 171-172
Corporation raiders, 55-256
Cost of living
    destination research, 51-52
    financial planning, 20-21
    Internet resources, 51-52
    publications, 51-52, 58
    quality of life factor, 18
    resources, 58
    trade-offs, 71, 73
Cost of living index for selected cities, 72-73
Covenants, conditions, and restrictions
        (CC & Rs), 157-158
Cover letters
    answering classified ads, 94
    headhunters, 103
    résumé writing, 81-82
Credit and financial planning, 21
Credit history, financing a home, 152
Crime, quality of life factor, 17
Crime rates
    FBI Uniform Crime Report per 100,000
        inhabitants, 48-49
    number of offenses known to police, 50
    publications, 47
    World Wide Web sites, 57-58
Cultural opportunities
    quality of life factor, 17
    quality vs. accessibility, 68-69
Curb appeal, 127-128
Customs, local
    Jaramillo, Debbie, 10
    fitting in, 237

D

Debt consolidation, 21

Debt ratio, 150
Demographics
  Internet resources, 51
  publications, 118
  quality of life factor, 18
  resources, 58
  starting a business, 108, 118
Destination research
  avoiding Caliphobia, 234, 235
  chambers of commerce, 32
  checklist, 54
  circle the city game, 30-31
  climate, 42-43
  company transfers, 85-86
  cost of living, 51-52
  crime rates, 47-51
  demographics, 51
  getting started, 29-30
  "Great Towns With Great Jobs," 6
  home-swapping groups, 52
  "Hottest Cities," 5-6
  Internet resources, 31-32, 33-37
  making the trip, 52-53, 55-56
  mapping software, 31
  newspapers, 44-45
  publications, 33, 41
  quality of life factors, 17
  resources, 32
  school districts, 45-46
  seasonal changes, 56
  telephone books, 43-44
  World Wide Web sites, 39-41
Destinations
  dissatisfaction with choice, 250-251
  expectations, 61-62, 74-76
  quality of life factors, 29-30
  see also States
Dickson, Pandra, involving your children in
    your relocation plans, 25-26
Directories
  destination research, 41
  finding employment out of state, 98
Disability insurance. *see* Insurance
Disclosure statement
  buying a franchise, 108, 110
  buying a home, 160
  selling your home, 119, 126
Dyer, Wayne, advice on idealizing, 61-62

E

E-mail, finding employment, 85, 97
Economic-development organizations, 257

Economy
  corporate relocation, 7
  quality of life factor, 17
Education
  changing careers, 101
  quality of life factor, 17
  questions to ask new school district, 46
  ratings by state, 38
  résumé writing, 78-79, 80-81
  World Wide Web sites, 47, 57
  see also Schools
Emigration
  most popular destinations, 5-6
  company reasons for leaving California,
    256-257
  personal reasons for leaving California,
    xiii, xv, 1, 2, 5-6
  statistics, 1-2, 3
Employee Relocation Council
  Real estate agents, 146
  relocation costs, 136-137
Employment
  assistance for spouse, 87
  buying a business, 110-111
  buying a franchise, 108-110
  Caliphobia, 91
  changing careers, 100-104
  finding employment in your field, 88-90
  Internet resources, 94-98
  interviewing techniques, 82-84
  methods for finding employment out of
    state, 77
  networking, 84-85, 90-91
  publications, 98, 104, 113
  quality of life factor, 17
  résumé writing, 78-79
  starting a business, 104-108
  state agencies, 99
  taking your job with you, 111-112
  telecommuting, 87
  testing of job market, 90-91
  transfers, 85-86
  the two-salary family, 77, 87-88
Environment/health World Wide Web sites,
    59
Escape Manual
  How to use, 11-12
  purpose of, xiv
  who should read, xiii
Escape plan
  elements of, 11-12
  establishing priorities, 14-15

financial planning, 19-23
involving your children, 23, 25-27
"Plan B," 18
quality of life, 15-17
real estate information, 140
Escrow companies, 165
Experience
changing careers, 101
résumé writing, 80

F

Federal agencies
moving, 181
small businesses, 110, 115-116
FHA loans, 155
Financial planners, Brubaker, Suzzanne,
20-22
Financial planning
business plans, 106
checklist, 19
cost of living, 20
insurance, 21
investments, 22
liabilities, 21
publications, 27
software, 20
wills, 22
Financial statements, buying a franchise,
109-110
Financing
formula, 135-136, 150
options when selling your home, 135
pre-approval, 152
qualifying factors, 150-152
types of loans and lenders, 153
Fitting in
avoiding Caliphobia, 235
community involvement, 238-239
local customs, 10, 237
local history, 10, 236, 238
local lingo, 237
making friends, 16, 243
small towns vs. big cities, 70
Fixed-rate mortgages, 154-155
Foreclosures, 162, 164
Fourth grade reading by state, 38
Franchises, 108-110
Frequently asked questions, starting a
business, 105-106

G

Geography, quality of life factor, 173
Goals
brainstorming, 14, 15, 16
business plans, 105
evaluation exercises, 16
Government
regulations and corporate relocation, 8
services trade-offs, 67-68
Groceries, cost of living for selected cities,
72-73
Growth
hazards of, 71
history of in California, 3-4
in Western states, 5-6
see also Population

H

Hawaii, profile, 196-197
Headhunters, 103-104
Health care
cost of living for selected cities, 72-73
facilities, quality of life factor, 17
Health/environment World Wide Web sites,
59
Help-U-Sell, 121
Hileman, Jack, corporate relocation and
regulation differences, 8
History
of growth in California, 3-4
learning about your new state, 236-237
Home loans. *see* Mortgages
Home price index for selected cities, 124-125
Home-based business resources, 111-112
Home-swapping groups
destination research, 52
World Wide Web sites, 58-59
Homesickness
moving back to California, 250-251
tips for curing, 247-250
House prices
average sales price for selected cities,
124-125
calculation for replacement in another
state, 125
Caliphobia, 9-10
on the Internet, 143-144
median price of existing single family
homes for selected cities, 163
real estate agent help with, 147
selling your home, 122-123

Household Goods Dispute Settlement
Program, 176
Housing
cost of living for selected cities, 72-73
costs and financial planning, 21
quality of life factor, 17
Housing ratio
financing a home, 150
selling your home, 135-136

I

Idaho
Boise, 215-216
profile, 214-217
Twin Falls, 216-217
visitor information addresses, 230
Idealizing
life changes, 74-76
relocation, 61-62
Incentives
company relocation, 258-259
real estate agents, 133-134
Income tax rates by state, 24
Inspections
buying a home, 159-161
real estate agent help with, 147
Insurance
gaps in life and disability coverage, 21
mover's liability, 171
rental trucks, 177
Insurance agents, destination research, 33
Interest rates, 153-155
Internet resources
buying a home, 142-144
city newsgroups, 94-95
cost of living, 51-52
crime rates, 57-58
demographics, 51, 108
destination research, 31-32, 33-37
education, 47
finding employment, 85
home-based businesses, 112
home-swapping groups, 52
Internet service providers, 39
job search, 95-98
pricing your home, 123
self-employment, 112
selling your home, 132-133
starting a business, 106
see also World Wide Web
Interviews
changing careers, 101

with real estate agents, 121-122
techniques for, 82-84
testing the job market, 90-91
Inventory
mover's list, 175
of personal belongings, 168
when unpacking, 176
Inventory, personal
changing careers, 101
résumés, 78
Investments, 22

J

Jandt, Fred, Internet job searching, 88, 94-95
Jaramillo, Debbie
respecting local customs, 10
Job market
changing careers, 101
testing of, 90-91
Jobs. *see* Employment

K

Kids' relocation package, 25

L

Labor union membership by state, 109
Lakein, Alan, goal evaluation exercises, 16
Larceny theft
number of offenses known to police by
city, 50
rates by city, 48-49
Lenders, types of, 153
Lewis, Marjorie, pricing your home, 123
Liabilities
buying a business, 110
financial planning, 21
Life insurance. *see* Insurance
Lifestyle changes, 16

M

Mailing lists
defined, 253
destination research, 40
Making friends and settling in Checklist,
244-245
Mapping software, 31
Maps
circle the city game, 30-31
on the Internet, 33
telephone books, 44

Metropolitan Statistic Areas (MSA), crime
    rates, 47
Miscellaneous goods and services, cost of
    living for selected cities, 72-73
MLS. *see* Multiple Listing Service
Montana
    Great Falls, 223-224
    profile, 221-223
    visitor information addresses, 230
Mortgages
    applying for, 150-152
    assumable, 136
    calculator on the Internet, 144
    real estate agent help with, 147
    types of, 153-155
Movers
    annual performance report, 171
    contracts, 171-172
    estimates, 169-170
    Household Goods Dispute Settlement
        Program, 176
    liability coverage, 171
    paying, 172
    Sutch, Cindy, 178
Moving
    cleaning out, 167-168
    cost considerations, 170-172
    dissatisfaction with destination, 250-251
    do it yourself, 177-178
    hybrid do it yourself, 178
    inventory of personal belongings, 168
    involving your children, 175
    packing, 172-175
    publications, 181
    sample schedule of events, 178-180
    software, 181
    unpacking, 175-176
Multiple Listing Service (MLS)
    advertising your home on the Internet,
        132
    browsing for homes, 143
    Internet search for home prices, 123
    selling your home, 120-121
Murder
    number of offenses known to police by
        city, 50
    rates by city, 48-49

N

Negative amortization loans, 154
Negotiations
    real estate agent help with, 147
    selling your home, 134-135

Neighbors, 239-241
Networking
    e-mail, 85
    finding employment, 84-85, 90
    through organizations, 88-89
Nevada
    Carson City area, 195-196
    Las Vegas, 193-194
    profile, 192-193
    Reno, 194-195
    visitor information addresses, 208
New Mexico
    Albuquerque, 198-199
    Las Cruces, 199
    profile, 197-198
    Santa Fe, 10, 199-200
    visitor information addresses, 208
Newsgroups
    defined, 253
    destination research, 39-40
    finding employment, 94-95
    real estate, 144
Newspapers
    destination research, 44-45
    finding employment, 92
    homesickness, 248
    selling your home, 131

O

Online. *see* Internet Resources; World Wide
    Web
Open house
    finding an out of state real estate agent,
        146
    selling your home, 130
Oregon
    Coos Bay/North Bend/ Charleston, 221
    Eugene, 220
    Portland, 218-219
    profile, 217-218
    visitor information addresses, 231
Organizations
    finding employment in your field, 88-89
    fitting in, 242-243
    résumé writing, 81
    small business, 117
    see also Associations

P

Packing
    considerations, 173-174

costs of, 172
do it yourself, 177-178
supervision of, 174-175
Per capita income by state, 93
Phone books. *see* Telephone books
Political trade-offs, 67-68
Pollution
quality of life factor, 17
reasons for leaving California, xiii, xv, 1,
2, 5-6
trade-offs, 66
Population
growth and predictions by state, 7
history of in California, 3-4
publications, 12-13
quality of life factor, 18
see also Growth
Priorities
cost of living, 51-52
crime rates, 17, 51
escape plan, 14-16
rethinking, 42
schools, 45-47, 55
Privacy, lack of in smaller towns, 70
Propane tank inspection, 159
Property crime rates by city, 48-49
Publications
buying a franchise, 109-110, 110
buying a home, 140-141, 148, 166
climate, 43, 57
cost of living, 51-52, 58
crime rates, 47
demographics, 118
destination research, 33, 41
financial planning, 27
finding employment, 98
finding a headhunter, 104, 113
on the Internet, 37
moving, 181
population figures, 12-13
selling your home, 138, 166
small business, 116-117, 118
trade-offs, 76
Pupil/teacher ratios by state, 38
Purpose of book, xiv, 11-12

Q

Quality of life
destination research, 29-30
driving forces, 16-18
"Plan B," 18

R

Rain statistics for selected cities, 64-65
Range Rover Syndrome, 10
Rape
number of offenses known to police by
city, 50
rates by city, 48-49
Real estate
associations on the Internet, 142
see also Buying a home; Selling a home
Real estate agents
advertising your home, 131
caravans, 129-130
closing, 164-165
defined, 122
destination research, 32
Dickson, Pandra, Raleigh, N.C., 25-26
Employee Relocation Council, 146
selecting, 121-122, 145-147
incentives for, 133-134
on the Internet, 33, 143
Lewis, Marjorie, 123
open houses, 130
pricing your home, 122-123
selling your home, 120-122
showing your home, 131-132
what a good agent should do for you,
120, 147
Recreation
quality of life factor, 17
trade-offs, 69
Referrals
finding employment, 94
follow ups, 85
résumé writing, 103
Regulations
corporate relocation, 8
starting a business, 104
taking your job with you, 112
Relocation
climate considerations, 62-63, 66
escape plan, 11-12
fastest growing states, 5-6
financial planning, 19-23
idealizing, 61-62
involving your children, 23, 25-27
job transfer, 85-86
priorities, 14-16
public services trade-offs, 66-67
quality of life, 16-18
reasons for, xiii, xv, 1, 2, 5-6, 15-16
seasonal changes, 27

statistics, 1-2, 3
the two salary family, 87-88
when the destination is predetermined, 18
see also Company relocation
Relocation costs
changing careers, 104
Employee Relocation Council, 136, 146
negotiation with employers, 93-94
Relocation policies
assistance from employer, 86-87
selling your home, 137
Relocation specialists
Certified Relocation Program, 146
Walker, Kathy, 137
Renting
Employee Relocation Council, 136
selling your home, 135
vs. buying a home, 140
Repairs, 126-127
Resources
buying a home out of state, 148-149, 166
climate for selected cities, 65
company relocation, 259-260
destination research, 40-41, 57-58
destinations, 207-209, 230-232
employment, 113
financial planning, 27
finding employment, 92, 98-99
home-based businesses, 112
moving, 181
Northwestern states, 230-232
selling your home, 138
small office/home office, 112
Southwestern states, 207-209
trade-offs, 76
Résumés
building blocks for, 79-81
cover letters, 81-82
headhunters, 103
Internet resources, 95-96
writing, 78
Retirement, 22
Robbery
number of offenses known to police by city, 50
rates by city, 48-49
Robinson, Keith, finding employment in your field, 92-94
Roller Route Map Measurer, circle the city game, 31

Rural
considerations when buying a home, 158-159
migration trends, 6

S

Salaries
interviews, 83
trade-offs, 71-73
Sales tax rates by state, 24
SAT. *see* Scholastic Assessment Tests
SBA. *see* Small Business Administration
Scholastic Assessment Tests (SAT) by state, 38
Schools
fitting in, 243
questions to ask a new district, 45-46
real estate agent help with, 147
sports programs, 55-56
see also Education
SCORE. *see* Service Corps of Retired Executives
Search engines
basics, 252
city networks, 35-36
defined, 254
web site addresses, 252-253
Seasons, destination research, 56
Self-employment resources, 112
Seller's market defined, 145
Selling your home
with an agent, 120-122
assistance from employer, 86-87
capital gains, 152
curb appeal, 127-128
days on the market, 123
exposure, 129-132
fundamentals, 119
job transfers, 136-137
keeping it clean, 128-129
mortgage options, 135-136
negotiations, 134-135
premiums and incentives, 133-134
pricing, 122
publications, 138, 166
repairs, 126-128
showing your home, 131-132
trades, 135
Septic tanks inspection, 158
Service Corps of Retired Executives (SCORE), starting a business, 106-107
Services, trade-offs, 67-88
Shopping, quality of life factor, 18

Small Business Administration (SBA)
    franchise failure rates, 110
    frequently asked questions, starting a
        business, 105
    Small Business Development Centers
        (SBDC), 106
Small business incubators, 112
Small office/home office (SOHO)
    resources, 112
Smith, Verenda, determining tax liability, 23
Software
    financial, 20
    home design, 181
    mapping, 31
SOHO. *see* Small office/home office
Start-up kits, 107
State agencies
    buying a franchise, 110
    finding employment, 99
    small business, 113-115
    starting a business, 107
    taking your job with you, 112
State population growth and predictions, 7
States
    Alaska, 211-214
    Arizona, 184-188
    Colorado, 188-192
    Hawaii, 196-197
    Idaho, 214-217
    Montana, 221-224
    Nevada, 192-196
    New Mexico, 197-200
    Oregon, 217-221
    Texas, 200-203
    top ten fastest growing, 5-6
    Utah, 203-206
    Washington, 224-228
    Wyoming, 228-229
    see also Destinations; Individual state names
Statistics
    climate, 64-65
    cost of living, 72-73
    crime, 48-49, 50
    education, 38
    house prices, 124-125, 163
    income, 93
    labor union membership, 109
    number of people leaving California, 1-2,
        3
    per capita income, 93
    population, 7
    reliability of, 183
    tax rates, 24

Sunny day statistics for selected cities, 64-65
Swann, Becky
    advertising your home on the Internet,
        143
    advice on prices, 139

T
Tables
    climate for selected cities, 64-65
    cost of living index for selected cities,
        72-73
    education ratings by state, 38
    FBI Uniform Crime Report per 100,000
        inhabitants, 48-49
    general information, 12
    home price index for selected cities,
        124-125
    labor union membership by state, 109
    median sale price of existing single family
        homes for selected cities, 163
    number of offenses known to police by
        city, 50
    number of people leaving California by
        age, 3
    per capita income by state, 93
    state population growth and predictions,
        7
    state tax rates, 24
    top ten fastest growing states, 5
Tax administrators, Smith, Verenda, 23
Tax rates by state, 24
Taxes
    company relocation, 7-8, 256
    financial planning, 20
    quality of life factor, 18
    retirement accounts, 22-23
    selling a home, 152
Telecommuting, 87
Telephone books
    destination research, 43-44
    employment resources, 91
Temperatures for selected cities, 64-65
Texas
    Austin, 201-202
    Bryan/College Station, 202-203
    profile, 200-201
    visitor information addresses, 208
Thompson, Judy, working with headhunters,
    103-104
Title insurance, 165
Trade-offs
    adjustable rate mortgages, increased rates

vs. lower initial payments, 154
buying a business, 111
climate, 60
community involvement vs. privacy, 69-71
cultural quality vs. accessibility, 68-69
pollution vs. climate, 66
public services, 66-68
salaries vs. cost of living, 71-73
small town vs. big city, 235
Traffic trade-offs, 66-67
Transfers, 85-86
Transportation, 213
cost of living for selected cities, 72-73
quality of life factor, 18
Travel bureaus
addresses in the Northwest, 230-232
addresses in the Southwest, 207-209
destination research, 32

U

Usenet newsgroups. *see* Newsgroups
Utah
Cedar City, 205-206
profile, 203-204
Provo/Orem, 204-205
Salt Lake City, 204
St. George, 206
visitor information addresses, 209
Utilities
company relocation, 256
cost of living for selected cities, 72-73
financial planning, 20
Utility companies, destination research, 33

V

VA loans, 155
Violent crime rates by city, 48-49

W

Walker, Kathy, buy-outs, 137
Washington
Bellingham, 225-226
profile, 224
Seattle, 224-225
Spokane, 227-228
visitor information addresses, 231
Weather. *see* Climate
Web. *see* World Wide Web
Wells, testing of water, 158
Western states, rural migration trends, 5-6
Wills, 22

World Wide Web
basics, 251-254
buying a home web sites, 141, 142
company relocation web sites, 259-260
cost of living web sites, 58
crime rate web sites, 57-58
demographics web sites, 58
destination research web sites, 34, 40-41
education web sites, 47, 57
employment web sites, 98-99
environment/health web sites, 59
federal agencies web sites, 116
financial planning web sites, 27
home-swapping web sites, 58-59
moving information web sites, 181
National Association of Governments web
    site, 37
real estate web sites, 148-149, 166
search engine web sites, 252-253
selling your home web sites, 138
small business publications web sites, 117
small business web sites, 116, 117
state agencies web sites, 114-115
terminology, 253-254
see also Internet resources
WWW. *see* World Wide Web
Wyoming
Cheyenne, 229
profile, 228-229
visitor information addresses, 231-232

Order Form

You may order a copy of the *California Escape Manual* directly from the publisher at $19.95 each.

For orders shipped to California, add 7.75 percent state sales tax.

_____ Books at $19.95 each . . . . _____

7.75% California sales tax . . . . _____

Shipping and handling . . . . _____
    ($4.00 for one; $1.00 for each additional book)

Total enclosed: . . . . _____

Please print clearly

Name _____

Address _____

City _____State____Zip _____

Send to: Archer & Clark Publishing
            Order Dept.
            P.O. Box 7327
            Redlands, CA 92375

Do not send cash. Make checks payable to: Archer & Clark Publishing.

If not satisfied, you may return the book within 30 days for a full refund.

Free Update Service

You can receive a free update bulletin containing additional resources including references to magazine articles and Web sites, plus other information of interest to future ex-Californians. To receive your update, send a stamped, self-addressed No. 10 (business size) envelope to the address below. Be sure to affix first class postage.

        Escape Update Bulletin
        Archer & Clark Publishing
        P.O. Box 7327
        Redlands, CA 92375